Morality and Objectivity

A Tribute to J. L. Mackie

International Library of Philosophy

Editor: Ted Honderich
Professor of Philosophy, University College London

A catalogue of books already published in the
International Library of Philosophy will be found
at the end of this volume

Morality and Objectivity

A Tribute to J. L. Mackie

edited by

Ted Honderich

ROUTLEDGE & KEGAN PAUL

London, Boston, Melbourne and Henley

First published in 1985
by Routledge & Kegan Paul plc,

14 Leicester Square, London WC2H 7PH, England,

9 Park Street, Boston, Mass. 02108, USA,

464 St Kilda Road, Melbourne,
Victoria 3004, Australia and

Broadway House, Newtown Road
Henley-on-Thames, Oxon RG9 1EN, England

Set in Press Roman
by Hope Services, Abingdon
printed in Great Britain

Library of Congress Cataloging in Publication Data

Morality and objectivity.
(International library of philosophy)
Bibliography: p.
1. Ethics – Addresses, essays, lectures.   2. Values –
Addresses, essays, lectures.   3. Mackie, J. L.
(John Leslie)   I. Honderich, Ted.   II. Series.
BJ1012.M6354 1985   170   84-17855

British Library CIP data also available.

ISBN 0-7100-9991-6

CONTENTS

INTRODUCTION

Five of the nine papers in this volume give a new understanding of that most fundamental issue in moral philosophy, the issue of whether our moral judgments are in some way objective. Or rather, these papers are concerned with the several related issues suggested by that question, as by the question of whether the correct account of moral qualities of acts and agents is given by a doctrine of what is called moral realism. This subject was rightly at the centre of the moral thought of the philosopher to whom this volume is a tribute, John Mackie. His own sceptical view is indicated by the subtitle of his principal work in moral philosophy, *Ethics: Inventing Right and Wrong*.

Mackie's philosophical strengths were great, and he used them unpridefully and with wonderful effect. His acuteness, his perfect orderliness, and above all his unfailing pursuit of clear truth and his entire disregard of lesser philosophical goals — these strengths could not conceivably be celebrated by a volume informed by philosophical piety. Certainly this one is not. As John McDowell remarks in his paper, Mackie would not have found it strange that tribute is paid to him by the continuing of strenuous disagreements with him.

Simon Blackburn's 'Errors and the phenomenology of value' is in part concerned with the idea that denials of the objectivity of morals call for an 'error theory', an account of why we mistakenly suppose that morality does have an objective character. R. M. Hare's 'Ontology in ethics' makes four distinctions that enter into the controversy about moral judgments and qualities, and argues that one of them takes us to the root of the matter. Susan Hurley, in 'Objectivity and disagreement', maintains that a certain conception of objectivity suggested by some of the work of Ludwig Wittgenstein and Donald Davidson escapes refutation by the undoubted fact of our moral disagreements. John McDowell's 'Values and secondary qualities' takes up a subject also treated in passing by other contributors, the extent to which our moral responses are like our experience of such secondary qualities as colour. Bernard Williams, in 'Ethics and the fabric of the world', carries forward an inquiry which is in part concerned with the consequences of the doctrine that what we require is a theory of our erroneous disposition to moral realism.

The other four contributors to this volume give their attention to problems which are as compelling. Philippa Foot, in 'Morality, action and outcome', defends two moral intuitions which conflict with what, in her view, can seem uniquely rational and therefore irresistible, which is utilitarianism. Steven Lukes, in 'Taking morality seriously', offers an account very different from Mackie's of the problem to which a central part of morality is our solution. Amartya Sen's 'Rights and capabilities', beginning from the limitations of Utilitarianism, defends a moral outlook based on a conception of our capabilities. In 'Claims of need', David Wiggins makes a rightly extended investigation of the conception of a need and of what follows from it.

The volume, I think, is indeed a proper tribute to the achievements of an exemplary philosopher. It ends with the addresses given by Simon Blackburn and George Cawkwell at a memorial service in the University Church at Oxford on 27 February 1982 and with a list of the publications of John Mackie, compiled by Joan Mackie. The memorial addresses, like the philosophical papers before them, are not encomiums, and have no need to be. The list of publications speaks for itself.

Ted Honderich

I

ERRORS AND THE PHENOMENOLOGY OF VALUE

Simon Blackburn

Oh Is there not one maiden breast
That does not feel the moral beauty
Of Making worldly interest
Subordinate to sense of duty?
W.S. Gilbert
The Pirates of Penzance

I

John Mackie described himself as a moral sceptic, and he described his theory of ethics as an error theory. The ordinary user of moral language wants to claim something which, according to Mackie, cannot be claimed without error: he wants to claim 'something that involves a call for action or for the refraining from action, and one that is absolute, not contingent upon any desire or preference or policy or choice, his own or anyone else's' (p. 33).[1] Again, someone in moral perplexity may want to know whether a course of action is wrong 'in itself' (p. 34), and 'something like this in the everyday objectivist concept' which is erroneous. For, according to Mackie, ordinary judgments and perplexities include an assumption that there are objective values, in a sense in which he denies that there are. This assumption is ingrained enough to count as part of the meaning of ordinary moral terms, but it is false.

Mackie did not draw quite the consequences one might have expected from this position. If a vocabulary embodies an error, then it would be better if it were replaced by one which avoids the error. Slightly more

1

accurately, if a vocabulary embodies an error *in some use* it would be better if either it, or a replacement vocabulary, were used differently. We could better describe this by saying that our old, infected moral concepts or ways of thought should be replaced by ones which serve our legitimate needs, but avoid the mistake. Yet Mackie does not say what such a way of thought would look like, and how it would differ in order to show its innocence of the old error. On the contrary, in the second part of the book, he is quite happy to go on to express a large number of straightforward moral views, about the good life, about whether it is permissible to commit suicide or abortion, and so on. All these are expressed in the old, supposedly infected vocabulary. Mackie does, of course, notice the problem. He explicitly asks (p. 49) whether his error theory rules out all first-order ethics, and when he returns to the question (p. 105) there is a real threat that ideally there would be no such activity as first-order moralizing. The threat is only averted, supposedly, by introducing the general Humean theme about the social function of morality: 'Morality is not to be discovered but to be made: we have to decide what moral views to adopt, what moral stands to take.' (p. 106) Yet from the standpoint of an error theory it is quite extraordinary that we should have to do any such thing. Why should we have to choose to fall into error? Surely it would be better if we avoided *moral* (erroneous) views altogether, and contended ourselves with some lesser, purged commitments which can be held without making metaphysical mistakes? Let us call these shmoral views, and a vocabulary which expresses them a shmoral vocabulary. Then the puzzle is why, in the light of the error theory, Mackie did not at least indicate how a shmoral vocabulary would look, and did not himself go on only to shmoralize, not to moralize. And in my view this is enough of a puzzle to cast doubt back on to the original diagnosis of error. In other words, it would obviously have been a silly thing to do, to try to substitute some allegedly hygienic set of concepts for moral ones; but that in itself suggests that no error can be incorporated in mere use of those concepts.

In reply to this it may be said that appearances notwithstanding, Mackie did actually only go on to shmoralize. He rids himself of the error, but uses the Humean reconstruction of practical needs and practical reasoning to advocate various shmoral views. These are only accidentally expressed in a vocabulary looking so like that of ordinary moralists: the identity of shape of words does not signify identity of concept, although there is sufficient overlap in function between

2

moralizing and shmoralizing to justify retention of the same words. This is certainly possible. But it leaves an acute problem of identifying just where shmoralizing differs from moralizing: what shows us whether Mackie is moralizing or shmoralizing? Does it determine the issue that he will say things like 'there is no objective prescriptivity built into the fabric of the world'? Troubles multiply. Firstly it is clear that not all moralists will deny this (many moralists will not even understand it). Secondly it seems gratuitous to infer that there are two different activities from the fact that there are two or more different theories about the nature of the activity. It would be much more natural to say that Hume and Mackie moralize, just as ordinary people do, but with a developed and different theory about what it is that they are doing. The error theory then shrinks to the claim that most ordinary moralists have a bad theory, or at least no very good theory, about what it is to moralize, and in particular that they falsely imagine a kind of objectivity for values, obligations, and so on. This may be true, but it does not follow that the error infects the practice of moralizing, nor the concepts used in ways defined by that practice.

Here, however, a fairly blanket holism can be introduced to rescue Mackie, or at least to urge that it is profitless to oppose him. Our theories infect our meanings; so a different theory about the nature of the activity of moralizing will yield a different meaning for the terms with which we do it; hence Mackie is right that the ordinary meanings do embody error. It becomes profitless to split things in two, so that on the one hand there is the error-free practice, and on the other hand a multiplicity of possibly erroneous theories about its nature. Indeed, the split appeals no more than the despised analytic-synthetic distinction, and if the opponents of an error theory need that, they will gain few supporters.

It is important, and not just to this philosophical issue, to see that this defence fails. To answer it, distinguish between the activity or practice of moralizing and the 'full meaning' of moral terms, where this is determined as the holist wishes, by both the practice and whatever theory the subjects hold about the nature of their practice. Then the holist may have the thesis about 'full meaning', with the consequence that Hume and Mackie may give a different full meaning to their terms, simply through having a different theory of their point and purpose. But it will not follow that their *practice* will differ from that of other people. Hence, it will not follow that other people's practice embodies error. For it is in principle possible that we should observe the practice of some subjects as closely as we wish, and know as much as there is to know about their ways of thinking, commending, approving, deliberating, worrying, and so on, yet be unable to tell from all that which theory they hold. The practice could be clipped on to either metaphysic. The holist will have it that this alters meanings throughout. But we can give him that, yet still maintain that no difference is discernible in the practice, and therefore that no error is embodied in the practice of those who hold the wrong theory. To use a close analogy, there are different theories about the nature of arithmetical concepts. Hence a holist may claim that a subject will give a different total meaning to numerals depending on which theory he accepts, and this difference will apply just as much when the subject is counting as when he is doing meta-mathematics. All that may be true, yet it would not follow that any practice of counting embodies error. That would be so only if one could tell just by observing it which of the competing metamathematical theories the subject accepts. In the arithmetical case this would not be true. Similarly, I maintain, in the moral case one ought not to be able to tell from the way in which someone conducts the activity of moralizing, whether he has committed the 'objectivist' mistake or not; hence any such mistake is better thought of as accidental to the practice.

Obviously there is *an* answer to this. It is that the objectivist error does so permeate the practice that you can tell, from the way people moralize, that they are in its grip. It is as if a strict finitist theory, say, of arithmetic led someone to deny that you could count certain sets which others can happily enumerate. But which features of the practice show this? They are to be features which lie beyond the scope of what I have called 'quasi-realism': the enterprise of showing how much of the apparently 'realist' appearance of ordinary moral thought is explicable and justifiable on an anti-realist picture.[2] According to me quasi-realism is almost entirely successful, and I do not think John Mackie provided reasons for thinking otherwise. In other words, proper shmoralizing is proper moralizing.

II

So far, I have tried to show that there is something fishy about holding an error theory, yet continuing to moralize, and I have argued that the 'holistic' or Quinean defence of such a position would fail. The argument can now move in different directions. Let us call the Humean picture of the nature of morality, and of the metaphysics of the issue, projectivism. On this view we have sentiments and other reactions, caused by natural features of things, and we 'gild or stain' the world by describing it as if it contained features answering to these sentiments, in the way that the niceness of an ice-cream answers to the pleasure it gives us. Then we could say that Mackie is right about the metaphysical issue, and ought to have been more thoroughgoing in replacing moral terms and concepts by different ones — in other words, that the projectivist in ethics should conduct his practical reasoning in a different way: his shmoralizing would not be moralizing. Let us call this a *revisionist* projectivism. By contrast, there is the quasi-realist identification of shmoralizing with moralizing. In effect the skirmishes in part I of this paper urge that quasi-realism needs to be taken seriously, because even projectivists are going to find themselves indulging in a practice which is apparently identical with moralizing. Of course, in opposition to each of these views, there is the realist charge that projectivism is false in any case; finally there is the 'quietist' view, urged for instance by Professor Hare, that no real issue can be built around the objectivity or otherwise of moral values.

If we are to say that the practices characteristic of moralizing are or are not available to a projectivist, we should be careful to identify the practices at issue. In previous papers I have tried to show how the realist-seeming *grammar* of moral discourse can be explained on that metaphysic. This involved, for instance, addressing the Geach-Frege problem of accounting for unasserted occurrence of sentences using moral terms, explaining the propositional form which we give to moral utterances, explaining why we may legitimately worry whether one of our moral views is correct, and hence explaining the role of a concept of truth in ethics, and so on. If this work is successful there is no way of arguing that the grammar of moral discourse either refutes projectivism, or forces it to take a revisionist course. This means, of course, that Mackie cannot properly use these aspects of our practice in support of the error theory. And sometimes he does just this. For instance, he cites Russell's feeling that on a particular moral issue (opposition to the introduction of bull-fighting into England) one does not just express a desire that the thing should not happen, but does so while feeling that one's desires on such a matter are *right*.[3] Mackie thinks that this is a claim to objectivity, and as such erroneous. The quasi-realist will see it instead as a proper, necessary expression of an attitude to our own attitudes. It is not something that should be wrenched out of our moral psychology; it is something we need to cultivate to the right degree and in the right places, to avoid the (moral) defect of indifference to things that merit passion. This actually illustrates a central quasi-realist tactic: what seems like a thought which embodies a particular second-order metaphysic of morals is seen instead as a kind of thought which expresses a first-order attitude or need. Perhaps the nicest example comes from counter-factuals which seem to assert an anti-projectivist, mind-independence of moral facts: 'even if we had approved of it or enjoyed it or desired to do it, bear-baiting would still have been wrong' can sound like a second-order, realist commitment directly in opposition to projectivism. But in fact, on the construal of indirect contexts which I offer, it comes out as a perfectly sensible first-order commitment to the effect that it is not our enjoyments or approvals which you should look to in discovering whether bear-baiting is wrong (it is at least mainly the effect on the bear).

For the rest of this paper I shall suppose that this aspect of quasi-realism is successful. So projectivism can accommodate the propositional grammar of ethics. It need not seek to revise that. On the contrary, properly protected by quasi-realism it supports and indeed explains this much of our ordinary moral thought. But in my experience this explanation is apt to leave a residual unease. People feel uncomfortable with the idea that this is the true explanation of our propensity to find and to respect values, obligations, duties and rights. They feel an unease perhaps rather like that of nineteenth-century thinkers who found it so difficult to do ethics without God. This unease is located in a tension between the subjective source which projectivism gives to morality, and the objective 'feel' that a properly working morality has. It is this objective feel or phenomenology which people find threatened by projectivism, and they may go on to fear the threat as one which strikes at the core of morality. We may scoff at those who thought that if God is dead everything is permitted. But it is harder to really shake off the feeling that if duties, rights, etc. come down to *that* — to the projectivist earth — then they do not have quite the power or force, the title to respect, which we were brought up to believe.

It is, I think, particularly the side of morality associated with *obligation* which is felt to be subject to this threat. Obligation needs to be 'peremptory and absolute', as George Eliot famously said; it often needs to be perceived as something sufficiently external to us to act as a *constraint* or bound on our other sentiments and desires. The chains and shackles of obligation must come from outside us. Can anything both be felt to have this power, and yet be explained as a projection of our own sentiments? The charge will then be that projectivism falsifies this aspect of morality; it will be unable to endorse this kind of perception of obligation, but must explain it away as a phenomenological distortion. It will be the result of an error, and realist opponents of projectivism will join with revisionists to urge that it marks a point at which quasi-realism fails.[4] The realists will trust the phenomenology, and revisionists will regret it. We can notice in this connection that when Mackie identifies the error of ordinary thought, it is the 'intrinsic' or 'absolute' to-be-done-ness which certain actions are felt to possess which he often points to.[5] It is not just the 'intrinsic' value of happiness or pleasure, because it is less surprising that these values should receive a projective explanation. It is as if the objectivists' error is to think of certain things as obligatory in a way which has nothing to do with us, and about which we can do nothing: a way which could in principle stand opposed to the whole world of human desire and need. Now admittedly from this it might seem that the error is to adopt a deontological rather than a teleological first-order morality. But surely this is wrong, for Mackie did not want the error to be purely one of adopting a defective or non-consequentialist first-order morality. Doing that may be a natural consequence of a metaphysical mistake but it is not in itself an 'error' intrinsic to the very nature of morality. I think instead that Mackie chose the word, and chose to concentrate upon obligation, because of the absolute and external 'feel' which he wanted to indicate, and which he felt was not explicable or defensible on a projective metaphysic. And if he were right, then by threatening this part of the feeling of obligation, projectivism would indeed threaten one of the most important and characteristic parts of morality. But is there any reason to believe that he is right?

The issue will look rather different depending on whether the difficulty is supposed to concern the explanation of moral psychology, or its justification. Consider a very pure case of someone in the grip of a duty. Mabel and Fred want to marry each other. The opportunity is there, the desires are aflame, the consequences are predictably acceptable or even desirable. There is only one thought to oppose it: they have a duty to do otherwise, so it would be wrong. And this feeling that it would be wrong can wrestle with and sometimes even overcome all the rest. Isn't this mysterious? Called conscience, it used to be mysterious enough to suggest an internal voice of God standing outside the natural world of sentiments and desires. On the present line of thought, it is mysterious enough to suggest perception of an external or objective moral fact, also standing outside the natural world of sentiments and desires. Unfortunately, neither of these explanations is more than a gesture. It is trivial to point out the gaps they leave. But there is a better explanation: Fred has been brought up in a certain way and a consequence of this upbringing is that he looks on certain courses of action with horror. He will only keep his self-respect, only be able to live with himself if he conducts his life in a particular way, and this is a range of feeling sufficiently strong to oppose immediate desire, and which gains expression when he describes the conduct as wrong. Whether it was a good thing that Fred was brought up like that is a matter of judgment, but it can hardly be doubted that it is a good thing that people should sometimes feel like that, for otherwise they are more likely to do the most awful things. It is of course a brute fact about human beings that our sources of self-respect are malleable in this way, but that is a matter of common observation. Equally, it is a matter of common observation that there are cultural ways of reinforcing such feelings in elements of the population which may be in particular need of them: traditionally soldiers and girls get strong injections of honour and duty.

At the level of explanation, then, it is hard to see why there is any problem for the projectivist. Indeed, it is hard to see how there *could* be. For many of the ingredients of his account will be needed by any other account. For instance, his observations on the plasticity of our sensibilities, and on the various devices which lead people to respect different sets of obligations and to value different aspects of things, will be simply copied by a realist, who will need to say that our perceptions of moral facts are similarly trained and adapted. As usual, however, the extra ingredients the realist adds (the values or obligations which, in addition to normal features of things, are cognized and the respect we then feel for these cognized qualities) are pulling no explanatory weight: they just sit on top of the story which tells how our sentiments relate to natural features of things. If Fred poses a problem, then, it cannot be one of the explanation of moral psychology, but must be one of justification.

If Fred is rational, can his virtue survive his own awareness of its origin and nature? If Mabel throws into her wooing a whole projective plus quasi-realist explanation of what Fred is doing when he maintains that it's wrong, and if Fred is rational, will this not destroy his resolve? Shouldn't he think something like this: that although he has been brought up to use moral categories and to think that there are moral obligations etc., *there are none really* — they are a fiction, or useful, regulative myth: hence — forget them? Once again we are reminded of those thinkers who felt that if there were no God or no afterlife, then it would be rational to ignore the claims of morality whenever self-interest suggested it. Their anxiety was grounded on a mistake about rationality, for the altruistic or principled man is no more nor less rational than the self-interested — he is just different in ways which affect his happiness and the happiness of communities composed of people like him. Rationality in itself does not force one sensibility or another on us *just* because we have some belief about the origin of that sensibility. This is obvious if we take a parallel: Mabel may be tempted to laugh at Fred's moustache; Fred may seek to dissuade her by telling a projectivist story about the judgment that something is funny, but there is no reason for him to succeed. Finding things very funny is perfectly compatible with believing that it is a tendency to laugh which we project on the world when we do so. It is not uniquely rational to try to smother our sense of humour because of this belief about its nature. So Mabel is not irrational if she accepts Fred's theory of laughter and continues to laugh at his moustache, and by analogy he may be perfectly rational to accept the projectivist account of morality, and to maintain his resolve just as forcefully as before.

I say that he may be rational to do this. But it is possible that he is not, for an explanation of the origin of a sentiment can diminish its force. For example, psychologists sometimes connect humour with sublimated or concealed aggression. Believing this explanation, and being ashamed of aggressive instincts, it would be rational for me to find fewer and fewer things funny. The explanation *coupled with* other values undermines the sentiment. Similarly a morality might contain values whose effect, coupled with a projective explanation, is to diminish a subject's respect for some obligations. For example, a child may be brought up to believe that things really matter only in so far as God cares about them; learning not to think of conscience as the voice of God would couple with this attitude to diminish the force with which he feels obligations. Or, someone might suppose that only commitments which describe the constitution of the real world have any importance and that all others are better ignored: a projective explanation of morality may then diminish the attention he is prepared to pay to it.[6] This latter attitude is actually quite common. For example, when people feel uncomfortable about trying to impose a morality on other people it is the idea that moral commitments lack real, objective truth values certified by an independent reality that troubles them. The hope of rehabilitating morality by making it an object of perception or reason, and thereby having a better claim on our attention, bears witness to the same idea. In each case however it is not the explanation of the practice *per se* which has the sceptical consequence. It is only the effect of the explanation on sensibilities which have been brought up to respect only particular kinds of thing. So when people fear that projectivism carries with it a loss of status to morality, their fear ought to be groundless, and will only appear if a defective sensibility leads them to respect the wrong things.

So far I have considered this problem only as it affects obligations. But similar remarks can be apposite in connection with values. It is not initially so surprising that we can go on valuing the good things of life whilst knowing that the valuing is an expression of our own subjective sentiments. This need be no more odd than that we should go on finding things funny or painful, or worthwhile or beautiful, although God is dead, or although we accept subjective responses as the source of these reactions. However, David Wiggins has found a problem even here for the position which he called non-cognitivism, which shares with projectivism the Humean theme that 'ends are supplied by feeling or will, which are not conceived either as percipient or as determinants in any interesting way of perception'.[7] The core of the charge is, I think, that projectivism cannot co-exist with the way in which we perceive values as residing in things outside ourselves. It is not entirely clear, because Wiggins associates with projectivism the repugnant (first-order) doctrine that the only things which possess any intrinsic value are human states of consciousness. But a projectivist's sensibility need not, and in my view should not, take this shape. He can admire features of things regardless of their effects on us: his first-order morality need no more be anthropocentric than it need be egocentric. Remember here that a projectivist who avails himself of quasi-realism can assert those tantalizing expressions of apparent mind-independence: it is not my sentiments that make bear-baiting wrong; it is not because we disapprove of it that mindless violence is abominable; it is preferable that the world should be a beautiful place even after all consciousness of it ceases. The explanation of what we are doing when we say such things in no way impugns our right to hold them, nor the passion with which we should do so. But if we dissociate ourselves from this target then at this point Wiggins seems to threaten projectivism no more than the attack deflected in the last paragraph. It might be that there are people who cannot 'put up with' the idea that values have a subjective source; who cannot put up with the idea that the meaning of their life and their activities is ultimately something they confer, and that even critical reflection on how best to confer them conducts itself in the light of other sentiments which must be taken simply as given. But this will be because such people have a defect elsewhere in their sensibilities — one which has taught them that things do not matter unless they matter to God, or throughout infinity, or to a world conceived apart from any particular set of concerns or desires, or whatever. One should not adjust one's metaphysics to pander to such defects.

There is still that nagging feel that on this metaphysic 'there are no obligations etc. *really*' (otherwise, why call the position anti-realist?). But urging this as a problem confuses two different contexts in which such a remark might occur. Protected by quasi-realism, my projectivist says the things that sound so realist to begin with — that there are real obligations and values, and that many of them are independent of us, for example. It is *not* the position that he says these for public consumption but denies them in his heart, so to speak. He affirms *all that could ever properly be meant* by saying that there are real obligations.[8] When the context of discussion is that of first-order commitment, he is as solid as the most virtuous moralist. It is just that the explanation of why there are obligations and the rest is not quite that of untutored common-sense. It deserves to be called anti-realist because it avoids the view that when we moralize we respond to, and describe, an independent aspect of reality. Again, a useful model for understanding this is provided by mathematics. There are anti-realist views of what we are doing when we practise arithmetic. But they need not and should not lead to anyone wondering whether $7 + 5$ is 'really' 12, for that would be an expression of first-order doubt which would not be a consequence of the second-order theory. Arithmetical practice would remain as solid and certain as could be, but explained without reference to an independent mathematical reality.

III

Thus far I have been using quasi-realism to protect the appearance of morality: to urge that there is no error in our ordinary ways of thought and our ordinary commitments and passions. This enterprise will interest a projectivist most, because it defends him against the most forceful attack he faces,which is that he cannot accommodate the rich phenomena of the moral life. But realist opponents of projectivism need to notice quasi-realism as well, since otherwise they do not know how to launch an attack on projectivism. They would not have correctly located its strengths or weaknesses. Nevertheless, they could concede that its defence is successful on these fronts, yet still maintain their hostility. They can urge that the metaphor of projection fails, or is better replaced by a comparison between our knowledge of ethics and our knowledge of other things, such as mathematics, or colours. It is this latter comparison which I now wish to explore. It is not, in my view, right to suppose that there is immediately an issue between two rival theories of morality. This is partly because some of the writers I shall mention, who might seem to be offering a perceptual account of morality, are at least half-inclined to deny that they wish to offer a theory at all, although that does leave the status of some of their remarks regrettably unclear. At any rate, as I see it there are in the beginning two invitations, but they are not so much rivals as complementary to each other. The one is to explore the idea of a projection upon the world of a sentiment which we feel. The other is to explore the idea of a perception of a real property, but one which is intimately related to our own sensibilities. These mark different directions of exploration, and it should not be obvious at first sight which will prove the more profitable. I believe that at the end the first provides illumination where the second runs into obstacles, disanalogies, and an ultimate inability to say anything. I also believe that the first can explain and soothe away the fears which lead people to the second — the fear I addressed in part II, that without obligations of a reality which he cannot aspire to, everything is permitted, for example. I shall try to make good these claims by presenting the 'perceptual' direction in the light of the writings of David Wiggins, Thomas Nagel and John McDowell, and more recently Hilary Putnam,[9] but as I mentioned, I am conscious that it is not easy to extract one theory, or just one theory, from those writings. However, at least they suggest a direction of thought, and it is this direction which I want to block.

The opposition understands that projectivism is an explanatory theory, which maintains that moral values are projections of sentiment because we have a better explanation of moral practices if we see ourselves as responsive only to a value-free world. But according to the opposition, a number of considerations make this an insufficient basis for projectivism. Disquiet can perhaps be focused under three headings.

(1) Consider secondary properties. Colours (etc.) are real properties of objects, and this is true even if the best causal explanation of how we detect them proceeds by mentioning primary properties. Colours really exist, although the reality which contains them is not independent of the fact that there also exist human modes of perception.

(2) The thesis just put forward will only appear surprising (i) because of a prejudice that only primary properties, or the properties of some 'ultimate' scientific theory of things, are real, or (ii) because we forget the truth that the world cannot be 'prised away from' our manner of conceiving it, nor from our interests and concerns when we do so. Since neither of these motives is legitimate, there is no obstacle to (1), and to using the parallel with colours to allow a reality to values etc.

(3) It is true that a training of a particular kind is needed to enable people properly to perceive values etc., but this is harmless: people need training to detect, e.g., features of tunes or shades.

I do not suppose that each of the writers I have mentioned would assent to each of these. For example, although the work of Nagel is prominent in opening up the idea of a reality which is yet subject-dependent, his own work on moral motivation is much more concerned with rationality than with any analogy to the perception of secondary qualities. And Wiggins thinks that the question of the truth of moral commitments looks very different if we consider values and if we consider obligations. But I shall put questions of attribution to one side, simply taking these three themes to form the core of a *perceptual* model of moralizing which at least appears to be a rival to projectivism. Is it a rival, and if it is, then how are we to tell which is better?

Wiggins writes that he has 'long marvelled' at the fact that philosophers have dwelt frequently upon the difference between 'good' and 'red' or 'yellow'. I do not think he should have, unless indeed it is marvellous that philosophers should emphasize things that are banal, and basic. At any rate, it is very easy to rattle off significant differences between secondary properties and those involved in value and obligation. Here are half a dozen.

(a) Moral properties supervene upon others in quite a different way from any in which secondary properties do so. It is a scientific fact that secondary properties supervene upon primary properties. It may even be a metaphysical fact, at least inasmuch as it would offend deep metaphysical commitments to imagine secondary properties changing whilst primary properties do not. But it is not a criterion of incompetence in the ascription of secondary properties to fail to realize that they must

13

supervene upon others. On the other hand, that moral properties supervene upon natural ones is not a scientific fact, and it *is* criterial of incompetence in moralizing to fail to realize that they must do so.

(b) The receptive mechanisms whereby we are acquainted with secondary properties are well-known objects of scientific study. For example, the kinds of damage to the retina or the ear or taste buds which result in defective perception of secondary qualities can be studied. These studies are not at all similar to studies of defects of character which lead to moral blindness: these latter studies have no receptive or causal mechanisms as their topic. This is just as well, for we need to put things in a particular moral light after we are told about their *other* properties; we do not *also* have to wheel a particular sensory mechanism up against them. Connected with this, and with (a), is the thought that if our secondary-property-detecting mechanisms fail we know that immediately: it presents itself as a loss of immediately felt phenomenal quality, just as it does when the light fails or we stick cotton wool in our ears. There is no such loss when we become, say, corrupt. We cannot become corrupt overnight, and usually we cannot tell when we have done so. Indeed, it would be a hallmark of many kinds of moral blindness that this is so. The really coarse man thinks that he is perfectly in order, but that other people are too fastidious (recognizing that you have become really coarse is in this way self-refuting: the realization itself shows some residual delicacy).

(c) It is not altogether simple to characterize the 'mind-dependence' of secondary qualities. But it is plausible to say that these are relative to our perceptions of them in this way: if we were to change so that everything in the world which had appeared blue came to appear red to us, this is what it is for the world to cease to contain blue things, and come to contain only red things. The analogue with moral qualities fails dramatically: if everyone comes to think of it as permissible to maltreat animals, this does nothing at all to make it permissible: it just means that everybody has deteriorated.[10]

(d) The way in which moral practices vary with the forms of life of a society is not at all similar to the way, if any, in which perceptions of secondary qualities can vary with those forms of life. Roughly, we expect such perceptions to vary in acuity depending on whether the property perceived is important to a culture. But once a predicate is located as expressing such a property, there is no prospect of finding that it has a radically different extension. Whereas many things are evaluated quite differently in different groups or at different times.

Similarly, apart from rare borderline cases, there is nothing in secondary quality ascription parallel to the 'essentially contested' character of many moral verdicts.

(e) It is up to a subject whether he cares about any particular secondary property in any way. If morality consisted in the perception of qualities, there would be a theoretical space for a culture which perceived the properties perfectly, but paid no attention to them. But however it is precisely fixed, the practical nature of morality is clearly intrinsic to it, and there is not this theoretical space.

(f) Evaluative predicates are typically attributive: a thing may be good *qua* action of a commander-in-chief, but bad *qua* action of a father, just as a man may be a good burglar but a bad batsman. Secondary properties just sit there: a red tomato is a red fruit and a red object just bought at the grocer's. (Wiggins notices this asymmetry after the passage quoted.)

Of course, the extent to which these constitute disanalogies can be debated. But perhaps by way of illustrating their strength in the moral case, we can notice that sometimes they will not present such a clear picture. For example it is very doubtful whether they apply with equal force to the perception of physical *beauty*. For at least (a), (c), (e) and (f) can be queried in this case. And this in turn connects with the sense we can have that sometimes the beauty of a thing needs perception, and cannot be told. Whereas when it cannot be told how good something was, this is always because some other fact about it resists communication — how happy we were, or how brave we needed to be. So unlike John Mackie I incline to find the projective nature of morality much better motivated than the projective theory applied to aesthetic evaluation. But applied to ethics the cumulative effect of these considerations seems to me to be great enough for it to appear a severe error of philosophical taste to expect a theory of moralizing to look very much like a theory of secondary quality perception. Nevertheless we cannot depend entirely upon this cumulative effect. For it will be retorted that mention of secondary qualities just provided an illustration of a combination, a shape of theory, which can also apply to ethics, however different the subject matter is in other respects. This is the combination or shape of theory illustrated by (1) − (3). So the disqualification of secondary properties wins one battle, but it does not by itself win the war against a 'perceptual' direction.

I will now try to show that once they are properly distanced from other perceptual analogues, (1) − (3) provide no theory of ethics at all, let alone one capable of standing up against projectivism. The first thing to realize is that there is nothing to prevent a projectivist *talking of* the perception of moral properties, of the world containing obligations, and so on. We talk of the perception of every single category of thing and fact which we ever communicate. We talk of perception of numerical truths, truths about the future, truths about the past, possibilities, other minds, theoretical entities of all kinds. We talk of perception whenever we think of ourselves as properly indicating the truth: in other words, whenever we feel able to say that 'if it hadn't been the case that p I would not be committed to p'. But this is not the end of epistemology, but its beginning, for the theorist's job is to reflect upon our right to hold such conditionals. Merely reporting that we hold them is not doing this. Now in the ethical case, the projectivist, protected again by quasi-realism, has a story to tell about this: he can explain why people who are satisfied that their moral sensibilities are functioning well express themselves in this way. But genuine cases of perception standardly demand stories with different ingredients. 'If it hadn't been the case that the shape was square, I would not have believed that it was' can be said because we are causally affected by shapes and can use those effects to deliver verdicts on them. 'If it hadn't been red, I would not have believed that it was' can be said because I know enough of my normality in relation to other people to know that only when a thing disposes most people, in good light conditions, to say that it is red, do I say that it is red. And of course I can be wrong about that on an occasion of bad light or bad brain state or whatever.

The important point is that talking of moral perception by itself provides no theory whatsoever of such conditionals. It provides only a misleading sense of security that somewhere there is such a theory. The theory is not causal, as in the case of shape, nor can it be a matter of conformity with a community, for that just misplaces moral reality, which is not created by community consensus, as (c) reminds us. So what is it? It just doesn't exist. But this means that the invitation to explore the perceptual direction has simply petered out. It is as if someone thought that they could seriously provide a theory of mathematical truth which based itself on the idea that we perceive that $7 + 5 = 12$, and then simply turned its back on the disanalogies between such knowledge and ordinary sense perception. It is obvious that until the question of the status of these conditionals, and our right to believe them, is prosecuted nothing has been said, or at any rate nothing that cannot be tacked on to the end of any genuinely successful account of arithmetic. Similarly with ethics.

The nub of the matter, then, is that the projectivist provides explanation, making moralizing an intelligible human activity with its own explanation and its own propriety, and the opposition provides none, but gestures at an evidently lame analogy. In his paper in this volume John McDowell counters both by claiming that the explanatory pretensions of projectivism are 'spurious', and by mounting an opposition case for being able to do something better. I take this last claim first. In effect it uses the 'interest-relative' nature of explanation to cite contexts in which proper explanations of various verdicts can be given by citing supposedly projected states of affairs. 'Why did I find that frightening/funny/appalling?' It can satisfy the interest behind such questions to answer 'Because it *merited* fright/mirth/horror'. 'Why do we find human happiness good?' 'Because it *is* good'. Citing the supposedly projected state of affairs here plays a part in an explanation, and one which in certain contexts can meet the need behind the question.

This is true, but by itself it is quite inert. Compare: 'why do we say that the cube root of 1728 is 12?' 'Because it *is* 12'. At least if the motive behind the question is fear that this is an anomalous, surprising thing for us to say, then the answer can allay it: we are, as it were, only running true to form in such a verdict. We are not in the grip of strange or local arithmetical error. This provides an explanation relative to an interest in whether the thing that we say shows us making a mistake: the reply says that it does not. Similarly in the first cases: a suspicion that there is something odd about, say, finding the dark frightening, can be allayed by saying that it is what you would expect, that darkness merits fear. But of course allowing all this goes no way to disallowing another, wider, explanatory interest which these answers quite fail to engage. This questioner may be asking why we find something frightening because he finds any such reaction puzzling: why do human beings ever feel fear, or get as far as supposing that anything merits fear? No doubt there is an answer to hand: one which talks of the behavioural consequences of the emotion, and their evolutionary advantages to creatures which have it. In a similar vein we try to place the activity of moralizing, or the reaction of finding things funny, or the practice of arithmetic. In particular we try to fit our commitments in these areas into a metaphysical understanding of the kinds of fact the world contains: a metaphysical view which can be properly hostile to an unanalysed and *sui generis* area of moral or humorous or mathematical facts. And relative to this interest, answers which merely cite the truth of various such verdicts are quite beside the point. This, again, is because there is no theory connecting these truths to devices whereby we know about them — in other words, no way of protecting our right to the conditionals I identified.

Could it be held that this explanatory interest is somehow unjustified: that explanations of a certain type cannot be had, or that the desire for them is the desire for an illusory, 'external' viewpoint outside of all human standpoints and perspectives? This is the justification for not having or wanting to have an explanatory theory along my lines at all. There are two reasons to resist this 'quietist' idea (again, I hesitate to attribute it directly, because the opponents to projectivism that I have mentioned tend to ride both the perceptual, explanatory line, and the suggestion that we need no line at all, in uncomfortable tandem). The first reason for rejecting it is that we know that it is a common human option to moralize about more or fewer things in greater or lesser strengths. The scope of morality can wax and wane, and this makes it urgent to find an explanation of the practice which goes some way to defining its *proper* scope. Secondly, there can never be an *a priori* right to claim that our activity in making judgments X permits of no explanation (except the gesture which says that we perceive X-type states of affairs). You just have to try the various explanations out. And of course it is particularly perverse to say that any explanatory attempt in a direction must fail when many appear to have succeeded well (I myself think that there is precious little surprising left about morality: its meta-theory seems to me to be pretty well exhaustively understood. The difficulty is enabling people to appreciate it). Could it be said that although these wider explanatory interests are legitimate, they mark a boundary between the philosopher and the natural scientist? The evolutionary explanation of the emotion of fear is not only empirical, but marks a recognizable divide between any enterprise of understanding fear as we all feel it and know it, and understanding it discursively, in terms of its origins or function. Can the philosopher rest with the phenomenology, and dismiss the rest as sociology, psychology, or someone else's science? The trouble then is that the philosopher gets to say nothing: Hobbes and Hume and Mackie become classified as natural scientists, and the only philosophical activity left is playing variations on the theme of everything being what it is and not another thing. The philosophical spade becomes by definition the one that is turned on the first shove.

IV

There is one final question I would like to raise, but not to settle. So far I have discussed the metaphysics as if it were exclusively a second-order issue, with no necessary consequences for first-order moral theory. But we saw in part II that when Mackie characterizes the mistake which according to my kind of projectivism need not be made, he found it natural to describe it by using a deontological moral vocabulary. And it is, I think, not a mistake to expect that a projective theory will consort with consequentialist first-order views. Since those views are generally downgraded today it will be important to get that connection a little bit further into focus, lest projectivism gets damned by association.

It should be said at the outset that there is no essential connection between projectivism and a consequentialist view in ethics. It could be that all human beings found it natural to feel certain sentiments, which gain expression as approval, when faced with some features of action, although those features have no consequences which explain the approval. This would be parallel to the way in which certain gestures or timings of actions are hugely funny, although for no apparent reason. If we had this kind of propensity, then it would not alter the metaphysics — it would not in itself make a realistic theory easier to define properly, or more likely to be true. But we would say that those features are good (or right, or whatever) and perhaps we would be unable to envisage admirable moralities which did not do so: we would have a deontological ethics. As a metaphysical view, projectivism explains what we are doing when we moralize. It does not follow that it can explain, or be asked to explain, all the features of the particular way we moralize. First-order quirks would be as mysterious to a Humean as they are to anyone else. Nevertheless. it is natural to associate projectivism with consequentialist moralities, in the following way. A projectivist is unlikely to take the moral sentiments as simply given. He will fill out the story by attempting an explanation of the practice of moralizing. This turns to its function, and particularly to its social function. In Mackie's terms, morality is an invention which is successful because it enables things to go well amongst people with a natural inheritance of needs and desires which they must together fulfil. Moral thought becomes a practice with a purpose. Saying this goes beyond the metaphysical view, as I have tried to explain, but it is a natural addendum to it. And if it is right, there must at least be a limit to the extent to which moral thought can oppose consequentialist, teleological reasoning. It will be unclear how wholeheartedly a moralist who understands this second-order theory can endorse deontological views which stand in the way of all human purpose or fulfilment. Perhaps this is part of the trouble with Fred and Mabel. Perhaps Fred has a psychology which motivates him one way, when his and Mabel's happiness would be found another way. So should he not regard this as an encumbrance: isn't he the victim of an upbringing, and should he not see his particular psychology as a defect, whether or not he can effectively work to change it?

This is another version of the problem of part II, except that this time it is the peculiarly deontological cast of mind which is threatened. But Fred need not regard himself as a victim, so long as he can endorse the general policy of producing human beings whose motivational states are like his. What we really have is a 'motive consequentialism' – a grown-up brother of rule-utilitarianism.[11] The motivations people obey are good in proportion as the consequences of people being like that (and knowing that other people are like that) are good.[12] Actions are then judged either in the light of the motivations that prompted them, or in the different dimension of their actual effects in the world, depending on the purposes for which we are judging them. But the position does not collapse into ordinary act-consequentialism, because for well-known reasons one would expect a society of people motivated solely by consequentialist considerations to do pretty badly. Nor need any such position share the other prominent feature of utilitarianism which causes dislike: the idea that all values are ultimately commensurable. The features of human life which we value, and which would be drawn into any remotely plausible sketch of human flourishing, very probably represent a bundle of ultimately incommensurable goods, amongst which there is no systematic way of making choices. In any case, there is ample room for a projectivist to respect the reasons which make this seem plausible. His explanatory project can start from the heterogeneity of ways in which life can flourish, or fail. On the whole, then, I regard the alliance with consequentialism as a strength rather than anything else – to put it another way, it is only an alliance with the best features of that direction in ethical thought. Of course, there may be features of some people's moralities which even this diluted motive-consequentialism cannot well explain, and these it will regret. But I hope I have said enough to show that none of them could possibly count as integral to moral thought itself.

20

NOTES

1   Unless otherwise stated page references are to *Ethics: Inventing Right and Wrong* (Penguin, 1977).

2   'Truth realism and the regulation of theory', in *Midwest Studies in Philosophy, vol. V (Epistemology)*, ed. French, Uehling and Wettstein; 'Rule following and moral realism', in *Wittgenstein: To Follow a Rule*, ed. Holtzman and Leich (Routledge & Kegan Paul, 1981); and chapter 6 of *Spreading The Word* (Oxford University Press, 1984).

3   p. 34.

4   See for instance the first paragraph of John McDowell's careful continuation of the realist-projectivist issue, in this volume.

5   *The Miracle of Theism* (Oxford University Press, 1982) p. 104, 115 ff.

6   Mackie mentions this kind of psychology on p. 24.

7   'Truth, invention and the meaning of life', British Academy Lecture (Oxford University Press, 1976).

8   Compare Evans on the unintelligibility of one way of thinking of colours as real ('Things without the mind' in *Philosophical Subjects*, ed. Z. van Straaten (Oxford University Press, 1980)). I want to maintain that any genuinely anti-projective attempt to think of obligations or values as 'real' is either similarly unintelligible, or marks a mistake about explanation. This is why I would deny that there is an aspect of moral *phenomenology* which gives morality an objective appearance which quasi-realism must regard as illusory (as McDowell claims in note 4 to his paper in this volume). For there is nothing in the appearances of morality to force us to make the mistake about explanation. Obligations and so forth appear in exactly the way I would predict.

9   Wiggins, 'Truth, invention and the meaning of life', op. cit.; T. Nagel, 'Subjective and objective', in *Mortal Questions* (Cambridge University Press, 1979); J. McDowell, 'Are moral requirements hypothetical imperatives?' (*Proceedings of the Aristotelian Society Supplementary Volume* 1978) and in this volume; H. Putnam, *Reason, Truth and History* (Cambridge University Press, 1981).

10   I stressed this in 'Rule following and moral realism'. McGinn concentrates upon the point in *The Subjective View* (Oxford University Press, 1983), p. 150.

11   And, fairly clearly, the one that Hume endorsed. Talking of motives is better than talking of rules (rule-utilitarianism can be charged with 'rule worship' when it tries to give the verdict to a rule rather than to utility in a hard case. But what charge is there of motive worship?), and as explained in the text, consequentialism is not subject to at least some of the main objections to utilitarianism.

12   Rule-utilitarianism is falsely supposed to collapse into act-utilitarianism partly through neglecting this qualification. (e.g.

B. Williams, *Utilitarianism For and Against* (Cambridge University Press, 1973), p. 118 ff). I am contesting what Williams calls the 'act-adequacy premise'. The consequences of a rule being embedded in a society go well beyond the consequences of definite commissions or omissions for which the rule is responsible. There is also the consequence of mutual knowledge that the rule is likely to order action. To illustrate the effect of this consider a rule that promises that dead people should be respected. The main part of the good such a rule does lies not in any surplus utility of acts performed in accordance with it, but in the dignity with which one can approach old age or death in a society where it is known that people have such respect. This value resides not in acts, but in states of mind for which respect for the rule is responsible.

II

MORALITY, ACTION AND OUTCOME

Philippa Foot

No decision is more important for practical ethics than that by which we come to embrace or reject utilitarianism. For although non-utilitarian principles are apparently deeply embedded in our ordinary morality, theoretical justification often seems hard to find; and some common intuitions are in danger of being disregarded on theoretical grounds. I want to consider two of these intuitions, and to defend them. The first is that there is a morally relevant distinction between what we do and what we allow to happen, and the second that there is a similarly relevant distinction between what we aim at and what we foresee as the result of what we do. I believe it is rather generally thought that the moral relevance of these distinctions is impossible to maintain. I shall, however, deny this, arguing that both differences are defensibly as well as widely recognised in the moral judgments we ordinarily make.

Let us consider first of all the distinction between 'doing' and 'allowing', the moral judgments which seem to depend upon it, and the nature of the distinction itself. It is implied, it seems, in many decisions about what it is right to do, e.g. in cases dealt with in medical ethics. So, for instance, if some medical resource is in short supply and it would be possible to deploy it either to save a number of patients or to save one, then the policy would be to save as many as possible. It does not follow, however, that any and every decision could rightly be taken which resulted in the same net saving of lives. For although it might be called a regrettable moral necessity that a smaller group should be left to die while a larger group was saved, the same could not be said in the case that the few were to be killed. It is not respectably believed that medical experimentation is justifiable so long as the benefit to some

23

outweighs the cost to others; nor do those doctors whose patients will die without organ transplants think that they should secretly kill one healthy person if his body could save several. And while it might be right to leave one injured person to die by the road if hurrying to the rescue of several, it would be outrageous to drive over a recumbent person in order to reach them in time. It seems, therefore, that the 'negative duty' of non-interference is stronger than the 'positive duty' of assistance.[1] The same distinction between 'doing' and 'allowing' appears again when we think of what someone is obligated to sacrifice, on the one hand to avoid being the agent of some mischief to another and on the other to prevent or remedy the same evil when it is in no way due to him. We are inclined to think that no one is required to bring financial ruin on himself in order to give funds to Oxfam, but to export poisonous food even to stave off ruin is clearly another thing.

So much is implied in our ordinary moral judgments; but it is not easy to see just what principle is at work. Is the operative difference the difference between act and omission, between what someone does and what he refrains from doing? Obviously this cannot be it. For then it would be possible to change the moral character of certain trains of events by such simple expedients as building respirators which needed to be turned on each day. The difference between act and omission is in fact irrelevant to any moral issue except in so far as it corresponds to the distinction between allowing something to happen and being the agent to whom the happening can be ascribed. The difference we should have in mind is roughly this: in the case of *allowing*, a train of events must already have started or be on the horizon; an agent who could stop or prevent it does not do so, and therefore allows it to go on. In the other case it is he who *initiates* a sequence, as for instance by shooting someone who dies of the shotgun wound, or by pushing into the water someone who then drowns.[2] No one who has worked on these questions in vexed areas such as medical ethics can think that the distinction between allowing something to happen and being its agent is simple or clear-cut, if only because what goes on in the world is not neatly divided into differentiated sequences.[3] Nevertheless it is from the moral point of view a different thing to start up a new train of events in someone else's life and to refuse to intervene to stop one. This may strike us again if we think about objections to paternalistic action. For while it is not normally permissible to seize an object from a man because he will harm himself with it, it does not follow that there is an obligation to help him to keep such a thing if it is falling out of his reach.[4]

It seems, then, that the moral character of an action is on occasion affected by the position of the agent in the causal nexus: by the fact that he is on the one hand the initiating agent of a sequence or happening, or by contrast merely one who does not intervene. But whether someone's role in a train of events is permissive or initiatory is something that makes no difference to its outcome. The good or harm for which the action is a necessary or sufficient, or necessary and sufficient, condition may be the same in either case. And therefore utilitarians, who place the whole moral significance of an action in its production of good or harm, must treat the difference between initiating and allowing as having no independent influence on morality.

So much, for the moment, about the first of the principles mentioned in the opening paragraph of the present piece as being inconsistent with utilitarianism. Let us now consider the second; namely the one that allows a moral distinction between what the agent 'directly intends', that is what he aims at either as means or end, and what he 'indirectly intends' in foreseeing it as a consequence of his action. The moral relevance of this distinction has often been challenged.[5] I think, however, that it must be allowed. To be sure it often makes no difference to the injustice of an action whether an injury which it causes is something the agent aims at or is something he foresees but has not made the object of his will. A merchant who sold food he knew to be poisonous in order to make money would be morally no better than an unemployed grave digger who deliberately killed to get trade. Nevertheless there are circumstances in which it is morally permissible to bring something about *without* aiming at it although it would not be morally permissible to aim at it; even though the balance of benefit and harm in the consequences remained the same. That this is so is proved, I think, by some facts about the permissibility of allowing an evil to come on some for the sake of saving others. For sometimes this is a regrettable moral necessity, as in our previous examples having to do with scarce medical resources and with the person lying injured by the roadside. But it does not follow that it would be morally unobjectionable deliberately to leave someone unattended because his death would allow us to save others. We said earlier that it would be objectionable to kill even for such a good purpose, and now we must add that it would also be wrong to serve that same purpose by deliberately allowing someone to die.[6]

There is, moreover, a very interesting and significant extension to the principle that bans direct intention in certain cases where indirect intention would be permissible. For it seems that what matters morally is not only how someone *acts*, which is what we have so far been considering, but also how his will is disposed even when this cannot affect the course of events. To see this one has only to think of a case in which someone is a spectator rather than a participant in a complex of circumstances where several lives might be saved through one man's death. For then one sees that while it is wrong to aim at the death of one in order to save others, and wrong of course to go along with the doing of this action by somebody else, it is also morally objectionable to be glad, as a spectator, if it is done; or indeed if such a thing comes to pass without human agency. No doubt some will deny this conclusion about the mere spectator's wishes; but simpler examples from more familiar surroundings might make them think again. For would it not be objectionable if, in a hospital where patients were dying for lack of a transplant, the death of someone in the hospital with several transplantable organs was automatically treated as good news?

It follows from what has been said in the last two paragraphs that the recognition of a moral distinction between allowing and initiating evil is not able by itself to take care of all our non-utilitarian moral intuitions. But would the other principle, the one telling us that indirect intention may be permissible where direct intention is not, be enough on its own to do all the work that needs to be done? It is perhaps tempting to think so, but would nevertheless be wrong. For although many cases of the initiation of harm are also cases of direct intention the example of the wicked merchants shows that it is not always so. Moreover when the evil is merely foreseen and so not directly intended the morality of the action of which it is an effect may vary according to whether the agent is or is not the originator of that effect. So, although we may have to allow an individual to die because we must use the scarce medical resources for others it would nevertheless be impermissible to manufacture a curative substance for the same number at the cost of sending fumes to poison one. It seems, therefore, that we need both the principles discussed in preceding paragraphs, and may of course need others as well, in order to bring moral theory into line with our ordinary moral thoughts.

There is, I think, no way of amending utilitarianism which will cure the discrepancies we have noticed. They will remain so long as the moral character of an action, motive, or any other subject of moral judgment is taken wholly to depend on its causal relation to the general welfare: whether welfare is conceived as pleasure, happiness, or preferential choice; whether maximum welfare is taken as an average or a sum

26

total; and whether it is supposed to be distributed more or less equally. It is another question, however, whether the trouble is endemic to welfare utilitarianism in particular or whether it rather belongs to consequentialist theories as a whole. Might the situation be remedied if some other form of consequentialism replaced utilitarianism? What if, for instance, the violation of rights should be recognised as one element in the goodness or badness of states of affairs; the general idea being that the moral character of an action should depend, as in utilitarian philosophies, on their outcome – on the goodness or badness of states of affairs in which they play a causal, or a constitutive, role – but that the judgment of these states of affairs should no longer be directed solely to welfare? By this amendment it would become possible to count any violation of rights as itself contributing an element of badness to the total outcome of an action, and in principle in this 'goal rights system' such badness could be supposed to outweigh any good the action might produce. Such a provision would take care of many of our recalcitrant examples because they do in fact have to do with the violation of rights.[7]

This interesting attempt to remain within the boundaries of outcome morality while throwing off the shackles of welfare utilitarianism has the great advantage of giving rights a more basic role than they can have within the latter theory. The theory fails, however, to accord with common morality in the verdict it implies in a special range of cases having to do with the causal interaction of one agent with another. Suppose, for instance, that you threaten (reliably) to kill or torture several people if I do not kill or torture one. Then it may be that by doing one of these actions I can lessen the total number done; and it would follow in such a theory that whatever weight of badness is given to this kind of action it could be my duty to do it.[8] We can therefore see that no amendment of utilitarianism which retains its consequentialism can get away from the following implication: that there is nothing so bad that it cannot be done to prevent others from doing more things of the same kind. Consequentialist systems have this implication because in basing moral judgment solely on the evaluation of states of affairs they allow of no distinction between what an agent does himself and what he allows others to do. Each contributes its quota of goodness or badness to the total, along with other elements such as happiness or pain.

So within a consequentialist system even of the goal rights kind a violation of rights such as murdering or torturing will be justifiable if the alternative is more murdering or torturing; and it follows that any powerful and ruthless person can make it right, can even make it our duty, to do these things, by threatening to do more of them himself. Some people may think that it would indeed be our duty to give in to him if *enough* were at stake; but if they are consistent consequentialists they must believe the more obviously bizarre proposition that any net balance of 'goodness' over 'badness' in the total outcome would do.

So far as I know the only way to meet this objection from common morality while staying within anything that could possibly be called a consequentialist system is to introduce 'agent-relativity' into the evaluation of states of affairs. By this expedient each agent would be enabled to value his own performance of an action differently from its performance by others; so that each could think it a worse total outcome when *he* killed or tortured than when someone else did, other elements of the situation always remaining the same. Amartya Sen has suggested this as a viable account of the matter.[9] But it seems to me that it is implausible. For it is not true that one thinks that a given act is worse when done by oneself than when done by another, unless of course there is some relevant difference between us, as when only one of us is a doctor or a parent or a friend. It is after all generally agreed that an action done by one individual is not, except in such cases, morally different from the same action as done by someone else. I do not refuse to kill or torture to prevent others from killing or torturing because I think that killing or torturing is, in the ordinary sense, worse when I do it than when they do. So what is it that one is supposed to think about one's own action as opposed to that of others? Sen speaks of 'evaluating' differently the states of affairs of which each is a part, suggesting as an illustration that if Othello and another gave a moral evaluation of the state of affairs in which Othello had murdered Desdemona the murderer himself would think it morally worse.[10] And he also uses the idea of an agent-relative moral judgment to explain, e.g., why someone with moral objections to a certain kind of work might refuse to do it himself though he felt no obligation to influence others similarly placed. The agent is supposed to think that it is *worse* if he takes the job than if someone else does, even when their situations do not relevantly differ.[11] It is to be morally worse from his point of view. But it is hard to know what this means. Sen suggests a comparison with an aesthetic proposition to the effect that an object is beautiful (he must surely mean 'looks beautiful') from a certain position.[12] But the comparison will not go through. Anything which is, visually, beautiful is so because it looks beautiful. This implies that it looks beautiful from some distances and from some angles but not that it must look beautiful from all; and the question therefore arises of whether it looks beautiful (or of how beautiful it looks) from some particular place. But it would be impossible even to start to give a similar explanation of moral badness *from an agent's point of view* because there is nothing that stands to being morally right or wrong as looking beautiful from certain positions stands to being beautiful. I believe therefore that Sen has failed to explain a concept which is central to his attempt to reconcile consequentialism with our moral intuitions.

It seems, then, to go back to the main line of the argument, that it is impossible to believe in utilitarianism or any other form of consequentialism and at the same time to hold on to more or less well entrenched moral ,opinions. And this naturally raises the question: why believe in those theories? Why do they seem to be plausible? Why in particular does utilitarianism seem to be so in spite of the difficulties it creates for practical morality? Different people no doubt have their own reasons for believing in utilitarianism, and some think that they have proof of its truth. But many more appear to embrace the theory because they are convinced that utilitarian morality is the only *rational* morality, and we should ask about the cause of this conviction. It lies, I think, first of all in the fact that utilitarians insist that moral goodness must somehow be connected with what is good to and for human beings. But it also lies in the utilitarian, or basically consequentialist, idea that it must always be right for an agent to bring about *the best state of affairs* that is within his reach. And it is this last thought that makes the theory discordant with our ordinary moral intuitions. For the question raised is why any action should not be done if the doing of it will produce the best state of affairs or total outcome; and it is exactly this which tends to make us think that it must be morally permissible, or even obligatory, to do to individuals anything that 'needs to be done for the general good'. How can it be right, we ask ourselves, to choose to produce a state of affairs less good or worse than another that is equally within our reach? If this state of affairs is the best state of affairs then we ought to produce it. To be sure we are not always able to do what would bring about what is *in other contexts* referred to as the best state of affairs, but that is because there may be restraints on our actions coming e.g. from law, morality, or etiquette. When it is a question of bringing about the 'morally best state of affairs' there can be no such restrictions because only moral restraints could operate against morality, and only an irrational moral rule could stand against the production of the morally best state of affairs.

It is such thoughts that tend to make utilitarianism seem uniquely rational and therefore irresistible. Those who hold out against it usually argue that it is not always right to produce, or try to produce, the best state of affairs; but naturally find it hard to see how indeed it can be right to prefer a worse over a better state of affairs. What does not occur to them is that with the posing of the question, which they thought to be on neutral territory, they are already deep within utilitarianism itself. This is what I shall now try to show.

Let me begin this part of the discussion by making some observations about the peculiar and problematic character of judgments about good states of affairs when construed as they are apt to be construed by both sides in this debate. For of what form are they supposed to be? Clearly 'state of affairs' is not a description like 'game' or 'holiday' or 'committee meeting' giving the possibility of what Peter Geach has called an attributive judgment of goodness of the ordinary 'good F', 'good G' form.[13] But nor, again, does the description 'a good state of affairs' refer to *a* good like pleasure, or health, or affection, or understanding. So where do propositions about good states of affairs belong in the language? And in particular how do they get the connection which they are supposed to have with human choice? In the case of the two other types of judgments the relationship, although complex, is usually in principle fairly clear. Good Fs and good Gs may in certain cases (such as good roots and good claws) have no particular connection with the human will; but where a connection does exist it is not magical, nor merely linguistic, but depends upon the way in which those in some standard position are interested in choosing that type of person, role, or thing. And for the case of *a* good the conceptual connection with choice or reasons for choice though hard to explain, and still very much of a philosophical problem, obviously exists. For the reason for calling pleasure and health and affection and understanding *goods* is clearly something to do with the fact that they are goods *to* or *for* people; and thus give these people a reason to seek them out.

How is it then with good states of affairs? We often speak of them in everyday life — such locutions are not the invention of philosophers — and nothing then seems clearer than the fact that we have reason to try to produce the states of affairs we call good and avoid the ones we call bad. But is not the explanation of this that in these pieces of everyday, non-philosophical, usage we use expressions such as 'a good state of affairs' and 'a good thing' as a way of saying how things fit in with our interests and with things we are interested in? And of course this makes these particular usages quite unsuitable as a pattern for the way in which the expressions might function in moral contexts, where a more impersonal reference would be required.[14] I do not know why these *impersonal* uses of 'good state of affairs' and likewise 'good thing' and 'It is good that . . .' are supposed to be unproblematic. It seems to me that there is every reason for being suspicious of them as they are talked about in philosophy, where it is supposed that judgments of this form, though having no original connection with anything that a particular agent sees as *a* good, or with any object of his interest or desire, are nevertheless held to compel, persuade, or at least give him reason for choice.

Let us consider, then, what use there can be in moral contexts for expressions such as 'a good thing' and 'a good state of affairs'. There seems to be no doubt that kindly people agreeing with each other in their attitudes will take for granted that certain occurrences — such as natural disasters for instance — produce 'a bad state of affairs'; and among those who accept morality a certain modicum of kindness will be assumed. It will also be taken for granted that the avoidance of suffering is among the ends which can determine what it is right to do. This must be so given any morality in which benevolence is recognised as a virtue; and a further end is implied by the acceptance of a morality in which the virtue of justice is held to include fighting against injustice as well as performing just acts. We find these ends, and perhaps others, deeply embedded in our morality, and for this reason there is a special way of talking about states of affairs as good and bad, particularly when a moral issue is actually being discussed. In such contexts, unlike those of which we spoke earlier, there is implicit reference to ends belonging to moral persons as moral persons, rather than to idiosyncratic or personal aims.

It is not, therefore, to be denied that there is a special way of talking about good and bad states of affairs in what we might broadly call moral contexts. But this in itself does not mean that we are back with the old puzzle about how it can be right *not* to do anything and everything which will be for most people's good. For it is one thing to think that morality dictates an end such as the happiness of others, and even directs us, on occasions, towards doing as much good as we can, and quite another to think that any action is morally permissible if directed

31

to this end. For what we have said so far does not give any reason why the pursuit of the end should not be restricted by moral rules forbidding e.g. certain kinds of interference with individuals even for the sake of the general good. The fact that benevolence is a virtue giving persons who possess the virtue certain ends does indeed determine a special use of expressions such as 'a good state of affairs' in moral contexts. (And as already mentioned the virtue of justice can also play its part.) But there is nothing in the virtue of benevolence licensing us to say that it is 'a good thing' when a benefit comes to many through injustice to a few. So benevolence gives us no reason to say, for instance, that it would be a 'good state of affairs' or 'good total outcome' if the sacrificing of a few experimental subjects allowed us to get cancer under control. The operation of benevolence is circumscribed by justice, and even the end which the virtue prescribes is qualified, in that we are not told to be glad that good should come to some when it comes through evil to others.

The fact that benevolence is a virtue, and a virtue which dictates attachment to the good of others, does not, then, give morality a universal end or goal; and the same is true of other parts of morality which have to do with what must be aimed at or desired. Thus the moral requirement to fight injustice does not imply that one must, or may, fight it by any means. And if there is a separate requirement having to do with the promotion of good action in others (which perhaps there is), this too can be circumscribed. So if, at this point, we return to consider the morality of doing some apparently bad action such as torturing, or killing innocent people, to stop someone else doing more acts of the same kind, and think that it *must* be right to do it, we can see where we have gone wrong. For whether we think of the moral objection to such actions in terms of suffering inflicted, injustice, or immorality, we have no reason to suppose that our sole moral duty is to minimise it. We are not even mandated to minimise immorality. For moral injunctions can be like orders which say not 'See to it that there is less shouting' (which might be obeyed *by* shouting) but rather 'don't shout'. There is thus nothing puzzling about the fact that many moral directives give rules for an agent's own conduct and tell him nothing about what he is to do about influencing the actions of others. In so far as one *is* required to see that other people behave well these requirements come from other parts of morality and have no priority over moral rules.

The argument of the last few paragraphs has suggested that the use of the notion of a good state of affairs is very limited in moral contexts.

This restriction may, however, be disputed, on the ground that any *reasonable* recognition of rules in morality must allow that they may sometimes be broken, and must therefore deploy the notion of better and worse states of affairs in deciding when that may be. This has recently been argued by Amartya Sen who insists that any theory which allows deontological restraints to be overridden in certain circumstances must collapse into a form of consequentialism, because if it is determined that a constraint may be overriden in specified circumstances (as e.g. a right violated when it will save lives) then the badness of the violation is being weighed against that of non-violation.

> For example, it can be specified that if the badness of the state of affairs resulting from obeying the constraint exceeds some 'threshhold', then the constraint may be overridden. Such a threshold-based 'constraint' system must rest ultimately on consequential analysis, comparing one set of consequences (badness resulting from obeying the constraint) with another (badness of violating the constraint itself, given by the threshold), and its distinguishing feature will be the particular *form* of the consequence-evaluation function.[15]

This is an interesting argument, but I think it is mistaken. To meet Sen on his own ground I shall assume that moral rules can indeed be broken on occasions, which is certainly true of some even if not of all. So why do we say that in *these* circumstances *this* rule but not *that* one could be broken, or that *this* rule could be broken in *these* circumstances but not in *those*? Sen supposes that we make the decision by estimating the goodness and badness in the total outcomes of the alternative choices. But this seems to me to be either vacuous or wrong. If it merely says that our decision may be put in terms of 'better' and 'worse' ('It is better to do without a cure for cancer than to perform this experiment') it is vacuous. But if it says something about the *way* in which the decision is arrived at it is dubious. For what entitles Sen to assume that this is how we judge rightness, i.e. by comparing total outcomes; when what is, or should be, at issue is the concept of a *good total outcome* as intended here?

It seems, then, that we can accept the idea that we talk in special ways in moral contexts about good and bad states of affairs without implying anything that could make the existence of non-utilitarian principles problematic. Some virtues do indeed give us aims, but nothing from within morality suggests the kind of *good state of affairs* which it would seem always to be our duty to promote. And why indeed should there be any such thing?

It will be helpful here to consider a parallel between the case of morality and the case of etiquette. Why is it, we may ask, that we do not have good and bad states of affairs from the point of view of etiquette? The notion seems incomprehensible. But why is it so? It is so because a good state of affairs from the point of view of etiquette would be one which from the point of view of etiquette it must be right to aim at or produce. But in fact there can be no state of affairs which stands in this position because even if there are aims prescribed by etiquette (as e.g. avoiding causing social embarrassment), etiquette is also a matter of following rules, and the rules circumscribe the manner in which the aims may be followed. So what of morality? A morally good state of affairs would, it seems, be a state of affairs which morally right or good action must aim at or produce. But since what is morally good or right is what a good moral system calls good or right there can *be* a state of affairs which stands in this position only if a good moral system contains no radically non-utilitarian rules. So if a good moral system does indeed contain rules of the kind we have been discussing then there cannot be a good state of affairs in the sense which consequentialism requires. There is, as we saw, a limited use for the concept *within* morality; but a virtue such as benevolence does not give an end to which all moral action must aspire.

So far, then, the argument has tended to resist the encroachment of any form of consequentialism on the 'mixed' aim-and-rule morality that we actually seem to have. But nothing has yet been said of the rationale of this partly deontological system. If we do in fact recognise virtues such as justice which consist mainly in adherence to rules of conduct, as well as those like benevolence which we might call virtues of attachment, why do we do so? Will utilitarianism not re-establish itself when it comes to defending the morality we have?

This is an important line of thought: it is responsible for the faith of many utilitarians, and the answer to it goes to the heart of the debate. So let us see why it is that a non-utilitarian morality might be thought to need a utilitarian defence. The idea is, I think that a morality can be shown to be a good morality only by being shown to *do better* than its rivals; that is to work better or produce a better state of affairs. And this generates the old problem about individual actions which do not, because of exceptional circumstances, have the usual effect. For then violation (perhaps secret violation) of the code could produce a better state of affairs than obedience, and it will seem irrational to insist on adherence nevertheless.

The crucial assumption in this argument is the one that links the goodness of a moral system to a prior goodness in states of affairs. For states of affairs are things that can be brought about or influenced by actions, and this is why we have only to suppose strange causal circumstances to get a violating action producing 'the best state of affairs'. The question we should ask is, therefore, why this criterion of goodness should be assumed for a moral system. Perhaps some think that there just *are* good states of affairs and that this is a fact which can hardly be ignored in moral judgment, but I hope that the argument in the early part of this paper has helped to make this seem more problematic. Others believe that *the moral point of view* relates to the unique purpose of maximising welfare, and try to prove it, but it is significant that the general line of argument outlined above seems irresistible to many who are not actually satisfied by any such proof, and therefore have no warrant such as Hare and Harsanyi believe themselves to have for operating with the idea of states of affairs which are good from the moral point of view.[16] But is it then so obvious that the criterion of goodness in a moral system must lie in its relation to a state of affairs that is judged to be good? Perhaps it will seem obvious so long as no alternative comes to mind. But of course there are alternatives which make a clean break with the idea of morally criterial 'good states of affairs'.

To see that this is true we have only to look at the way in which Rawls, for instance, sees the distinction between a good moral system and a bad one. For in his moral philosophy any good moral system is necessarily a fair one, and a fair system one which operates on principles which would be chosen by rational agents in the original position. Thus a good moral system will be one that has a certain characteristic which is not a causal property, and there need be no place in this theory for an original judgment about good states of affairs.[17] The same is true of Scanlon's more thoroughgoing contractarianism, under which a moral rule's justification depends on its acceptability (a rather complex kind of acceptability) by, or on behalf of, every individual whatever his position in the world.[18]

It is not necessary to commit oneself to either system to see in outline how a justification might be produced for the two principles of non-utilitarian morality discussed earlier in the present paper. Suppose for instance that we simply start from the rough idea that a good moral system must be one that could use a demand for reciprocity to urge conformity on any individual; and that the necessity that it produce benefit to him should be linked to this condition if to no other.[19] Then it would be intelligible that the more a morality rendered benefits from which each and every person stood to gain, the more acceptable, and so far forth the better, the system would be. And of course there are such benefits from the existence of a morality which refuses to sanction the automatic sacrifice of the one for the good of many because it secures to each individual a kind of moral space, a space which others are not *allowed* to invade. Nor is it impossible to see the rationale of the principle that one man should not want evil, serious evil, to come on another even to spare more people the same loss; it seems to define a kind of solidarity between human beings, as if there is some sense in which no one is to *come out against* one of his fellow men.[20] In both cases the good of the rule is a good that comes from having the system. But the justification is not, as with rules that limit the direct pursuit of the general good in rule utilitarian systems, that those who accept them will be most likely actually to bring about the best result. For if this were it the supposition of exceptional circumstances would give cases in which the agent would be obliged to break the rule.

What I am suggesting is that the concept of 'the best state of affairs' should disappear from moral theory, though not, as explained earlier, from all talk in moral contexts. If this would allow some of the insights of rule utilitarians to be validated, so much the better. But the starting point would be so different that the results would be unlikely to be the same. It has been suggested here that one criterion for a good moral system is that it should be possible to demand reciprocity from every individual because of the good the system renders to him. But I am sure that this is not the only condition for a good moral system. It has also, for instance, to be such that *anyone* can conform to it and still live well in the ordinary, non-moral, sense.[21] This condition may well be what limits the demands of altruistic action, and a whole new non-utilitarian enquiry should open up here.

ACKNOWLEDGMENT

I want to thank Warren Quinn and David Sachs who have helped me by criticising a draft of this essay.

NOTES

1 I have discussed this idea more fully in 'The problem of abortion. and the doctrine of the double effect', *Oxford Review*, no. 5, 1967. Reprinted in Philippa Foot, *Virtues and Vices* (Blackwell, 1978).

2 In some cases the agent will not start a sequence but rather keep it going when it would otherwise have come to an end. Then he initiates a new stage of the sequence rather than the sequence itself.

3 One interesting complication is that diverting a harmful sequence from one victim to another seems not to be viewed in the same way as starting one up. A pilot whose plane is going to crash should steer from a more to a less inhabited area, and the principle apparently holds even in case it should be certain that someone will die. It does not follow, however, that one could, as it were, start a flood to stop a fire.

4 Cp. Foot, 'Killing, letting die, and euthanasia: a reply to Holly Smith Goldman', *Analysis*, vol. 41, no. 4 (June 1981).

5 See, e.g., H. L. A. Hart, 'Intention and Punishment', *Oxford Review*, no. 4, Hilary 1967. Reprinted in Hart, *Punishment and Responsibility* (Oxford, 1968).

6 In 'The problem of abortion and the doctrine of the double effect' I argued (wrongly as I now think) that the distinction between direct and indirect intention was irrelevant to moral judgment. Not surprisingly I was then in difficulties about the wrongness of deliberately allowing a beggar to die in order to use his body for medical research.

7 Amartya Sen discusses goal rights systems in his excellent article 'Rights and agency', *Philosophy and Public Affairs*, vol. 11, no. 1. It would also, I suppose, be possible to recognise other non-welfarist values within a theory of this general type, saying for instance that there is more badness in the direct than in the indirect intention of harm.

8 Samuel Scheffler has an interesting discussion of this kind of case in *The Rejection of Consequentialism* (Oxford, 1982), especially chapter IV.

9 Op. cit., sections VI and VII.

10 Ib., pp. 29–30.

11 Ib., pp. 24–6 and 32.

12 Ib., pp. 35–6.

13 Peter Geach, 'Good and evil', *Analysis*, vol. 17, no. 2 (December 1956).

14 I have discussed this topic at more length in 'Utilitarianism and the virtues'; Presidential address to the American Philosophical Association, Pacific Division, 1983. *Proceedings and Addresses of the A.P.A*, vol. 57, no. 2, (November 1983).

15 Op. cit., pp. 6–7, note 8.

16 See R. M. Hare, *Moral Thinking* (Oxford, 1981) and John C. Harsanyi, 'Morality and the theory of rational behaviour', *Social Research*, Winter 1977, vol. 44, no. 4. Reprinted in Amartya Sen and Bernard Williams (eds), *Utilitarianism and Beyond* (Cambridge, 1982). Hare's position has been criticised, to my mind effectively, by Thomas Nagel in *The London Review of Books*, 1–15 July 1982.

17 John Rawls, *A Theory of Justice* (Harvard, 1971).

18 T. M. Scanlon, 'Contractualism and utilitarianism', in Sen and Williams, op. cit, pp. 103–28. I find this a bold and very suggestive piece.

19 Cp. Scanlon, op. cit., pp. 118–19.

20 Perhaps it is this idea that is partly responsible for the peculiar outrage that we feel about torture.

   The principle must obviously be qualified to take care of the case of guilty men. Yet witnesses to judicial executions have reported a primitive reaction of horror at the fact that *no one went to help* the man in the electric chair, as if it was impossible really to believe that the assembled company *wanted* him to die.

21 Nietzsche's suggestion that some men's lives are necessarily deformed by obedience to morality is not, I think, one that we could see as leaving morality intact.

III

ONTOLOGY IN ETHICS

R. M. Hare

There is a long-standing dispute between two main types of ethical theory, which, nevertheless, is not always stated in the same terms. It is the purpose of this paper to ask whether it matters in what terms we formulate it. I shall argue that one way of posing the issue has advantages over the others, if we want to get to the root of the matter. This is because all the others pose it in terms which, for want of clarity and other reasons, leave it undecidable unless in the end we have recourse to the preferred way.

Here is a list of the formulations that I shall be considering, with, in brackets, indications of the type of distinction that each purports to be.

(1) Realism vs. anti-realism (ontological)
(2) Moral judgments as expressing beliefs vs. moral judgments as expressing attitudes (psychological)
(3) Cognitivism vs. non-cognitivism (epistemological)
(4) Descriptivism vs. non-descriptivism (logical or conceptual)

In his splendidly invigorating book *Ethics: Inventing Right and Wrong*, John Mackie opted on the whole for the first way of stating the issue, though he did not favour the *words* 'realism' and 'anti-realism', preferring such names for his own theory as 'subjectivism' and 'scepticism'. This choice of words is perhaps to be regretted; for 'subjectivism' has many different meanings between which people will go on being confused in spite of Mackie's ample explanation; and a 'sceptic' is hardly what he was, since, like Hume, he allowed plenty of room in his theory for the holding of moral opinions, and certainly had strong ones himself, which guided his conduct more firmly than those of many of us. He explains his use of 'scepticism' too; but it is hardly the usual one. However that may be, he undoubtedly thought of the main issue as ontological. He says, 'What I have called scepticism is an ontological thesis, not a linguistic or conceptual one' (p. 18)*; and he would surely have insisted that it was not an epistemological nor a psychological nor a logical one either, though it might have close relations with such theses.

It is to be noted that it is not necessary to take the same side in all formulations of the dispute, as might be thought by one who was confused by the use of the muddling words 'objectivist' and 'subjectivist' to label the two sides regardless of the different formulations. To take different sides can, however, in view of the close relation between the formulations, lead to difficulties. Mackie himself illustrates this. He adheres to the left-hand side of the fourth formulation, although he has adhered to the right-hand side of the first; he is, that is to say, a descriptivist but an anti-realist. 'If second order ethics were confined, then, to linguistic and conceptual analysis, it ought to conclude that moral values at least are objective; that they are so is part of what our ordinary moral statements mean; the traditional moral concepts of the ordinary man as well as of the main line of western philosophers are concepts of objective value' (p. 35). The fact that Mackie takes different sides on these two formulations is in fact the root of his 'error theory'; for he has attempted to saddle the ordinary man with moral concepts such that nothing said in terms of them could possibly be true if anti-realism were correct.

The ontological way of posing the issue is now the most popular, and is also the most primitive. It goes back to Plato at least, and has recently come back strongly into fashion after a period of neglect, so that many people now use the expressions 'realist' and 'anti-realist' as if it were perfectly plain what they mean (which is far from being the case). This is in conformity with a similar recent trend in philosophical logic generally, where the words are now much used. I shall not be so bold as to express any opinions about their use in other fields such as the philosophy of mathematics, although I suspect that it has caused trouble there too. The trouble it has caused in ethics is enough for one paper.

What then does 'ethical realism' mean? On the face of it, it means the view that moral qualities such as wrongness, and likewise moral facts such as the fact that an act was wrong, exist *in rerum natura*, so that, if one says that a certain act was wrong, one is saying that there

*All page references are to the first edition of titles.

existed, somehow, somewhere, this quality of wrongness, and that it had to exist *there* if *that* act were to be wrong. And one is saying that there also existed, somewhere, somehow, the fact that the act was wrong, which was brought into being by the person who did the wrong act (or should we say that the fact that the act *would* be wrong *if* he did it existed even before he did it?)

It is easy and perhaps even legitimate to caricature ethical realism in this way; for it is not clear what else the term could mean. But we are not much the wiser. First of all, there is a quite general problem about the existence of qualities and facts of all kinds. The word 'exist' is, admittedly, notoriously treacherous. There are said to be both different senses of the word, and different kinds or levels or even orders of existence or being. We have to distinguish at least two ways in which we can speak of senses of 'exist' or kinds of existence. One of them need not detain us for long. For a cow to exist is obviously not the same as for a horse to exist; but this is merely because a cow is a different sort of thing from a horse. We do not need, in order to account for this difference, to distinguish between senses of 'exist' or kinds of existence (see W. V. Quine, *From a Logical Point of View*, pp. 2ff.). It is possible to extend this move in order to deal with kinds of things that differ from one another much more than cows and horses do. So, if one philosopher claims that numbers exist in a different sense from cows, or that the existence of numbers is a different kind or order of existence from that of cows, another philosopher may well reply that no distinct senses or orders are required; it is simply that numbers are different from cows.

However, even if we agree with this second philosopher, there remains a way in which we can usefully distinguish between senses of 'exist'. (1) In one of these senses it is all right (e.g.) to say 'The quality of redness exists', if we can *meaningfully* say of something that it is red. (2) In another, somewhat stronger, sense, it is all right to say that it exists, if we can *truly* say of something that it is red. (3) There is also a sense of 'exists', not the same as either of these, in which it is all right to speak of something existing, if it can be *referred to*. This is so (to speak roughly) if an expression referring to it can occur in the subject-place in a true, or even a false, statement. This sense does not for our purposes need to be distinguished from a closely related sense in which it is all right to speak of things of some kind existing if variables which range over things of that kind can be quantified over in true affirmative existential statements, or even in false ones. Thus the Queen of England exists if we can say something true or even false about her, and the King of France does not exist because we cannot; and cows exist because we can begin true statements or false ones with the words 'Some cows'. In this sense, the property redness exists because we can say 'Redness is a colour-property', and properties exist because we can say 'Some properties are not instantiated'. This is obviously a very weak sense. It would take a hardened anti-realist to say that wrongness does not exist in this sense; for we can certainly refer to wrongness, as when we say 'The wrongness of Smith's act is such that he ought not to be allowed to profit from it'.

It is to be noticed that all these three senses of 'exist' (which we might call formal senses) have been defined in terms of what we can or cannot rightly say — which means, here, what the logical rules governing the words or concepts allow us to say. This in itself ought to give the ontologist pause. For it may turn out that the problem of whether wrongness exists is after all a conceptual one — a problem in philo-sophical logic not metaphysics. Or it may turn out that *all* ontological problems are really conceptual ones, and that metaphysics is not to be distinguished from philosophical logic. Without entering into this old general question, I will merely express the hope that in ethics it might turn out that this is so — that is, that when we are discussing so-called ontological questions in ethics, we are really discussing the same questions as can also be put in conceptual or logical terms; and then it would have to be asked which were the most perspicuous terms to put them in. That indeed is the question I wish to pose in this paper.

But it is not clear that any of these formal senses of 'exist' is being used when the ethical realist claims that wrongness exists *in rerum natura*, or the anti-realist denies this. At the beginning of his book, Mackie uses, not this expression, but the phrase 'part of the fabric of the world' (p.15, cf. p.21). I am sorry to say that he gets this expression from me, but from a passage in which I explicitly say that I cannot attach a sense to it in this context ('"Nothing Matters"', in my *Applications of Moral Philosophy*, p.47). It raises all the same questions. It is probable that most anti-realists, perhaps including Mackie, would not mind saying that wrongness exists in one of these formal senses, and would wish to deny it existence only in some more 'material' sense. Reverting to the two philosophers mentioned above, it might be that the anti-realist is like the first of them: he thinks that, even if wrong-ness exists in *some* sense, it exists in a different sense from cows. A realist follower of the second philosopher might reply that it exists in the same sense, but is a different sort of thing from cows.

But if this is what they say, there is really no reason why they should quarrel. There would be a substantial dispute between them if the realist were claiming that wrongness was like cows, tangible and spatially located; or, to use the alternative formulation in terms of existence, that wrongness exists in the way that cows exist, by being encounterable. But he is not claiming either of these things. He may be claiming that we might somewhere encounter someone doing a wrong act; but the anti-realist, unless, unlike Mackie (p. 16), he is also an amoralist who refuses to make the moral judgment that any act is wrong, will not deny that.

In other words, if expressions like '*in rerum natura*' and 'part of the fabric of the world' are taken in a strong sense which lets cows in but keeps numbers out, the realist can admit that wrongness is not *that* sort of thing, or does not exist in *that* sense. But if these expressions are being used in some weaker sense which lets numbers in as well as cows, then I can see no reason why the anti-realist should not admit that in *that* sense wrongness exists, at any rate provided that he admits that some acts are wrong (cf. sense (2) above), or that he at least admits that it makes sense to say that they are (cf. sense (1) above), or that one can say something about wrongness, putting the word in the subject-place (cf. sense (3) above).

It might be objected that in defining senses (2) and (3) above, I made essential use of the notion of truth. For redness to exist (sense (2)) we had to be able to say *truly* of something that it was red; and for redness to exist (sense (3)) 'redness' had to admit of being a subject-term in a true or false statement. So, it might be claimed, wrongness will not exist on either of these definitions if statements containing the words 'wrong' and 'wrongness' cannot be true or false; and they cannot be true or false if the notion of truth does not apply to them. So an anti-realist could insist that wrongness did not exist in either of these two senses, because the statements in question cannot be either true or false. He might add, in view of the close connection between the notion of truth and that of meaning, that in that case it would not exist in sense (1) either.

This objection, however, is not to the point when we are discussing, as we now are, whether there is an *ontological* issue of substance between the realist and the anti-realist. For even if the question whether moral judgments can be called true or false is a fundamental question in ethics (as some think it is), it is not an ontological but a conceptual question. It is not a question about the existence or non-existence of anything. So, if the realists and the anti-realists were to claim that the issue between them is a serious one because it hangs on the answer to this serious conceptual question, they would be admitting that the issue is not really ontological but conceptual. They might as well give up calling themselves realists and anti-realists, and start calling themselves descriptivists and non-descriptivists instead. This is what I shall in fact be proposing, though I do not think that the most perspicuous way of stating the issue between the descriptivists and the non-descriptivists is by asking whether moral judgments can be true or false (on this, see my Lindley Lecture 'Some confusions about subjectivity', in *Freedom and Morality*, ed. J. Bricke).

To sum up so far: it is unlikely that the formal senses of 'exist' are going to be of any use in setting up an ontological dispute between the realist and the anti-realist, because the latter can agree that in those senses moral qualities exist; but nor is the supposed stronger 'material' sense, because in that sense the realist would be unwise to claim that they exist, and does not need to.

It is now time to turn briefly to the other possible formulation of realism, that which insists on the existence of moral facts. The dispute is likely to collapse in the same way as before. Consider again the three formal senses of 'exist'. There seems to be no sense of 'exist' analogous to sense (1) above in which facts can be said to exist, because we do not establish the existence of facts, as we do of properties in this sense of 'exist', by making meaningful statements, but only by making true ones (or by its being the case that they could be made). In a sense analogous to sense (2), the fact that an act was wrong can be said to exist, if someone can truly say that that act was wrong. In a sense analogous to sense (3), the fact that an act was wrong exists, if the fact can be referred to by putting, e.g., 'the fact that it was wrong' into the subject-place in a true or false statement.

But the realists and the anti-realists have no reason to fall out over any of this, unless they are really disputing about the conceptual, not ontological, question of whether moral statements can properly be called true or false — in which case they should rename themselves descriptivists and non-descriptivists, as suggested already. By all means let them, if they wish, formulate their dispute as one about whether moral statements are factual or not; but let them recognize that this is not an ontological question but a conceptual one about the logical character, or role in our discourse, of these statements.

As to the question whether moral facts are part of the fabric of the world, or exist *in rerum natura*, that is a question that could be asked about *any* facts, and I shall not go into it. Actually, I agree with those who have argued *contra* the *Tractatus* that 'the world is the totality of things, not of facts' (cf. P. F. Strawson *Supplementary Proceedings of the Aristotelian Society*, 24 (1950), pp. 133 ff.). I do not believe that we encounter facts in the world, spatially located. But since this is a general question in metaphysics, and what we say about it will apply to the fact that there is a cow in the field as well as to the fact that Smith's act was wrong, any dispute about it is not going to divide *ethical* realists and anti-realists in particular. If an ethical anti-realist is against admitting the existence of moral facts because he is against admitting the existence of any facts, his dispute with the realist is not a dispute in ethics. For there to be a dispute in ethics, one side must say that some facts exist, but not moral ones, and the other side must say that both sorts exist. In that case, the dispute is disposed of by what I have said already.

So far we have been talking about the property of wrongness, and the fact that an act was wrong, in just the same terms as the property of redness, and the fact that a thing is red. Everything that I have said about one of these pairs of expressions could be said about the other. Now it is time to ask whether there are things we should say about moral properties and facts which we should not say about 'ordinary' properties and facts. There is an old move, and an old answer to it, which used to be current in moral philosophy. The move has been revived; and perhaps the answer should be too. It is not my present business, however, to decide whether the answer is effective, but only to point out, what is fairly obvious, that neither the move nor the answer to it is ontological, both being epistemological or conceptual.

It is tempting, and initially useful, to compare moral qualities with what, following Locke, have been called 'secondary' qualities. Redness, which I have been using as an example, is one of these. The move is to claim that all the reasons given by anti-realists for singling out moral qualities as special in some way can equally be given for singling out secondary qualities as special in the same way. Thus, if the wrongness of an act is said to be the 'product' of an attitude on the part of the person who thinks it wrong, so also the redness of a thing can be said to be a 'product' of the visual reactions of a perceiver. In neither case, of course, is it the product solely of the attitude or reaction; in both, the primary or the non-moral qualities of the act or thing are partly involved. In both cases, on this view, the wrongness or the redness can be said to be the joint product of properties of the object or act (which are themselves not identical with the quality of wrongness or of redness) and of reactions in the perceiving or thinking subject.

The usefulness of this move to a realist is thought to be the following. If the anti-realist claims that so-called moral 'qualities' are nothing but reactions in an observer or thinker produced by the non-moral properties of an act, in conjunction with his prior dispositions or attitudes, the same can be said of all secondary qualities. So the distinction which the anti-realist is trying to make between moral properties and qualities like redness disappears.

The answer to this move has two parts. The first is to point out that, on this interpretation of what they are saying, both parties are misconceiving the issue between them in a common but by now inexcusable way. They are both speaking as if the anti-realist were advocating an 'old-fashioned' subjectivism of a kind which Mackie rightly disavows (p. 17). This is the consequence of talk about moral qualities being the 'products' (in part) of attitudes, dispositions or reactions of a thinking subject. Many people, because they have not even begun to understand the issue, seem unable to conceive that the anti-realist could mean anything else but this; but there is no reason why we should follow them. They only think this because they have not rid themselves of the prejudice that everything we say of anything has to be the ascription of some sort of descriptive property to it: if not an 'objective' quality of the thing, then a 'subjective' property consisting in some relation the thing stands in to a subject (e.g. that of arousing an attitude in him). This is an old and tedious mistake, which it was the achievement of the early non-descriptivists to expose; when we say something moral, we do not have to be ascribing any kind of property, subjective or objective.

It is worth while pointing out, in this connection, that realists who make this move are in acute danger of falling into a most implausible type of relativism. For if they treat wrongness as fully analogous to redness, the statement that an act is wrong will be refutable by showing that it is not called wrong by people, conversant with the language, who view it under normal conditions. This is what we do with the statement that a thing is red. In the latter case, there is no room for anything as an explanation of deviance, except either a mistake about the meaning of a word or a fault in observation. If 'wrong' were treated in the same way, we should be able to squash a person who said it was wrong to eat meat by pointing out that everybody else, all those conversant with the use of the word, see nothing wrong in it even when fully informed about the character of the act. So the vegetarian will have to accept that he either is morally colour-blind or does not know English. The only way to get our moral judgments right is to say what others who speak our language say in the same circumstances.

This brings us to the second part of the answer to the realist's move. Even if there is an analogy between moral qualities and secondary qualities, those who press the analogy will fall into this kind of relativism unless they notice that there is also an important difference. The reactions which, according to this sort of phenomenalist view of morality, 'produce' the moral quality are attitudes such as approval and disapproval. But these, unlike the perception of something as red, are subject to our reasoned choices. We can ask, and rationally answer, the question 'What attitude shall I take up to meat-eating?'. There is nothing corresponding to this in the case of redness. This fact is reflected in another, that to call an act wrong is to condemn it, and thus to engage our wills and those of any who agree with us in antagonism to the act.

The difference between moral and 'ordinary' properties lies not in any supposed difference in what 'produces' them, but in the different kinds of semantic or linguistic conventions which determine when we can ascribe them. The ascription of redness, for example, is governed by conventions which do not allow two people, faced with the same object in the same light in normal circumstances, to say, one of them that it is red and the other that it is not. One of them must be in breach of the conventions. He is in breach of them even if his mistake is due to colour-blindness. But the ascription of wrongness is governed by conventions which do allow you and me, confronted by the same act in normal and identical circumstances, to go on saying, one of us that it is wrong and the other that it is not wrong, if that is what we respectively think. We can reason about it in the hope that one will convince the other; but neither of us is constrained by our observation of the facts of the case and the correct use of words.

But we have now got right away from the supposedly ontological question which allegedly divided the realist and the anti-realist, and on to questions about language and the conventions for the ascription of properties. It is not my purpose in this paper to settle these questions by coming down on one side or the other in any of the issues (realist/ anti-realist, cognitivist/non-cognitivist, etc.) that I have listed, although

47

it is well known what side I in fact support. I aim only to indicate which of these formulations best locates the main issue and gives us some hope of understanding it. I have said enough, perhaps, to show that the ontological way of putting the issue, which is associated with the names 'realist' and 'anti-realist', is *not* the best way of putting it. As soon as we start discussing the question in any penetrating way, it collapses into questions of a non-ontological sort. We cannot understand what on earth the parties to the ontological dispute are claiming until we restate the issue in terms which are not ontological.

In the light of what I have said, it appears that we do not need to worry about whether moral facts or moral qualities exist. Doubtless they exist in some of the senses I have listed, but not in others. At least, they are not part of the fabric of the world, and do not exist *in rerum natura*, if those terms are used in the strict sense that they certainly are by Mackie. I have heard realists agree that they do not: 'Of course,' they say, 'moral properties are not physical properties and moral facts are not physical facts; but all the same they are real properties and facts'. An anti-realist, on his part, can easily agree that they exist in some of the other senses, or even exist *in rerum natura*, if that term is taken more liberally. That is not the way to get to the bottom of the problem.

What should concern us, rather, is how we should rationally determine, or satisfy ourselves, whether an act is wrong. People become realists, and insist that the quality of wrongness has to be part of the fabric of the world, because they think that, unless this is so, there will be no way of rationally deciding such questions. But are they right to think this? They think it, only because they are the victims of a prejudice which is almost universal among moral philosophers.

The prejudice is one about rationality. It is thought that only procedures leading to the making of statements can be rational. Hume summed up this prejudice in his famous remark that

> Reason is the discovery of truth or falsehood. Truth or falsehood
> consists in an agreement or disagreement either to the *real* relations
> of ideas, or to *real* existence and matter of fact. Whatever, therefore,
> is not susceptible of this agreement or disagreement, is incapable
> of being true or false, and can never be an object of our reason
> (*Treatise*, III, 1, i).

Mackie, in this as in so much else, seems to have been a follower of Hume. That this is a mere prejudice should be apparent to anybody who reflects that we can rationally decide what to do, or what to ask or

advise others to do. In other words, thought-processes which have as
their end-products prescriptions can be rational (or irrational). There
will be factual elements in the reasoning (i.e. rationality demands
cognizance of the facts – see my *Moral Thinking*, esp. p. 88); but even
given this cognizance, whether the whole process is rational or irrational,
or whether the conclusion is rationally or irrationally arrived at, does
not depend solely on the rationality of the fact-finding part of the
process. What Hume calls 'the relations of ideas' have to be rationally
ordered too, and these ideas will include some prescriptive ones. Indeed,
they must, if the conclusion is to be prescriptive. It is thus entirely
possible to arrive rationally at a moral conclusion even though that conclusion is not a statement of fact about what is the case *in rerum natura*.
Ethical rationalism does not, therefore, demand ethical realism.

If this is once understood, we are free from the need to engage in
ontology of any sort in order to do ethics. The ontological issue has
dissolved into an epistemological or logical one: how to give an account
of moral thinking which allows it to arrive in a rational way at conclusions which are practical and prescriptive. We can admit that there
exist moral qualities and facts in some of the senses listed above, but
see that this is beside the main point. A philosopher who affirms that
they exist has done absolutely nothing to solve the main problem,
namely how we determine that they exist in a particular case – in
plainer words, how to determine, for example, that an act *is* wrong.

I started by listing various ways in which the distinction between
types of ethical theory could be put. Of these, we can perhaps
now leave behind the terms 'realism' and 'anti-realism', as concealing
the main issue. We are left with the distinctions in psychological
terms (beliefs/attitudes), in epistemological terms (cognitivism/non-
cognitivism) and in logical or conceptual terms (descriptivism/non-
descriptivism).

The psychological way of putting the distinction can perhaps be set
aside fairly rapidly. This is because the beliefs and attitudes in question
will share the property of intentionality which all mental states have.
It will be impossible to characterize them fully and perspicuously without introducing a proposition or 'that'-clause which gives the content of
the mental state. For example, it is commonly and rightly held that to
describe a desire we have to characterize it as the desire *that* such and
such a thing should happen. This is obviously so with moral beliefs or
attitudes. Whether we speak of the belief that an act would be wrong,
or of an attitude of disapproval of the proposed act, we have, in order

to characterize the mental state in question (say what in particular the person who is in it is thinking, or what is going on in his mind) to say that he is thinking *that* the act would be wrong.

Thus the full explanation of these psychological states demands a logical or conceptual or linguistic explanation of the words in which what he is thinking would be expressed if it were expressed, or of what he would be saying if he said that the act would be wrong. This can be illustrated by the controversies between the early emotivists and their opponents. Suppose that an emotivist (Professor Ayer for example in *Language, Truth and Logic*) were to say that 'It would be wrong' is to be analysed as an expression of disapproval of the act. And suppose that an opponent protested that at least this sentence has the grammatical form of an indicative and therefore must express a belief. This will not serve to refute the emotivist or even put him off his stride. In order to determine the issue between those who say that this grammar is only superficial and those who maintain that it truly represents the logical character of the judgment, we shall have to engage in conceptual study, and only when that is complete shall we know whether, when the man said it, he was expressing a belief or an attitude. The psychological way of putting the distinction, therefore, will always for its full explanation require the logical or conceptual.

I wish to say in passing that in my own view the grammar is *not* superficial, but that those who rely on it for an argument are. There are descriptive elements deeply embedded in moral statements, along with the prescriptive, and they need a full account of what Stevenson called the descriptive meaning of the statements to explain them. An initial dogmatic insistence that the statements are descriptive in form gets in the way of this necessary explanation, whose upshot is that moral statements are a hybrid, sharing some of the characteristics both of pure descriptions and of pure prescriptions. All this I have treated of elsewhere; and it needs to be understood if we are justly to assess Mackie's view that people making moral judgments claim to be 'pointing to something objectively prescriptive' (p. 35; see my *Moral Thinking*, pp. 78 ff.).

If, then, the psychological way of putting the distinction, like the ontological, collapses into the logical or conceptual, we are left with the epistemological and logical-conceptual ways as the only remaining possibilities. I shall now argue that the epistemological in turn collapses into the logical-conceptual, and that for clarity we should cease to speak of cognitivism and non-cognitivism and use instead the terms 'descriptivism' and 'non-descriptivism'. The reason for this is that a solution to the epistemological problem of how we can determine rationally whether an act would be wrong depends on a solution to the logical or conceptual problem of what we are saying when we say that it would be wrong. One does not have to be an old-fashioned verificationist, nor even (which is different) hold a purely truth-condition theory of meaning, to be sure that the logical character of an utterance, and the rules which govern our reasoning about it, are closely linked. If it is by reasoning that we determine whether we should accept what has been said, the epistemological question of how we determine this must be inseparable from the logical question of what we are saying and its implication-relations with other things we might say. This could be denied only by a very extreme intuitionist who thought that we needed no reasoning, no rational thinking, to determine the moral character of acts, but just saw intuitively that they were right or wrong. But even he would have taken a stand on the logical character of moral judgments, assimilating them to judgments of perception immune to thought. The issue between him and a rationalist would still be a logical one.

There is, however, a danger to be guarded against here, signalled by the reference in the last paragraph to the verification and truth-condition theories of meaning. It is right to say, as I have, that the logical character, even the meaning, of moral statements is closely tied to ways of reasoning about them. But it is wrong to say that their meaning, in conjunction with the non-moral facts, determines their truth or falsity. The ways of reasoning which their logical character imposes on us do not consist simply in comparing a moral statement with the non-moral facts and then pronouncing it true or false in accordance with truth-conditions or verification-rules. To think this is to be a descriptivist. A prescriptivist like myself will think that we have first to understand the statement (its logic and conceptual character as well as its content), and thus the forms of thought which are appropriate to determining whether to accept it, and then do some thinking in accordance with these forms of thought. They may require much more than a bare comparison with the non-moral facts. I have tried to explain elsewhere what they do require (*Moral Thinking*, chapters 5, 6).

My conclusion is that, for any penetrating thinker, both ontological and psychological questions about ethics are bound to give place to a combination of logical and epistemological questions intimately related to one another. The reason why I much prefer the term 'descriptivism' to the term 'cognitivism', and somewhat dislike being called a non-cognitivist, is that this term would seem to imply that I recognize no rational procedure for deciding moral questions. It depends on how much one reads into the word 'cognitive'. For many psychologists, belief counts as a cognitive state. The psychological argument, just set aside, between those who call moral convictions beliefs and those who call them attitudes was superficial, not only for the reason given (intentionality), but because one could very well call them beliefs and yet maintain that they were radically different from ordinary factual beliefs. The same trouble will infect the word 'cognitive' if a belief is to count as a cognitive state. Even an emotivist might hold that in this wide sense of 'cognitive' moral attitudes were cognitive states. But in a narrower sense of 'cognitive', in which a mental state is not cognitive unless it consists in *knowing* something, an emotivist could not be a cognitivist, for he denies that there can be knowledge of moral truths.

My own position is that we can certainly speak of knowing that an act is wrong, just as we can speak of someone saying truly that someone did something wrong. But I would immediately add that this is because such utterances have in most societies a fairly firm descriptive meaning attached to them, so that we know at once what non-moral properties would be accepted as substantiating the claim that an act was wrong, and can therefore, when we know that an act would have these properties, readily say that we know that it would be wrong and that it is true that it would be wrong. But to recognize this should not lead us to ignore the much more important question of how we are to decide whether society is right to give the word this particular descriptive meaning, thereby selecting certain kinds of act and not others for condemnation.

It is this latter question (how to decide) which should engage us. It is an epistemological question − a question in the theory of knowledge in a wide sense of 'knowledge'; not a question of how to find out facts, but one of how to determine questions (in this case prescriptive questions) rationally. If to think that they can be determined rationally is to have an epistemology or theory of knowledge, then one who thinks this, as I do, should perhaps be labelled a cognitivist. But I do not recommend the label, because those who are unable to envisage any other kind of reasoning than factual will think that if I am a cognitivist I must be a descriptivist, which I am not.

In conclusion, I should like to defend briefly my use, here and above, of expressions such as 'logical and conceptual'. I belong to the school of thought which holds that to study the logical properties of words and to study concepts are the same study. Formal logic, on this view, is the formalization of the rules governing words (especially but not only the so-called 'logical' words) which partly determine the meanings of those words (determine it wholly if they are purely logical words like 'all'). I would wish to maintain that 'ought' and 'wrong' are in this way purely logical words, being natural-language versions of deontic-logical signs. But a lot of this could be given up, without abandoning the essential point, that to understand what someone who has made a moral statement was saying we have to understand what he was implying, what would be consistent or inconsistent with what he said, and the like. In this field at least, logical and conceptual analysis are inseparable, and that is why I have not tried to separate them.

It was John Mackie's great contribution to ethics to display clearly the absurdity of realism. But because he put his argument in ontological dress he prevented himself from going on from this achievement to an account of the rational defence of moral convictions to which he was certainly, and deeply, committed. Because he took what seems to me a mistaken descriptivist view of the logical character of the moral words in ordinary speech, he was left saying that ordinary people, whenever they use these words, are in error (which is implausible); and he was not able to turn his valuable account of how we think morally into a convincing elucidation of moral rationality. He first said that moral judgments are all false, and then told us how to decide which moral judgments we should accept. This seems self-defeating. If he had not mistaken conceptual confusion for factual error, he might have gone on to say more clearly than he did how to get our moral thinking right.

ACKNOWLEDGMENTS

I am grateful to Professor J. J. C. Smart, who saw this paper only just before I had to send it off, for saving me from a number of mistakes, though he still dissents from some things that I say. John Mackie's criticisms of my own published views are to be found in *Utility and Rights*, ed. R. G. Frey, with a reply by me, and I also discuss his views at some length in *Moral Thinking*, pp. 78–86.

IV
OBJECTIVITY AND DISAGREEMENT

S. L. Hurley

In his lucid and influential book, *Ethics: Inventing Right and Wrong*, John Mackie appealed to the existence of moral disagreement as one of two major sources of support for moral scepticism. The view that disagreement undermines claims to objectivity, however, is not independent of the way in which objectivity is conceived; one of the many salutary effects of Mackie's scepticism has been to stimulate explicit consideration of conceptions of objectivity. A distinctive conception of objectivity is suggested by Wittgenstein's later work and by certain of Davidson's writings. In this essay I shall sketch the way in which a view about practical reason may be in this sense objectivist, and shall go on to challenge the view that disagreement undermines an objectivism conceived along these lines.

Three caveats are in order: First, I shall distinguish a certain conception of objectivity from other conceptions that cut across it and shall try to defend it against arguments from disagreement, but I shall here take the general interest of such an objectivism for granted. I hope elsewhere to develop such an objectivist view more fully. Second, I shall not here offer a systematic exposition or defence of the views of the later Wittgenstein and of Davidson which I invoke. I assume that these views are of sufficient currency, influence and power for the availability of a view about practical reason that develops out of them to be of interest, although it is subject to whatever objections the original views are subject to. What I hope to show is that the view about practical reason is not subject to a further difficulty, special to itself, on the score of disagreement. Third, my development of a view about practical reason out of certain views of the later Wittgenstein and of Davidson is

54

not intended to describe a position that might be attributed to these philosophers.

At least two issues have frequently been treated as bearing on the objectivity of the values that govern action. The first, the issue of *cognitivism*, turns on whether evaluative judgments carry assertoric force or imperatival force, whether they express beliefs about the way things are that may be true or false or express attitudes of some other kind. The second, the issue of *realism*, turns on whether evaluative judgments have explanatory primacy, that is, whether they feature in ideal causal theories of the world,[1] including our uses of evaluative concepts. If causal explanation of the world, including our uses of certain concepts, itself depends on uses of such concepts, then a realistic view is warranted of the properties such concepts refer to; if such concepts do not feature in ideal theories of the world, then realism is not warranted.

The issue of *objectivity*, in the sense I shall be concerned with, cuts across the issues of cognitivism and realism. Though denials of objectivity in this sense are often made in the wake of arguments against cognitivism or realism, when the three issues are distinguished it is not obvious why the success of such arguments should be assumed to support the denial of objectivity. At least *prima facie*, it is possible to maintain the objectivity of claims about what ought to be done while admitting that such claims are logically tied to action, entail imperatives, express attitudes other than belief, and do not employ explanatorily primary concepts.

The possibility of objectivity, in the sense I am concerned with, is closely connected to an issue of logical priority. Issues of logical priority involve alternative accounts of the relationships between two concepts or sets of concepts, which follow from the choice of whether or not to take one as prior to the other. In general, to say that one concept or set of concepts is logically prior to another is to say that the latter is properly accounted for and understood in terms of the former and not *vice versa*; someone could grasp the prior concept without grasping the concept understood in terms of it, but not *vice versa*. To deny a claim of logical priority is to deny that someone could correctly understand one without understanding the other. Someone need not be invariably correct in his applications of a concept in order to be said to understand it, but he does need to be able to use it correctly in some cases. So, a denial of priority involves saying that correct uses of the concepts denied to be posterior are not irrelevant to the question of

55

whether someone understands the concept denied to be prior. And a denial of priority need not involve an assertion of the reverse priority; the two concepts or sets of concepts may be interdependent.

A feature common to many philosophical accounts of ethical concepts is that the general concepts, *right* and *ought*, are taken to be logically prior to and independent of the specific concepts, such as *just* and *unkind*. According to such accounts, the general concepts carry a core meaning, which may be associated with either assertoric or imperatival force, that also provides the specific concepts with reason-giving status, relating, for example, to their tendency to pick out the right thing to do or to provide evidence about the right thing to do. I shall refer to accounts that take the general concepts in some category to be logically prior to and independent of the specific as *centralist*.[2] Non-centralism about reasons for action rejects the view that the general concepts *right* and *ought* are logically prior to and independent of specific reason-giving concepts such as *just* and *unkind*. Instead it may take the identification of discrete specific values such as justice and kindness as a starting point, subject to revision, and give an account of the relationships of interdependence between the general concepts and specific reason-giving concepts. Coherentist views provide examples of non-centralism.[3] According to such a view, to say that a certain act ought to be done is to say that it is favoured by the theory, whichever it may be, that gives the best account of the relationships among the specific values that apply to the alternatives in question; such a view must, at least implicitly, characterise the conditions that must be met by a theory about the relationships among specific values.

Note that a non-centralist coherence account is not a form of reductionism, and that it avoids reductionism while respecting the logical requirement and evaluative concepts supervene on non-evaluative concepts. In fact, such an account provides a natural explanation of the compatibility of supervenience and irreducibility, which some have found puzzling: according to a coherence account to claim that a certain act ought to be done is not to say that it is favoured by any given theory, or to say which theory does the best job of displaying coherence, but rather that the act is favoured by *the theory that best displays coherence*; which theory this is must be discovered *a posteriori*. It is a concomitant of the theoretical status of the general concepts that they supervene on the concepts whose applications provide the subject matter of the theory in question. Theories must supervene on descriptions of what they are theories about; to the extent they fail to do so, they do no explanatory work. If the general concepts express claims about what is required by the best theory about the relationships among specific values in the circumstances at hand, then we should expect the general concepts to supervene on specific evaluative concepts and the concepts needed to describe the circumstances in which they apply. If in turn specific evaluative concepts supervene on (or perhaps reduce to as well — I need not take a position on the issue of reductionism for specific values) non-evaluative concepts, then we should expect the general concepts to supervene on non-evaluative concepts. Supervenience is the mark of the theoretical. But since the appeal to theory does nothing in itself to answer the question of which theory is in fact the best theory, a requirement of supervenience whose source is an appeal to theory has no need of reductionist (or non-cognitivist[4]) underpinning. It is always a further, substantive question which theory is the best theory, and the answer to it is no part of the sense of a concept that merely appeals to the best theory, whichever that may be.

To make the point more formally, by means of a scope distinction: A coherentist holds that when we say that a particular alternative would be right, it is part of what we mean that there is some theory which is the best theory about the specific values that apply to the alternatives at hand and that this theory favours a particular alternative. This claim must be distinguished from the stronger, reductionist claim that there is some theory which is the best theory about the specific values that apply to the alternatives at hand and such that, when we say that a particular alternative would be right, it is part of what we mean that it is favoured by this theory. The former claim preserves supervenience without entailing the reductionism of the latter claim by exploiting the distinction between the claim that necessarily there is some theory such that . . . and the claim that there is some theory such that necessarily . . .: in each logically possible world there may be some theory that does the requisite job, while there is no one theory (except, perhaps. a gimmicky disjunctive theory or list of theories, which provides a reduction of little concern) such that in every logically possible world that theory does the requisite job.

For present purposes, we must recognise that one of the attractions of centralism is that it facilitates an account of the criticism of particular ethical standards: the unparadoxical status of 'It may have been rude/unchaste/unpatriotic, but it wasn't wrong' is readily accounted for along such lines if right and wrong are logically independent of specific values. One of the challenges for non-centralism is to frame its account of the logical relationships between specific reason-giving concepts and the general concepts so as to avoid rendering such claims paradoxical. The challenge is met, however, by the coherentist view that right and wrong reflect status under the best theory about the relationships among various values. There is no appearance of contradiction in claims to the effect that some specific value condemns an alternative but that the best theory about the relationships among all the relevant specific values does not.[5]

The crucial difference between centralism and non-centralism, then, is over the priority of the general: whereas the centralist takes the general evaluative concepts to be logically prior to and independent of the specific, and explains the reason-giving status of the specific in terms of the general concepts, the non-centralist rejects this claim of priority and independence and as a result must give an account of the logical relationships between specific reason-giving concepts and the general concepts. In the case of coherentist views in particular, the relationships given by logic are held to be those of subject matter and theory; elsewhere I consider precisely how these relationships should be characterised. But from the denial that the general concepts are prior it doesn't follow that the specific must be prior, any more than it follows that data must be entirely independent of theory because theory is not independent of data. Data may be theory-laden; reflective equilibrium may be wide; the specific and the general concepts may be independent.

In what follows I shall be concerned to make out a point of view from which the priority issue may be seen in Wittgensteinian terms and its resolution in favour of non-centralism seen as a kind of objectivism. While we might compare centralism about reasons for action to several other kinds of centralism, including centralism about colours and legal centralism, for present purposes it will be most helpful to consider logical centralism, Wittgenstein's opposition to it, and the possibility of analogous opposition to centralism about reasons for action.

Logical centralism would take the general concepts of validity and truth-preservingness to be prior to and independent of specific characterisations of calculations and inferences, such as . . . *is a case of modus ponens*. The status of specific characterisations of calculations and inferences as validating them would be understood in terms of the prior general concept, which might, for example, express the community's endorsement, as a matter of convention, of all instances of a certain pattern of thought. Wittgenstein's view that meanings are determined by practices, applied to the logical constants and to mathematical

58

concepts, leads to what Crispin Wright describes as the doctrine of the antecedence of logic and mathematics to truth, which entails the denial of such logical centralism. According to the antecedence doctrine, '. . . there is . . . no content to the idea of something's *really* being a consequence of some set of statements over and above its following from them by *our* procedures of inference'; '. . . there is no ulterior concept of correct inference lurking behind our actual procedures of inference to which they are answerable.'[6] Thus Wittgenstein writes:

> The steps which are not brought in question are logical inferences.
> But the reason why they are not brought in question is not that
> they 'certainly correspond to the truth' — or something of the sort,
> — no, it is just this that is called 'thinking', 'speaking', 'inferring',
> 'arguing'. There is not any question at all here of some correspon-
> dence between what is said and reality; rather is logic *antecedent*
> to any such correspondence; in the same sense, that is, in which the
> establishment of a method of measurement is antecedent to the
> correctness or incorrectness of a statement of length.
>   — "But isn't there a truth corresponding to logical inference?
> Isn't it *true* that this follows from that?" — The proposition: "It is
> true that this follows from that" means simply: this follows from that.
>   . . . 'calculating right' . . . means calculating *like this*.[7]

While the doctrine that logic is antecedent to truth entails the denial of logical centralism, Wittgenstein holds the view that practices determine all meanings, and not only the meanings of logical and mathematical concepts. The view that practices determine meanings admits of no residue or slack in terms of which a practice can be challenged or justified by applications of the very concept whose meaning it determines: 'If you measure a table with a yardstick, are you also measuring the yardstick? If you are measuring the yardstick, then you cannot be measuring the table at the same time.'[8] The question does not arise whether our conceptual scheme, our determination of meanings corresponds to the facts conceived as including not only the objects we talk about but also whatever it is we can truthfully say about them.[9] It does not arise because it is no part of a defensible theory of truth and correspondence that 'meanings take care of themselves'; 'truth conditions are necessarily given by us, in a language that we understand'.[10]

> The words "right" and "wrong" are used when giving instruction in
> proceeding according to a rule. The word "right" makes the pupil go

on, the word "wrong" holds him back. Now could one explain these rules to a pupil by saying instead: "this agrees with the rule — that not"? Well yes, if he has a concept of agreement. But what if this has yet to be formed? (The point is how he reacts to the word "agree".)

One does not learn to obey a rule by first learning the use of the word "agreement".

Rather, one learns the meaning of "agreement" by learning to follow a rule.[11]

It makes no sense to suppose that there is some criterion of using an expression in the same way that is independent of all our particular ways of going on, some standard of meaning the same thing which is external to our practices and which they strive to approach.

In what follows I shall try to explain how a conception of practical reason as objective is connected with resolution of the logical priority issue in a Wittgensteinian spirit, in favour of non-centralism about reasons for action. In doing so I shall be drawing out the implications of the thought that the way in which meaning guides linguistic utterances may fruitfully be regarded as a special case of the way in which reasons guide action more generally. Thus I shall be trying to apply Wittgenstein's considerations about the way in which meanings are determined and their normative relation to linguistic action in particular to the way in which reasons in general are determined and their normative relation to action in general. I shall also pursue the analogy Davidson suggests between the problem of the interdependence of belief and meaning in interpreting linguistic action and the problem of the interdependence of belief and desire in interpreting action in general. And I shall draw connections between the Wittgensteinian and Davidsonian concerns: the conception of objectivity that emerges is represented by a generalised principle of charity; I address the problem that disagreement poses for a Wittgensteinian view of practical reason by interpreting the need for agreement in form of life in terms of the necessary role of charity.

The way in which considerations about meaning and its relation to belief may be applied to questions about desire and its relation to belief is brought out by the following claim: non-cognitivism is not inconsistent with non-centralism. The view that, as a matter of logic, claims about what ought to be done entail imperatives, express attitudes toward action which are preferences rather than beliefs, does not settle the further question, what is the relationship of this whole logical complex (of what ought to be done, preference and action) to specific values. Consider the way in which this claim might be developed.

Michael Dummett has suggested that there is an alternative to the interpretation of Wittgenstein as denying '. . . the idea, common to most philosophers who have written about meaning, that the theory of meaning has some one key concept', '. . . that there is some one feature of a sentence which may be identified as determining its meaning'. The alternative is the less radical view that Wittgenstein does not reject the idea that there is a key concept, but takes '. . . the key concept not to lie, as it were, on the side of the grounds for an utterance, as do the concepts of truth, verification, confirmation, etc., but, rather, on that of its consequences. To know the meaning of a sentence, on such a theory, would be to know what the conventional consequences of uttering it are, both in the sense of the appropriate response, linguistic and non-linguistic, to it by the hearers, and in that of what the speaker commits himself to by uttering it.'[12]

Similarly, the view that reason-giving concepts are unified by their consequences, for example, by the entailment of imperatives, at least under certain conditions, might be urged as an alternative to the rejection of centralism about reasons for action altogether. Of course the view that reason-giving concepts entail imperatives may take a centralist form. It does not have to, though; a non-centralist need not deny that reason-giving concepts entail imperatives which express attitudes toward action. What follows, however, is that the very concept of action that informs expressions of imperatival force is not logically prior to and independent of specific reason-giving concepts.

But this is not a surprising or outlandish view. It amounts to a rejection of the assumption that the concept of intentional action is primitive and unproblematic in a way that, say, linguistic action in particular is not. We must interpret the world in order to see events as intentional action, expressive of preference, no less than we must interpret the world in order to see events as linguistic action, expressive of belief. As Christopher Peacocke writes: 'Preferences as expressed in behaviour yield actions, that is, token events: and these token events, being each one an instance of ever so many types, in advance of a theory of interpretation give no clue as to the type (or indeed believed type) for which the behaviour expresses preference . . . .'[13]

The question then is whether theories of interpretation necessarily import normative considerations. A familiar answer is given by David

61

Lewis, who explains that a principle of charity constrains the relationship between the agent as a physical system (described in terms of bodily movements and the like, not yet in terms of his intentional actions) and the attitudes we ascribe to him: he 'should be represented as believing what he ought to believe, and desiring what he ought to desire. And what is that? In our opinion, he ought to believe what *we* believe, or perhaps what we would have believed in his place; and he ought to desire what we desire, or perhaps what we would have desired in his place. (But that's only our opinion! Yes. Better we should go by an opinion we *don't* hold?)'[14] Thus, the concepts of desire and intentional action, rather like those of meaning, belief and linguistic action and unlike those of bodily motion and brain processes, are normatively constrained concepts; susceptibility to the influence of certain values is a constitutive feature of intentional action, intelligible in terms of the agent's beliefs and desires, in the same sort of way that susceptibility to the influence of truth-related reasons is a constitutive feature of linguistic action, intelligible in terms of the speaker's beliefs and meanings. If this view is correct, we should expect that just as the interpretation of a particular linguistic action as deviant, reflecting an unfamiliar concept or an intention to deceive, is parasitic on charity at large, so interpretation of a particular intentional action as deviant, reflecting an unfamiliar value or an intention to do evil, is parasitic on charity at large.

Such a normative conception of action is supported by considerations Davidson adduces in commenting on Ramsey's proposal about the roles of belief and desire in the interpretation of behaviour. Davidson holds that 'an event is an action if and only if it can be described in a way that makes it intentional.' We interpret an agent's behaviour as action by ascribing beliefs and desires to him in terms of which it may be understood as intentional; happenings that cannot be rendered intelligible in this way do not count as actions. However, the possibility of rendering action intelligible by ascribing beliefs and desires to agents requires that we have some way in principle of sorting out the contribution of beliefs to determining behaviour from the contribution of desires; many possible combinations of beliefs and desires could explain the same behaviour. Holding behaviour constant, we can infer beliefs from desires or desires from beliefs; but since behaviour is 'the resultant of both factors, how can either factor be derived . . . until the other is known?'[15]

Ramsey's proposal is that we can tell that someone believes an event is as likely to happen as not if he does not care whether an attractive or an unattractive outcome is tied to it.[16] For example, his behaviour may reveal his indifference between option 1 and option 2:

	option 1	option 2
If it rains, you get:	$10	nothing
If it doesn't rain, you get:	nothing	$10

Having fixed the agent's belief about the probability of this one event, the theory goes, we can use it to measure his desires, and then fill in his other beliefs.

However, built into Ramsey's proposal that someone believes an event is as likely to happen as not if he is indifferent between option 1 and option 2 is the assumption that the attractiveness of the outcomes used to construct the options does not vary with the occurrence of the event. Consider option 3 and option 4:

	option 3	option 4
If it rains, you get:	an umbrella	no umbrella
If it doesn't rain, you get:	no umbrella	an umbrella

If we assume that an umbrella is more attractive to someone if it rains than if it doesn't, then his indifference between option 3 and option 4 does not suggest that he believes it is as likely to rain as not to rain, but that he believes it is more likely not to rain. This assumption is natural to make, but any behavioural basis for it that doesn't in turn depend on other assumptions about the agent's desires is obscure. (In another case we might interpret on the assumption that winning some reward under circumstances such that one deserved to win would be more attractive than winning under circumstances such that one did not deserve to win.) If we make this assumption, we arrive at a different description of the agent's indifference: it is indifference between a small chance of winning the prize when it would be more needed and a large chance of winning it when it would be less needed, rather than indifference between equal chances of winning it in each of two cases when it would be equally useful. In order to apply Ramsey's method of interpreting behaviour we must already be making assumptions about what is attractive to the agent, namely, that the options we construct to determine his beliefs are like options 1 and 2 and not like options 3 and 4.[17]

Davidson claims that '. . . if we are intelligibly to attribute attitudes and beliefs, or usefully to describe motions as behaviour, then we are committed to finding, in the pattern of behaviour, belief, and desire, a large degree of rationality and consistency.'[18] The nature of the assumptions we must make in order to apply Ramsey's method of ascribing beliefs and desires and hence to entitle ourselves to apply the concept of action to certain happenings warrants a strong interpretation of this claim. We must make assumptions about the substance of the agent's desires as well as their consistency. Such assumptions warrant the claim that the interpretation of action is dependent on a principle of charity that reaches to the substantive rationality of desires as well as to their consistency.[19] In order to conceive of happenings as action, we must make assumptions about the agent's susceptibility to the influence of certain specific values. As Davidson writes, in interpreting someone's action we 'will try for a theory that finds him consistent, a believer of truths, and a lover of the good (all by our own lights, it goes without saying).'[20]

Davidson urges that the problem of the interdependence of belief and desire in interpreting action has an analogue in the problem of the interdependence of meaning and belief in interpreting utterances, and that the latter problem is to be solved by assigning meanings to alien sentences '. . . that make native speakers right as often as plausibly possible, according, of course, to our own view of what is right'. Charity here reaches to substance as well, in that it imports our conception of truth and truth-related reasons for belief into the enterprise of ascribing meaningful assertions to others. Davidson cautions:

> The methodological advice to interpret in a way that optimizes
> agreement should not be conceived as resting on a charitable assump-
> tion about human intelligence that might turn out to be false. If we
> cannot find a way to interpret the utterances and other behaviour
> of a creature as revealing a set of beliefs largely consistent and true
> by our own standards, we have no reason to count that creature as
> rational, as having beliefs, or as saying anything.[21]

A non-centralist might hold, similarly, that the charitable ascription of desires informed by familiar specific reasons in interpreting the behaviour of others does not rest on an assumption about human motivation that could turn out to be false. On such a view, the ascription of preference, like that of belief, is essentially value-laden; the will, like the intelligence, can fall short only against the right sort of background, recognition of which is a condition of conceiving someone as a rational agent at all.

Thus, the view that claims about what ought to be done entail imperatives which express attitudes toward action does not rule out the view that the very concept of intentional action we invoke in deploying imperatival force is responsible to a set of specific values; decentralisation might proceed through action to imperatival force itself.

If the general concept of what ought to be done, all things considered is not logically prior to and independent of specific reason-giving concepts such as *just* and *unkind*, then what one ought to do, all things considered, must stand in some relationship to specific values that is logical, not merely epistemic, in nature. Thus, while non-centralism allows that our concepts give us the freedom to deny, for example, that one ought to do the just thing, it does imply that our freedom is limited. If what one ought to do, all things considered, is, a matter of logic, some function of specific values, then in order to deny that one ought to do what a particular value demands one must depend in some way on those specific values; the concept of what one ought to do does not afford a content to the denials of the global or arbitrary sceptic, but only to those of the limited sceptic who operates within the system of specific values. The limitation is not avoided by insistence on some form of logical link between claims about what ought to be done and action, as the concept of action itself may not be logically independent of specific values: if charity is not an option in interpreting events as intentional action by attributing meanings, beliefs and desires, then the concepts of objective values, no less than '. . . the concepts of objective truth, and of error, necessarily emerge in the context of interpretation.'[22]

What can we say about this function from specific values to what one ought to do, all things considered? What properties do we assume it has, and are they consistent with one another? I argue elsewhere that what at first looks an alarmingly strong case for their inconsistency, and hence for the non-existence of such a function, does not in the end succeed.[23] We can at least make the cautious claim that, if efforts to show that such a function does not exist fail, then an obstacle to believing that there is such a thing as what one ought to do, all things considered, that there are right answers to questions about what ought to be done, has been removed. In this sense, by proceeding from a non-centralist position we may take a step toward objectivism.

However, another obstacle must be overcome if we are to make out an objectivist position. Even if we agree that a function from specific values to all-things-considered evaluations must meet certain conditions and that the existence of a function that meets those conditions is not threatened, we nevertheless disagree widely in our all-things-considered evaluations, or, according to a non-centralist coherence account, about which of the possible functions that meet these conditions constitutes the best theory about the relationships among the relevant specific values in the circumstances at hand. Moreover, we may not even agree about which specific values are in play. What, then, guarantees that we are seeking the same thing to begin with? Isn't the attempt to found a decentralised account of what one ought to do, all things considered, on Wittgensteinian considerations vitiated by this disagreement? After all, it is a central tenet of the philosophy of the later Wittgenstein that '. . . the practice has to speak for itself'.[24] Can the Wittgensteinian conception of practices, in virtue of which we are able to use words with determinate meaning, accommodate the disagreement that is characteristic of issues about what one ought to do so as to allow us to be talking about the same thing, even though we disagree? If not, the existence of a function that meets the agreed-on conditions will not be enough to support the view that there are right answers; those who appear to be disagreeing about the right answer to a question would in fact be answering different questions.

The concepts that provide us with reasons for action permit us to communicate, disagree, and sometimes even argue, across the boundaries between paradigms of the good life for human beings. Members of different cultures or subcultures may in normal circumstances participate in rather different specific reason-giving practices, and yet they do stand substantively opposed to one another when one claims that an action is right and another claims that it is wrong. Thus, as Bernard Williams has put it, there must be some element of their claims 'which can be identified as the *locus* of exclusivity', such that they are not from every point of view incommensurable.[25] How is this *locus* of substantive disagreement to be accounted for?

On a centralist view of reason-giving concepts disagreement is located in some general evaluative concept that is prior to and independent of specific reason-giving concepts. But on the non-centralist view that the general evaluative concepts are not prior to the specific and that claims about what ought to be done, all things considered, are claims about the relationships among specific values, then if one person does not share the specific reason-giving concepts of another the minimal element of conceptual congruence that is a prerequisite of substantive disagreement between them may fail to obtain. Non-centralism claims that there are logical connections between claims about what ought to be done, all things considered, and a list of specific values; the sense of *ought* that is a function of the specific values on the list can be used to challenge and revise views about the relationships among those values, but it cannot be used to endorse an entirely unfamiliar list. Thus, non-centralism threatens to deprive us of a sense in which to disagree about things we seem to want to disagree about. In what sense can we disagree with someone who does not share our specific reason-giving practices? Even if someone does share our specific reason-giving practices, in what sense are we talking about the same thing when we disagree about what ought to be done, all things considered, when our specific values conflict?

Wittgenstein holds that a certain kind of disagreement, disagreement in form of life, precludes the use of language as a means of communication. He illustrates disagreement in form of life by describing people who go through motions that are puzzling in the following way: while we can understand the descriptions, which contain no hidden contradictions, and thus we must admit that what is described is possible, we cannot understand what reason anyone could have to act in the particular ways described. The procedures described do not make sense, and yet we are reluctant to dismiss them as perverse or idiotic. Disagreement in form of life is not substantive disagreement, which is a kind of communication, but conceptual disparity; it precludes substantive disagreement by ruling out the possibility of identifying what a particular dispute is about in a manner common to the different forms of life.[26]

According to Barry Stroud, the point of Wittgenstein's examples of peculiar behaviour is to show 'only that "the formation of concepts different from the usual ones" is intelligible to us; but it does not follow from this that those concepts themselves are intelligible to us.' The possibilities of language and communication, calculation and inference depend on certain contingent facts, such as the fact that we have certain mathematical and logical concepts, that we naturally continue a series or go on from examples in certain ways. But

. . . we can understand and acknowledge the contingency of this fact, and hence the possibility of different ways of calculating, and so forth, without understanding what those different ways might have been. If so, then it does not follow that those rules by which calculating, and so forth, have been carried out constitute a set of genuine alternatives open to us among which we could choose, or even among which we could have chosen.[27]

The possibility of language and communication, dependent as it is on our conceptual agreement, our shared sense of the necessity of going on in some ways rather than others, is not incompatible with the contingency, for each way of going on, of the fact that we do share a sense of its necessity.

The contingency claim supported by Wittgenstein's examples is: for any of our concepts, it is possible that others do not share it. It does not follow from this, as I shall emphasise below, that it is possible that others share none of our concepts but have an entirely alien conceptual scheme. It does follow, however, that agreement in form of life need not be sheltered or isolated from knowledge of or contact with other forms of life; the notion of a form of life admits of a conception of the world in which there is variation among forms of life. If it is a contingent fact that we do find it natural and necessary to go on in a particular way, then it is possible that others do not. If recognition of this possibility does not undermine our agreement in form of life, it is hard to see how recognition of the actual existence of others, who do not find it natural and necessary to go on in this way, could do so. Nor should the determinacy of our concepts be undone by contact with those whose concepts differ from ours; we might observe regularities in their unintelligible procedures that enable us to interact with them profitably, without thereby eroding our own forms of life.

Given that the conception is available of a world in which there is variation among forms of life, should we say that this conception is instantiated by our world, in which various schemes of reason-giving concepts co-exist? What are the consequences of the view that reason to act, like meaning, is '. . . embedded in its situation, in human customs and institutions',[28] that the way in which meaning guides linguistic action is a special case of the way in which reasons guide action generally? As linguistic practices rather than some central intention to go on in the same way determine that we mean *blue* and not *grue*, *plus* and not *quus*,[29] and constitute the 'bedrock' of logical necessity, so, on such a view, specific reason-giving practices, rather than some central commitment to do *this*, to go on in the same way, constitute the 'bed-rock' of practical necessity. The existence of certain shared practices, any of which might not have existed, is all that our having determinate reasons to say or do anything rests on. Still, it is compatible with their existence that other practices, different forms of life, also exist.

The price of regarding distinctive reason-giving schemes as different forms of life, however, may be to deprive ourselves of a sense in which they are in competition with one another, and of the *locus* of substantive disagreement that we started out to account for. It may be correct to regard some apparent disagreements about what ought to be done, all things considered, as differences in form of life, and our opponents as '. . . different sorts of beings from us',[30] with whom we do not stand in substantive disagreement because we do not have the concepts in common necessary to contradict one another. There may also be borderline cases between differences in form of life and substantive disagreement. However, some disputes about what ought to be done are substantive, and if the practice account is to succeed, it must make clear logical space for them. That is, it must make it possible to distinguish substantive disagreement within a given form of life from disagreement in form of life.

A closely related problem arises in other areas for Wittgenstein's views: there is tension between the doctrine of the antecedence of logic and mathematics to truth and the intelligibility of the supposition made by Wittgenstein that we can describe practices that are in some sense of the same general kind — logical or mathematical — as our own practices, yet constitute alternatives to them, that embody competing views about how to do the same thing. As Wright explains, '"Calculating", "inferring", "measuring" are, for us, determined by the methods we use; there is no residue in these concepts in terms of which the adequacy of our methods might be questioned.' But, he asks, '. . . if there is nothing further to our understanding of these concepts, how can it be coherent to suggest that other people might measure *differently*, might calculate in accordance with other rules, etc?'[31]

Wittgenstein is well aware of this tension. By focusing on his discussions of the problem I shall try to develop a framework in which many of his remarks about agreement and disagreement may be located and which makes a place within a non-centralist view of reasons for action for disagreement about the right answer to a given question. Although my purpose is interpretative, the interpretation is admittedly speculative: it does, I think, help to account for many of Wittgenstein's remarks taken together, but it goes well beyond anything that can be explicitly attributed to him, most obviously with respect to the connections suggested between a practice account and Davidson's views on interpretation.

Critics of what is taken to be Wittgensteinian 'conceptual relativism' have tended to assume that the practice account must assimilate persistent disagreement to difference in form of life, and hence be landed with the unacceptable consequence that such disagreement does not amount to substantive disagreement at all, so that argument is futile, misconceived in principle.[32] But it cannot be a consequence of the role of practices, customs, or institutions in determining meaning that all disagreements and mistakes threaten conceptual divergence; substantive disagreement and argument may themselves be practices or customs, as in ethics and law. I shall argue that to attribute such an assimilation to Wittgenstein is to make a fundamental mistake in interpreting his views. As well as his remarks rejecting the identification of agreement in form of life with substantive agreement, we have strategic reasons not to make this identification if we are to make sense of Wittgenstein's central concerns.

The identification would seem to be the result of an attempt to account for such remarks as:

> If language is to be a means of communication there must be agreement not only in definitions but also (queer as this may sound) in judgments. This seems to abolish logic, but does not do so. — It is one thing to describe methods of measurement, and another to obtain and state results of measurement. But what we call "measuring" is partly determined by a certain constancy in results of measurement.[33]

> We say that, in order to communicate, people must agree with one another about the meanings of words. But the criterion for this agreement is not just agreement with reference to definitions, e.g., ostensive definitions — but *also* an agreement in judgments. It is essential for communication that we agree in a large number of judgments.[34]

However, the correct interpretation of these remarks must at least reconcile them with remarks such as the following:

> "So you are saying that human agreement decides what is true and what is false?" — It is what human beings *say* that is true and false;

70

and they agree in the language they use. That is not agreement in opinions but in form of life.[35]

The agreement of humans that is a presupposition of logic is not an agreement in opinions, much less in opinions on questions of logic.[36]

It is obscure how we are to regard these remarks on any interpretation that identifies agreement in form of life with substantive agreement.

Indeed, the role that the notion of agreement in form of life is invoked to play in Wittgenstein's thought cannot be played by substantive agreement. Wittgenstein challenges the private language theorist to show how it is possible for a concept to have determinate meaning, such that mistaken attempts to apply *it* can be distinguished from the results of a failure to grasp its meaning and from applications of *other* concepts:

What is the difference between inferring wrong and not inferring? between adding wrong and not adding?

What I always do seems to be — to emphasize a distinction between the determination of a sense and the employment of a sense.[37]

Someone can only be mistaken in his use of a concept, however, if he stands in substantive disagreement with one who applies it correctly, as someone who is trying to apply a different concept does not. Thus, the challenge to the private language theorist is to distinguish same-meaning-different-belief cases, cases of substantive disagreement, from different-meaning cases, cases of conceptual difference; only if this distinction can be made out is it possible to regard the use of language as a rational activity, one that permits us to speak of right and wrong ways of going on. Private ostensive definition is incapable of meeting this challenge, not simply because of the inaccessibility of the crucial intentions to go on in the same way, but because we do not and cannot have intentions the content of which establishes, rather than presupposes, logical determinacy; our minds do not and cannot race ahead to decide of each possible case whether or not it falls under the concept whose meaning is supposedly thus determined. Not only can we not peer into our own minds in order to fix our meanings, but 'If God had looked into our minds, he would not have been able to see there . . .' what we meant.[38] This claim is not based on any behaviouristic premise that dismisses the inner, but rather on a proper respect for what inner life is really like. The difficulty it raises does not stem from a denial that there is something that it is like in there; rather, what it is like in there does not answer the question, as we do not have special inner experiences of meaning this or that. Nowhere in the contents of a mind is there to be found a rule that applies itself, an interpretation that does not permit of interpretation; and no such thing could determine our meanings or guide our uses of concepts.[39]

Moreover, we do not need such a thing in order to meet the challenge; it is by assuming that such a thing is needed that we arrive at the conception of meaning which gives rise to the problem. This is, a conception of meaning as implicitly guided by idealised interpretations of rules is what prompts the view that all disagreements or mistakes are symptoms of conceptual difference. It is this conception of meaning that Wittgenstein repudiates:

> This was our paradox: no course of action could be determined by a rule, because every course of action can be made out to accord with the rule. The answer was: if everything can be made out to accord with the rule, then it can also be made out to conflict with it. And so there would be neither accord nor conflict here.
>
> It can be seen that there is a misunderstanding here from the mere fact that in the course of our argument we give one interpretation after another, as if each one contented us at least for a moment, until we thought of yet another standing behind it. What this shews is that there is a way of grasping a rule which is not an interpretation, but which is exhibited in what we call "obeying the rule" and "going against it" in actual cases.
>
> Hence there is an inclination to say: every action according to the rule is an interpretation. But we ought to restrict the term "interpretation" to the substitution of one expression of the rule for another.
>
> And hence also 'obeying a rule' is a practice. And to think one is obeying a rule is not to obey a rule. Hence it is not possible to obey a rule 'privately': otherwise thinking one was obeying a rule would be the same thing as obeying it.[40]

Clearly, any account that Wittgenstein proposes in place of the private language theory must be able to make some progress toward meeting the challenge the private language theory fails to meet, or no ground is gained. This is true even if the solution Wittgenstein proposes is sceptical in the sense Kripke suggests, namely, that it concedes that we cannot '. . . speak of a single individual, considered by himself and in isolation, as ever meaning anything', and goes on to claim that we don't need to after all.[41] Wittgenstein suggests that the way to meet the challenge is to reject the assumption that gives rise to the problem. That is, we do not need to speak of an individual meaning something privately because what an individual means is not determined by some implicit idealised interpretation, but by shared practices, customs, institutions. Such an appeal to practices must be viewed as an attempt to meet the challenge despite the concession, not as an admission that it cannot be met. Otherwise the arguments against a private language lose their point, which derives from the assumption that the rational use of language *is* possible. For Wittgenstein to succeed in showing how it is possible by reference to practice and without invoking psychological states conceded to be mythical, the view that meanings are determined by practices must allow us to distinguish substantive from conceptual difference, to answer the question: 'In what does your having meant this in particular, rather than nothing in particular, or something slightly different, consist?', in terms of participation in the relevant practice. It is this participation that Wittgenstein calls agreement in form of life.

If agreement is form of life, identified in terms of practices, is to provide the conceptual common ground on the basis of which we may be entitled to regard ourselves as standing in substantive disagreement with someone who has made a mistake, it cannot amount to substantive agreement. The point of invoking practices is to account for the possibilities of substantive *dis*agreement and mistake, as distinct from the possibility of conceptual difference. Davidson makes a related point on the method of charity in interpreting behaviour: 'The method is not designed to eliminate disagreement, nor can it: its purpose is to make meaningful disagreement possible, and this depends entirely on a foundation – some foundation – in agreement.'[42] Thus, the problem that disagreement presents for a non-centralist coherentist view of practical reason is an instance of the general problem of how to accommodate the possibility of substantive disagreement and mistake among participants in a common form of life. If the notion of agreement in form of life is to do the work it is intended to do, it must accommodate the possibility of substantive disagreement wherever our concepts admit of it.

Above I described Wittgenstein's doctrine that logic is antecedent to truth as the rejection of logical centralism, and I noted the tension between this doctrine and the intelligibility of the supposition made by Wittgenstein that we can describe logical practices that are in some sense alternatives to our own, that embody different views about how to do the same thing. Crispin Wright has described this tension between two strands of Wittgenstein's thought in detail. He complains that '. . . Wittgenstein's soft-ruler people are merely *stipulated* as doing a kind of measuring; and the wood-sellers likewise are stipulated as determining quantity by area . . . .' '. . . what is not clear', he says, 'is what justifies the description of such people as employing different concepts of *length*, or of *quantity*. Where are the analogies anchored? What are the points of similarity?' '. . . it has still to be made out that there is in what they do anything which may rightly be regarded as the use of *any* such concepts; nothing has been done to distinguish their performance from mere ceremony.'[43] How can we admit that alternative practices may compete with our own, let alone that we are able to have substantive disagreements about the correct application of a given concept and to criticise mistaken attempts to apply it, without positing some logically central concept, prior to and governing specific practices, to carry the content of our disagreement?

In noting this tension we are noting that we have yet to see how the challenge to distinguish substantive from conceptual difference is to be met. Participation in practices that constitute a common form of life was invoked, in lieu of the mysterious intentions by which the private language theorist purported to anticipate reality, with the aim of meeting the challenge; but it is not yet clear how practices and forms of life do enable us to meet the challenge.

Wittgenstein explicitly recognises this tension and is crucially concerned to resolve it; he considers the problem in detail in relation to colour concepts and to logical and mathematical concepts. Since the identification of agreement in form of life with complete agreement in application gains appeal from consideration of concepts such as *red* and *green*, I shall first examine Wittgenstein's remarks about specific colours.

That someone groups a green object in good light and plain view with a series of red objects in good light and plain view is the best kind of evidence one could want that he is not applying our concept *red*. We do not articulate reasons for applying *red* or *green*. Hence, it is difficult to conceive of questions about someone's reasons for his grouping the answers to which would reveal him to stand in substantive disagreement with us about the redness of the green object, rather than not to be talking about its redness at all,

> Someone asks me: What is the colour of this flower? I answer: "red". — Are you absolutely sure? Yes, absolutely sure! But may I not have been deceived and called the wrong colour "red"? No. The certainty with which I call the colour "red" is the rigidity of my measuring-rod, it is the rigidity from which I start. When I give descriptions, *that* is not to be brought into doubt. This simply characterizes what we call describing.
>
> (I may of course even here assume a slip of the tongue, but nothing else.)[44]

It is simply the normal case, to be incapable of mistake about the designation of certain things in one's mother tongue.[45]

Nevertheless, Wittgenstein goes on to ask:

> Is it not difficult to distinguish between the cases in which I cannot and those in which I can hardly be mistaken? Is it not always clear to which kind a case belongs? I believe not.[46]

It is clear that we are not entitled to regard ourselves as disagreeing with someone about whether or not a red object is red, so long as both have a plain view of the object in good light. If he does not recognise that it is red he must not have the concept *red* or the ability to perceive redness. It is less clear that we are not entitled to regard ourselves as disagreeing with someone who groups a green object with a series of red ones about the colour of the object. It depends on further circumstances, on how much of the structure of the relationships among various specific colours he recognises. But if we were to stand in substantive disagreement with him, it would not be because the general concept *colour* is logically prior to and independent of the specific concepts *red* and *green* — it is not. Specific colour concepts are secondary, but they have logical ties to distinct qualities of experience, not to some central colourish quality. Rather, colour has an abstract and theoretical status in relation to specific colours that allows us to discuss, for example, the relationships among the primary and secondary colours, or to consider whether reddish-green is a possible colour. It is because we conceive colour to have an articulable structure that Wittgenstein is able to claim that there is 'a geometical gap . . . between green and red', and that the sentence '"There is no such thing as a reddish green" is akin to the sentences that we use as axioms in mathematics' in its contribution to the logic of colour concepts.[47] The articulability of the concept of colour in terms of the relationships among specific colour concepts, rather than some uniform colourish component in the meaning of the specific concepts, makes it intelligible for Wittgenstein to consider the possibility of unfamiliar colours and on what grounds we might attribute experiences of them:

> "Can't we imagine certain people having a different geometry of colour than we do?" That, of course, means: Can't we imagine people having colour concepts other than ours? And that in turn means: Can't we imagine people who do *not* have our colour concepts but who have concepts which are related to ours in such a way that we would also call them "colour concepts"?
>
> We will, therefore, have to ask ourselves: What would it be like if people knew colours which our people with normal vision do not know? In general this question will not admit of an unambiguous answer. For it is by no means clear that we *must* say of this sort of abnormal people that they know other *colours*. There is, after all, no commonly accepted criterion for what is a colour, unless it is one of our colours.
>
> And yet we could imagine circumstances under which we would say, "These people see other colours in addition to ours."
>
> The difficulty is, therefore, one of knowing what we are supposed to consider as the analogue of something that is familiar to us.[48]

Wittgenstein is well aware of the lack of definitive criteria for circumstances that support the alternative colourist hypothesis. Nevertheless, he does think it conceivable that such circumstances might be found, and suggests that we might identify them in terms of the relationship between the 'geometry' of our colour concepts and the geometry of the alternative colour concepts: for example, is the latter isomorphic to the former, or perhaps even a refinement of it?

> But even if there were also people for whom it was natural to use the expressions "reddish-green" or "yellowish-blue" in a consistent manner and who perhaps also exhibit abilities which we lack, we would still not be forced to recognize that they see *colours* which we do not see. There is, after all, no *commonly* accepted criterion for what is a colour, unless it is one of our colours.

76

'The colours' are not things that have definite properties, so that one could straight off look for or imagine colours that we don't yet know, *or* imagine someone who knows different ones than we do. It is quite possible that, under certain circumstances, we would say that people know colours that we don't know, but we are not forced to say this, for there is no indication as to what we should regard as adequate analogies to our colours, in order to be able to say it. This is like the case in which we speak of infra-red 'light'; there is a good reason for doing it, but we can also call it a misuse.

Can't we imagine people having a geometry of colours different from our normal one? And that, of course, means: can we describe it, can we immediately respond to the request to describe it, that is, do we know *unambiguously* what is being demanded of us?

The difficulty is obviously this: isn't it precisely the geometry of colours that shows us what we're talking about, i.e. that we are talking about colours?[49]

Let *colour'* be the predicate used by a group of people who may have an alternative set of colour concepts, and let *primary colours'* be colours' that cannot be obtained by combining other colours'. Circumstances that would support the claim that they are alternative-colourists rather than colour-blind might include, as a limiting case, those in which they typically assert that no colour' can be the result of combining more than two primary colours'. Since our primary colours are red, blue and yellow, the parallel claim for us would imply that there is no such colour as reddish-green, yellowish-purple, or bluish-orange. Now we might be unable to learn to apply the specific colour' concepts these people use, and yet be able to identify the predicates R, B and Y, which they use to stand for colours' they regard as unobtainable by combination, or primary. If they were in fact to assert that there is no such colour' as R-ish-B-Y, Y-ish-R-B, or B-ish-R-Y, the isomorphism might be regarded as providing some, though rather weak, support for the alternative colourist claim — at least, say, in the context that members of the group display interest in which particular combinations of R, B and Y occur in cloth, paintings and flower gardens.

Stronger support would be found in the circumstances Wittgenstein describes, in which members of some group make all the specific colour discriminations we make, but more as well, so that the geometry of their colour concepts is a refinement on that of ours:

Let us imagine men who express a colour intermediate between

77

red and yellow, say by means of a fraction in a kind of binary notation like this: R, LLRL and the like, where we have (say) yellow on the right, and red on the left. — These people learn how to describe shades of colour this way in the kindergarten, how to use such descriptions in picking colour out, in mixing them, etc. They would be related to us roughly as people with absolute pitch are to those who lack it. *They can do* what we cannot.[50]

The logic of the concept of colour is just much more complicated than it might seem.[51]

Members of such a group would bear the same relation to us as we bear to persons who are blind to some colour distinctions but not others. Just as we are able to disagree with someone who is red-green colour-blind about whether two purple objects are the same colour or not, we would be able to have substantive disagreements with the alternative colourists. Any disagreement about colour requires that there be some conceptual *locus* of disagreement, but there need not be one conceptual *locus* of all disagreements about colour. Thus, just as we are also able to disagree with someone who is blue-orange colour-blind about whether two purple objects are the same colour or not, we would be able to have substantive disagreements with two different groups of alternative colourists, whose candidate colour concepts bore different similarities to ours.

In looking for circumstances that would support the alternative-colourist claim, we are looking for examples of cases in which agreement in form of life with respect to the use of the concept *colour* is compatible with substantive disagreement about particular applications of it. That is, we are trying to discover the nature of the agreement in form of life that characterises the use of our concept *colour* and makes it possible to distinguish agreement over its proper use from use of another concept. We have found that this agreement in form of life is not monolithic; several practices, which need not go hand in hand, contribute to it. Among them are our applications of specific colour concepts such as *red* and *green* as well as our claims about the relationships among certain specific concepts. To be a colour is to be one of the things on our list of specific colours, related to one another as they are. The example of isomorphism we considered occupies a borderline position at best between conceptual and substantive difference; the relationships among specific concepts were familiar, but the specific component concepts were not. If we change the example so that most of the specific component concepts are familiar as well, as in Wittgenstein's example, the alternative colourist claim gains support; we could have a substantive disagreement with these people about whether two objects are the same colour — and we might well be mistaken. Such people are not failing to perceive colour at all, but are better at perceiving colour than we are.

In fact, Wittgenstein explicitly suggests that the distinction between conceptual and substantive difference with respect to the general concept of colour is not absolute but admits of differences of degree, and that this is also the case for the general concepts of *calculation* and *thinking*:

> Does it make sense to say that people generally agree in their judgments of colour? What would it be like for them not to?
> — One man would say a flower was red which another called blue and so on. — But what right should we have to call these people's words "red" and "blue" *our* 'colour-words'? —
> How would they learn to use these words? And is the language-game which they learn still such as we call the use of 'names of colour'? There are evidently differences of degree here.
> This consideration must, however, apply to mathematics too. If there were not complete agreement, then neither would human beings be learning the technique which we learn. It would be more or less different from ours up to the point of unrecognizability.[52]

> (There is a continuum between an error in calculation and a different mode of calculating.)[53]

> ... it is for us an essential part of 'thinking' that — in talking, writing, etc., — he makes *this sort* of transition. And I say further that the line between what we include in 'thinking' and what we no longer include in 'thinking' is no more a hard and fast one than the line between what is still and what is no longer called "regularity".[54]

I claimed above that the practice account ought to be viewed as an attempt to meet the challenge to distinguish conceptual and substantive difference and thus to show how language conceived as a rational activity is possible, rather than as a concession that the challenge cannot be met. To hold that the distinction between conceptual and substantive difference admits of degrees and borderline cases is not to

79

concede that the challenge cannot be met. Rather, it is another aspect of the strategy of rejecting assumptions that give rise to the problem. The importance of Wittgenstein's exercises in imagining strange ways of going on is not that they reveal a sharp boundary between conceptual and substantive difference or some deep underlying basis for the distinction. Rather, they show us that the distinction does *not* depend on such sharp boundaries or some deep underlying basis. And they help us to develop a sense of how to place instances of strange ways of going on on a spectrum that ranges from cases of radical conceptual disparity at one extreme to cases of purely substantive disagreement at the other. We learn to place cases on the spectrum by looking at the variety of ways in which the use of words can be different from ours and akin to ours, and thus to deploy the distinction Wittgenstein emphasises '. . . between the determination of a sense and the employment of a sense'. By contrast, the concept-determining intentions invoked by the private language theory to go on using a word *like this*, according to some implicit idealised interpretation, are no less mythical for purposes of developing such means of placement than for purposes of fixing absolutely clear conceptual boundaries.

Thus, '. . . it is not clear that the general agreement of people doing calculations is a characteristic mark of all that is called "calculating".'[55] This admission is compatible with the antecedence doctrine, that calculating means calculating *like this*, because calculating doesn't only mean calculating like *this*, but like *that*, and like *this*, and like *that* as well; Wittgenstein compares derivation to an artichoke:

> . . . we told ourselves that this was only a quite special case of deriving; deriving in a quite special garb, which had to be stripped from it if we wanted to see the essence of deriving. So we stripped those particular coverings off; but then deriving itself disappeared. – In order to find the real artichoke, we divested it of its leaves. For certainly [a case considered in a previous section] was a special case of deriving; what is essential to deriving, however, was not hidden beneath the surface of this case, but this 'surface' was one case of the family of cases of deriving.[56]

Thus, practices of articulating the relationships among specific criterial instances of calculation may also contribute to the meaning of *calculation*.

The concept of calculation is related to the concept, say, of adding 1 to 4 as is the concept of colour to the concept of redness: just as someone's grouping a green object with a series of red objects shows that he is not applying *red*, someone's getting a result other than 5 shows that he hasn't understood what it is to add 1 to 4:

> Thus the truth of the proposition that 4 + 1 makes 5 is, so to speak, overdetermined. Overdetermined by this, that the result of the operation is defined to be the criterion that this operation has been carried out.
>
> The proposition rests on one too many feet to be an empirical proposition. It will be used as a determination of the concept 'applying the operation +1 to 4'.[57]

The concept of redness and of adding 1 to 4 are among those that do not admit of substantive disagreement. I shall refer to such concepts as *uncontestable concepts*. Concerning uncontestable concepts it is correct to say that complete agreement in application characterises agreement in form of life. Strange ways of extending a series of applications of such a concept are located at one end of the spectrum we are concerned to fill out, and indicate conceptual disparity. People who persist in these strange ways of going on are not making mistakes, or disagreeing with us; rather they do not have our concepts, our perceptual capacities. With respect to these cases, the sense in which the practice 'speaks for itself' in enabling us to distinguish conceptual from substantive difference is clear: no persistent substantive difference, or mistake, is logically possible; persistent differences must be conceptual.

Further along the spectrum we find strange ways of extending series of applications of concepts such as *colour*, *calculation*, *thinking* and *measurement*. These are concepts that do not normally, but might conceivably, admit of alternative conceptions or substantive disagreement. I shall refer to them as *conceivably contestable concepts*. While uncontestable concepts include specific sensory concepts and the concepts of particular calculations, conceivably contestable concepts are categorial concepts that subsume uncontestable concepts of one or another sort, in the way that *colour* subsumes *red*, *green*, etc. and *calculation* subsumes *4 + 1*, *add 2*, etc. With respect to conceivably contestable concepts, it is normal for complete agreement in application to characterise agreement in form of life, and hence difference in application constitutes *prima facie* evidence of conceptual difference. However, such evidence is conceivably defeasible; we can imagine circumstances, as Wittgenstein does, in which we would hesitate to claim that the deviant application is not an attempt to apply our concept.

That such circumstances are conceivable is due to the complex and articulable structure of conceivably contestable concepts: Someone can make certain criterial applications of such a concept correctly and construct a theory about the relationships that obtain among his applications. Yet he may go on to make eccentric applications of it, based, perhaps, on extrapolation from the relationships he recognises. That such circumstances are not normal is due to the fact that the criteria for applying conceivably contestable concepts do not conflict among themselves: Correct uses of *red* do not compete with correct uses of *green* to tell us the colour of an object in the way that correct uses, for example, of *just* may compete with correct uses of *unkind* to tell us what we ought to do, all things considered. The laws of arithmetic reflect harmony among particular calculations rather than the resolution of conflict.

Again, it is by reference to practices that we attempt to identify circumstances in which contest is conceivable and to locate contested applications on the spectrum from conceptual to substantive difference. Extent of agreement or disagreement in form of life is signalled by a variety of uses. If complete agreement in application is the normal expression of agreement in form of life, nevertheless it might conceivably be expressed by agreement about certain criterial applications of a concept and the relationships among them, which provides a springboard for intelligible mistakes:

> In order to make a mistake, a man must already judge in conformity with mankind.
> Can we say: a mistake doesn't only have a cause, it also has a ground? i.e., roughly: when someone makes a mistake, this can be fitted into what he knows aright.[58]

> Whether a thing is a blunder or not — it is a blunder in a particular system. Just as something is a blunder in a particular game and not in another.[59]

And again, the admission that the division between conceptual and substantive difference is not sharp does not undermine the point of Wittgenstein's enterprise, which is to understand how meanings are determined to the extent they are, to an extent that makes communication possible. If meanings are not in fact completely determinate, we want our account to reflect this, without thereby going to the other extreme and making it impossible ever to distinguish conceptual from substantive difference. The practice account allows some concepts a measure of indeterminacy, as their uses and possible uses indicate. But this is indeterminacy with a good conscience, and concomitant with the firm determinations that practices also effect. The indeterminacy the private language theory involved, on the other hand, was disguised by the pretence that we have general pre-linguistic intentions capable of determining meanings to the extent they are determined; when this pretence is exposed as false, the private language theorist has no explanation of how meanings are determined at all.

At the other end of the spectrum we find divergent applications of what I shall call, following W. B. Gallie, *essentially contested concepts*. These are concepts that characteristically admit of substantive disagreement.[60] Gallie describes essentially contested concepts as appraisive and applicable to objects of an internally complex character that may be described in various ways of altering one's view of the significance of descriptions of their component features.

In my taxonomy, essentially contested concepts differ from conceivably contestable concepts in that correct descriptions of component features characteristically compete with one another to influence applications of the former. Examples of essentially contested concepts are the general concepts of what ought to be done, all things considered, and of what the law requires, all things considered, as well as many specific moral and legal concepts. (The concepts of equality, for example, may be tied to both a conception of equality of welfare and a conception of equality of resources.) Conceivably contestable concepts may be appraisive, but it is not characteristic of the criteria to which they are responsible to conflict with one another. Consider, for example, the concept *valid* as applied to inferences. We require any given formalisation of logic to be consistent. Nevertheless, disagreement exists, based on theoretical considerations, about the validity of the law of the excluded middle.

Gallie asks how we are able to distinguish cases in which the correct application of a single concept is contested from cases in which the dispute only serves '. . . to confuse two different concepts about whose proper application no one need have contested at all'.[61] A variety of practices contribute to agreement in form of life; Gallie makes two suggestions. First, each party to a disagreement about the correct application of an essentially contested concept '. . . recognises the fact that its own use of it is contested by those of other parties, and . . . each party must have at least some appreciation of the different criteria in

83

the light of which the other parties claim to be applying the concept in question', even though they differ as to the relative contribution made by the different criteria to an all-things-considered judgment. Second, a substantive disagreement about the correct application of an essentially contested concept involves appeals to exemplary applications that display relationships, which the disputants claim to be extrapolating, among the criteria that conflict in the case at hand.[62]

If there is some list of specific values such that what ought to be done, all things considered, is some function of those specific values, then both specific reason-giving practices and practices of theorising about specific values contribute to agreement in form of life. Accordingly, Gallie's two suggestions about how to recognise agreement in form of life may be applied at both levels. That is, in attempting to distinguish divergences that indicate substantive disagreement from divergences that indicate conceptual difference we may ask the following four questions.

(1) Do our opponents recognise the force of the various conflicting criteria our essentially contested concept is responsible to? When they conflict as well as when they apply in isolation? Do they recognise the force of specific reason-giving concepts in the cases in question?

(2) Can we agree with our opponents on an exemplary application of the essentially contested concept, in an instance in which the various conflicting criteria that apply to the cases in question also apply? Can we agree on the resolution of conflicts among the relevant specific reason-giving concepts in some actual or hypothetical cases?

(3) Are our opponents able to deliberate when criteria conflict, and do they recognise the force of the theoretical considerations that we bring to bear in arguments about the proper relationships among conflicting criteria? In constructing ethical theories, for example, do they respect the rule of dominance and the requirements of supervenience and transitivity? Do they recognise that the simplicity and comprehensiveness of an account of the relationships among specific values count in its favour?

(4) Can we agree with our opponents on an exemplary instance of an account of the relationships among some group of conflicting criteria (preferably criteria to which the same essentially contested concept is responsible in different circumstances so that the exemplary account is subject to the same theoretical constraints as the one we are

concerned with in the case at hand)? Can we find an example of ethical or legal deliberation and theorising that we agree is decisive?

If we were to limit ourselves to questions (1) and (2), the question of whether there exists a practice of theorising that 'speaks for itself', in addition to the specific practices it is about, would remain open; both types of practice contribute to agreement in form of life with respect to an essentially contested concept. But once again, the distinction between conceptual and substantive difference is drawn by reference to practices. By participating in such practices, our opponents reveal their competence at using the concept our applications of which they contest. Moreover, the practices that contribute to agreement in form of life need not go hand in hand. Any disagreement about what ought to be done, all things considered, requires that there be some conceptual *locus* of disagreement, but there need not be one conceptual *locus* of all such disagreements.

It might be objected that the challenge to distinguish substantive from conceptual difference can be raised again with respect to the claim to theoretical favour, which a non-centralist coherence account associates with the central concepts *right* and *ought*. The appeal to theory only puts the threat to the possibility of substantive disagreement at one step's remove, but does not really avert it. We can only understand substantive disagreement about applications of essentially contested concepts by reference to theoretical coherence if we share a conception of theoretical coherence; but the challenge we started out to meet may be raised again at the level of theory. How can someone's mistaken perceptions of theoretical coherence be distinguished from his failure to understand what he is supposed to be doing, or from an intention to do something else? What keeps theoretical differences in particular from threatening conceptual divergence? For example, suppose that we share specific reason-giving concepts and that we agree on certain conditions that a theory about the relationships between specific values and what ought to be done must meet, in order to be in the running as a theory. Nevertheless, we may differ about which of the possible theories that meet this description do the best job of accounting for the settled cases of conflict whose resolution we agree about. What guarantees then that we have the same interpretation of what it is to do the best job of accounting for the cases?

This objection misconstrues the role of the appeal to theory. Theoretical coherence does not permit us to resurrect the repudiated conception of meaning as determined by implicit idealised interpretations and go on to solve the problem of distinguishing substantive from conceptual difference in terms of this conception of meaning. Even at the level of theory, the way to meet the challenge is to reject the assumption which underwrites the suggestion that any difference threatens conceptual divergence. But the objection we are considering adheres to the assumption that there must be matching implicit interpretations guiding our efforts to achieve theoretical coherence if we are to be capable of substantive theoretical disagreements. It is this assumption that a practice account rejects; not only are there no such implicit interpretations guiding our behaviour about which we can ask: 'do they match up?', but they are not needed. At the level of theory again, the conceptual *locus* of disagreement is participation in practices and customs and the criterion of conceptual divergence is inability to participate. There is a spectrum ranging from participation to inability to participate, on which we may learn to place instances of different ways of going on. By rejecting the assumption that there needs to be some other kind of basis for the distinction between substantive and conceptual difference we undermine the suggestion that any difference threatens conceptual divergence.

However, the response to this first objection to the role of theoretical coherence may prompt a second objection. It may be objected that there is a general tension between Wittgenstein's views about following rules and the role given by a non-centralist coherence account to theoretical coherence. The thrust of the Wittgenstein's considerations of what it is to follow a rule is to deny that anything like implicit idealised interpretations are needed to determine our meanings or guide our uses of concepts. But isn't the pursuit of theoretical coherence the pursuit of just such an interpretation, an interpretation of what we have done in the past that will guide our efforts to go on in the same way? How can the view that interpretation is not needed be maintained in the face of such an account?

Wittgenstein's views about what it is to follow a rule apply no less to the second-order concept of coherence, as applied to sets of linguistic practices, than to any other concept; they apply both to the understanding of reasons and to the understanding of the relationships among reasons. Our exercise of the technique of bringing considerations of coherence to bear in difficult cases is itself a practice, a custom. Theorising when we are in doubt about what ought to be done, all things considered, is one of the things we 'simply . . . do'.[63] It is one thing to admit that by making claims about what ought to be done we leave ourselves susceptible to the influence of deliberation and theorising, which involve explicit interpretation of past claims about what ought to be done, and another to claim that implicit interpretations must guide our uses of any concept. Sometimes we simply do go in for interpretation; a denial that we have interpretative practices is no part of Wittgenstein's views about what it is to follow a rule. In allowing efforts at interpretation their proper place among our practices we do not concede that implicit idealised interpretations guide us at every step, even when we simply go on without such efforts, or that they determine our conception of what it is we are doing when we interpret; application of the rule-following considerations to our efforts at interpretation themselves averts any danger of a fruitless regress.

Wittgenstein's examples of strange ways of going on involve extending a series of applications of an uncontestable or conceivably contestable concept; they provide us with exercises in delimiting our own form of life from within. Bernard Williams writes: '. . . the business of considering them is part of finding our way around inside our own view, feeling our way out to the points at which we begin to lose our hold on it (or it, its hold on us), and things begin to be hopelessly strange to us. The imagined alternatives are not alternatives *to* us; they are alternatives *for* us, markers of how far we might go and still remain within our world — a world leaving which would not mean that we saw something different, but just that we ceased to see.'[64] We might think that comparable exercises in delimiting our own form of life with respect to essentially contested concepts are not far to seek, that we have only to look in the daily papers to find the moral analogues of the student learning to add 2, the soft-ruler people, the woodcutters, the people with absolute colour vision. However, if we seek a *locus* of substantive disagreement by asking questions (1) through (4) above, we find that examples of the sort provided by current events and recent history — crimes of passion, mercy killings, acts of political terrorism — rarely require us to ascribe concepts that approach the horizon of intelligibility. Indeed, as particular acts in our midst move toward this horizon our sense of the futility of attempts to communicate that the acts are wrong increases, as does our tendency to regard them as lacking the elements of intent required for responsibility, as manifestations of insanity; consider persons who go to great lengths for no intelligible reason: to acquire saucers of mud, to get parsley to the moon, to avoid even very mild pain on days other than Tuesday at the cost of agony on Tuesdays.[65]

87

A practice account allows us to place particular examples of divergent series of applications on a conceptual/substantive difference spectrum. Questions (1) through (4) seek out shared practices that might underwrite substantive disagreements about applications of an essentially contested concept. Such practices might underwrite disagreements, for example, about political terrorism, marital fidelity, vegetarianism. The conceptual *locus* of substantive disagreement is not constant from example to example. We are free to move around within a form of life and to criticise one aspect of it on the basis of another; indeed, it is characteristic of certain forms of life that we do so. The responsibility of essentially contested concepts to structured sets of conflicting criteria makes deliberation, argument and criticism not only intelligible but inevitable. On a coherentist view, deliberation requires abilities of more than one kind. We should expect for some people to be better at the sympathetic and imaginative scrutiny of alternatives that is needed to discover and illuminate the values at stake in the first place, to see all that it is possible to see about how an alternative might make sense, and others to be better at the more abstract and theoretical thinking that is needed to arrive at all-things-considered judgments.

A practice account does not allow us to have things both ways: it does not allow us to imagine ourselves as standing in substantive disagreement on certain points with those whose concepts differ sufficiently from ours. Moreover, we cannot stand in substantive disagreement of any kind with those whose forms of life are entirely alien to us. We cannot make sense of the supposition that they make mistakes in virtue of the fact that their forms of life are mistaken, and ours correct.[66] A practice account denies that there could be a residual content to the meanings of our concepts that transcends all the uses to which we put them, a slack that carries a claim about these uses themselves: that, as a matter of fact, they collectively succeed in delineating the contours of reality, contours which they do not collectively define. Jonathan Lear writes: '. . . we cannot step outside our form of life and discuss it like some *objet trouvé*. Any attempt to say what our form of life is like will itself be part of the form of life; it can have no more than the meaning it gets within the context of its use.'[67] Some such slack would be needed to make sense of the supposition that our forms of life are right and alien forms of life are wrong, to serve as the conceptual *locus* of their purported opposition to one another. No such slack is needed to make sense of substantive disagreements; the articulable complexity of our concepts and their susceptibility to theorising fills this need. The agreement in form of life that bears the weight of substantive disagreement may be preserved through various permutations of perspective on the criteria to which essentially contested concepts are responsible and the relationships among them.

To reject this sense of the claim that our concepts succeed in delineating the contours of reality is to reject what Davidson has called the third dogma of empiricism: the dualism of conceptual scheme and empirical content, of organizing system and something waiting to be organized. The effect of this rejection is a large-scale version of the effect of a non-centralist view of reason-giving concepts which I described above: namely, to deny a sense to the challenges of the global sceptic. Thus, in constraining scepticism to operate within the conceptual scheme we have we achieve a kind of objectivism. Davidson writes:

> In giving up dependence on the concept of an uninterpreted reality, something outside all schemes and science, we do not relinquish the notion of objective truth — quite the contrary. Given the dogma of a dualism of scheme and reality, we get conceptual relativity, and truth relative to a scheme. Without the dogma, this kind of relativity goes by the board. Of course truth of sentences remains relative to language, but that is as objective as can be. In giving up the dualism of scheme and world, we do not give up the world, but reestablish unmediated touch with the familiar objects whose antics make our sentences and opinions true or false.[68]

Support for the view that an objectivism of this kind rather than some form of relativism is the result of Wittgenstein's views about the determination of meaning by practices is provided by Bernard Williams's comments about the way in which the transcendental idealism of the *Tractatus* is implicit in pluralised form in the later work of Wittgenstein. He contrasts Wittgenstein's transcendental solipsism, which 'coincides with pure realism' and is expressed by the idea that 'the limits of my language are the limits of my world', with idealism '. . . regarded just as a kind of aggregative solipsism', which might be expressed by '. . . the confused idea that the limits of *each* man's language are the limits of *each* man's world' and which '. . . is indeed ridiculous.' He goes on to point out that relativism represents an aggregative solipsism of the pluralised form that might be expressed by the similarly confused idea that the limits of each society's language are the limits of its world. Relativism is likewise to be contrasted with the later Wittgenstein's transcendental idealism, which shares the characteristics of the solipsism of the *Tractatus*: that we are '. . . driven to state it in forms which are required to be understood, if at all, in the wrong way', and that it, '. . . when its implications are followed out strictly, coincides with pure realism.'[69]

Davidson rejects the third dogma on grounds that 'charity is not an option' when doing interpretation; 'whether we like it or not, if we want to understand others, we must count them right in most matters.' 'Given the underlying methodology of interpretation, we could not be in a position to judge that others had concepts or beliefs radically different from our own.'[70] Before reaching anything that would count as a radically different conceptual scheme, we lose our grip on the very idea of a conceptual scheme, on the very notion of belief; we might come across beings whose alien forms of life we cannot interpret at all, but then we would have no grounds for attributing a conceptual scheme and beliefs to them at all. Thus there are limits to conceptual difference, to the possibility of conceiving of alternative concepts. Alternatives must be local; we cannot make sense of the possibility of an entirely alien conceptual scheme. *A fortiori*, we cannot stand in substantive disagreement with those who do not share our conceptual scheme:

> It would be wrong to summarize by saying we have shown how communication is possible between people who have different schemes . . . . For we have found no intelligible basis on which it can be said that schemes are different. It would be equally wrong to announce the glorious news that all mankind — all speakers of language, at least — share a common scheme and ontology. For if we cannot intelligibly say that schemes are different, neither can we intelligibly say that they are one.[71]

To hold, as Wittgenstein does, that for any of our concepts, it is possible for language users not to have it but some other concept or concepts, is not to hold that it is possible for language users to have none of our concepts but an entirely alien conceptual scheme. Given Wittgenstein's prolific efforts at interpretation, of the soft-ruler people, the woodcutters, and so on, it is not surprising that he should anticipate the view that we do not choose to be charitable:

> To say: in the end we can only adduce such grounds as *we* hold to be grounds, is to say nothing at all.[72]

I argued above that, if the interdependence of belief and meaning is analogous to the interdependence of belief and desire in the way

Davidson suggests, then charity constrains our efforts to interpret events as action generally, as well as our efforts to interpret events as linguistic action in particular. Our response to the challenge to distinguish same-value-different-belief cases from different-value cases must be of the same form as our response to the challenge to distinguish same-meaning-different-belief cases from different-meaning cases: Alternative reason-giving concepts must be local alternatives; we cannot make sense of the possibility of an entirely alien scheme of reasons for action. To be a reason just is to be one of our reasons, related to one another in roughly the ways they are. The problem that essentially contested concepts present for a practice account is that of explaining the sense in which those with whom we disagree actually do share our reason-giving practices, our forms of life; a problem of how to justify our forms of life to those who do not share them cannot arise. Far from leading to relativism, a practice account denies the availability of a detached standpoint from which judgments about what ought to be done might be relativised. We cannot disagree or argue about whether something ought to be done with those to whom we cannot attribute the reason-giving concepts that would make the doing of it intelligible as intentional action rather than, say, as a series of muscular contractions. The very concept of the will and hence expressions of intention are logically if holistically tied to the specific reasons that make it possible for us to understand others as wanting, intending and doing at all.

ACKNOWLEDGMENTS

For helpful comments on various drafts and remarks in conversation, I am indebted to Simon Blackburn, John Broome, Ronald Dworkin, Elizabeth Fricker, Richard Hare, John Mackie, Derek Parfit, Christopher Peacocke, David Pears, Paul Seabright, Charles Taylor, and especially John McDowell. Needless to say, all remaining errors are my own.

NOTES

1 See David Wiggins, 'Truth, invention, and the meaning of life', *Proceedings of the British Academy* LXII (1976), pp. 331–78, at pp. 361–2.
2 See, for example, R. M. Hare, *Freedom and Reason* (Oxford,

Oxford University Press, 1963) (but compare *Moral Thinking* (Oxford, Clarendon Press, 1981)); Jaakko Hintikka, 'Some main problems in deontic logic', in *Deontic Logic: Introductory and Systemic Readings*, Risto Hilpinen, editor (Dordrecht, Reidel, 1971), pp. 59–104, at p. 99, and '"Prima Facie" Obligations and Iterated Modalities', *Theoria* 36–37 (1970-1), pp. 232–40, at pp. 232-3; and compare, John R. Searle, '"Prima Facie" Obligations', in *Philosophical Subjects*, Zak van Straaten, editor (Oxford, Clarendon Press, 1980), pp. 238–59, at p. 248; Peter K. Scotch and Raymond E. Jennings, 'Non-Kripkean deontic logic', in *New Studies in Deontic Logic; Norms, Actions, and the Foundations of Ethics*, Risto Hilpinen, editor (Dordrecht, Reidel, 1981), pp. 149–62, sections 4 and 5; E. J. Lemmon, 'Deontic logic and the logic of imperatives', *Logique et Analyse* 29 (1965), pp. 39–71, at pp. 50-1; Hector Neri-Castaneda, 'On the semantics of the ought-to-do', in *Semantics of. Natural Language*, Gilbert Harman and Donald Davidson, editors (Dordrecht, Reidel, 1982), pp. 675–94, at pp. 687-9.

3 See, for example, John Rawls, *A Theory of Justice* (Cambridge, Mass., The Belknap Press, 1971); Norman Daniels, 'Wide reflective equilibrium and theory acceptance in ethics', *Journal of Philosophy* (1979), vol. LXXVI, pp. 256–82; Ronald Dworkin, *Taking Rights Seriously* (London, Duckworth, 1977), pp. 87, 104–109, 119-122, 126-7, 159-68, 283, and 'No right answer?', in *Law, Morality and Society*, P. M. S. Hacker and J. Raz, editors (Oxford, Clarendon Press, 1977), pp. 58–84.

4 *Pace* Simon Blackburn in 'Moral realism', *Morality and Moral Reasoning*, John Casey, editor (London, Methuen, 1971), pp. 101–24. Indeed, the source of the supervenience of attitudes on the characteristics of their objects may itself be the theoretical or explanatory role of attributions of attitudes; see and compare Colin McGinn, *The Character of Mind* (Oxford, Oxford University Press, 1982), pp. 29-36.

5 See and compare Hilary Putnam, *Reason, Truth and History* (Cambridge, Cambridge University Press, 1981), pp. 206-8.

6 See Crispin Wright, *Wittgenstein on the Foundations of Mathematics* (Cambridge, Mass., Harvard University Press, 1980), chapters 4 and 5, esp. pp. 58, 61. On the parallel point for calculation, see pp. 68-9.

7 Ludwig Wittgenstein, *Remarks on the Foundations of Mathematics*, G. H. von Wright, R. Rhees, G. E. M. Anscombe, editors, G. E. M. Anscombe, translator (Oxford, Blackwell, 1978), I:156; I:5; VII:31. See also I:4, VI:16; and see *Philosophical Investigations*, G. E. M. Anscombe, translator (Oxford, Blackwell, 1976), I:164, and *On Certainty*, G. E. M. Anscombe and G. H. von Wright, editors, Denis Paul and G. E. M. Anscombe, translators (Oxford, Blackwell, 1977), section 47.

8 Wittgenstein, *Remarks on the Foundations of Mathematics*, *op. cit.* n. 7, III:74.

9 See Donald Davidson, 'True to the facts', *Journal of Philosophy* (1969), vol. LXVI, pp. 759–60.

10 See John McDowell, 'Wittgenstein on following a rule', *Synthese* 58 (1984), pp. 325–63, at pp. 351, 352.

11 Wittgenstein, *Remarks on the Foundations of Mathematics*, *op. cit.* n. 7, VII:39; see also VII:40. See and compare Saul A. Kripke, *Wittgenstein on Rules and Private Language* (Cambridge, Mass., Harvard University Press, 1982), p. 59n and *passim*; and Willard Van Orman Quine, *Word and Object* (Cambridge, Mass, MIT Press, 1960), pp. 24–5.

12 Michael Dummett, *Frege*, first edition (London, Duckworth, 1983), pp. 360, 362. See also pp. 352ff, and Wright, *op. cit.* n. 6, p. 70ff.

13 Christopher Peacocke, *Holistic Explanation: Action, Space, Interpretation* (Oxford, Clarendon Press, 1979), p. 215.

14 David Lewis, 'Radical interpretation', *Philosophical Papers*, vol. 1 (New York, Oxford University Press, 1983), p. 112; see also his 'New work for a theory of universals', *The Australasian Journal of Philosophy* (1983), vol. 61, pp. 343–77, at pp. 371–7. For comments about the normative constraints on the concept of belief, see Bernard Williams, 'Deciding to believe', *Problems of the Self* (Cambridge, Cambridge University Press, 1973), p. 148ff. Compare David Wiggins, 'Freedom, knowledge, belief and causality', in *Knowledge and Necessity*, Royal Institute of Philosophy Lectures, vol. 3, 1968–1969 (London, Macmillan, 1970), pp. 132–54, at p. 143ff; and Roy Edgley, *Reason in Theory and Practice* (London, Hutchinson University Library, 1969), chapters 3, 5. See also Wittgenstein, *Remarks on the Foundations of Mathematics*, *op. cit.* n. 7, I:131, 133.

15 Donald Davidson, 'Psychology as philosophy', *Essays on Action and Events* (Oxford, Clarendon Press, 1980), pp. 229, 234.

16 See F. P. Ramsey, 'Truth and probability', *The Foundations of Mathematics* (London, Kegan Paul, 1931), p. 177ff.

17 Here I am indebted to Paul Seabright and Huw Dixon. See Davidson, 'Psychology as philosophy', *op. cit.* n. 15, p. 236, and Seabright's discussion of Davidson's criticism of Ramsey in his Oxford MPhil thesis in economics, *Uncertainty and Ignorance in Economics*, 1982, p. 17ff. See also Daniel C. Dennett, 'Intentional systems', *Brainstorms* (Montgomery, Vermont, Bradford Books, 1978), at p. 19.

18 Davidson, 'Psychology as Philosophy', *op. cit.* n. 15, p. 237.

19 See and compare Peacocke, *Holistic Explanation; op. cit.* n. 13, pp. 31, 54, 190–1. Peacocke claims that an assumption of rationality, however broadly construed, is not sufficient to enable us to apply the concepts of belief and desire, but that we need 'a theory of regularity of such nonrational factors as the constancy and change of underived desires (desires that are not derivative from

other desires) over time, and the connection of sensory stimuli physically characterized with the formation of beliefs': '. . . the supposition of rationality and what is believed at a given time have no particular consequences for empirically possible sequences of actions until we adjoin a theory of the agent's underived desires over time, and have also an account of such matters as the connection of his beliefs with sensory stimuli' (pp. 190-1). We seem to be differing not so much over the content of the necessary assumptions as about whether it is correct to describe them as assumptions about rationality. Assumptions about the content of the agent's underived desires I am describing as assumptions of their substantive rationality. Assumptions about the connections of an agent's beliefs with sensory stimuli are among those that must be made if we are to follow Davidson's methodological advice to interpret so as to 'make native speakers right as often as plausibly possible, according, of course, to our own view of what is right'. 'Radical interpretation', *Dialectica*, XXVII (1973), pp. 313-27, at p. 324. Assumptions of both these kinds ought to be included in any conception of the charity that Davidson urges on us.

20 Davidson, 'Mental events', *Essays on Action and Events*, op. cit. n. 15, p. 222.
21 Davidson, 'Radical interpretation', op. cit. n. 19, p. 324.
22 Donald Davidson, 'Thought and talk', in *Mind and Language*, Samuel Guttenplan, editor (Oxford, Clarendon Press, 1975), pp. 7-23, at p. 22. See also Wright, op. cit. n. 6, p. 329.
23 'Supervenience and the possibility of coherence', article in preparation.
24 Wittgenstein, *On Certainty*, op. cit. n. 7, section 139.
25 Bernard Williams, 'The truth in relativism', *Moral Luck* (Cambridge, Cambridge University Press, 1981), p. 135.
26 See, for example, Wittgenstein, *Philosophical Investigations*, op. cit. n. 7, I:185; *Remarks on the Foundations of Mathematics*, op. cit. n. 7, I:149ff; *The Blue and Brown Books*, (Oxford, Blackwell, 1975), p. 97; compare Richard Norman, *Reasons for Action: A Critique of Utilitarian Rationality* (Oxford, Blackwell, 1971), p. 128.
27 Barry Stroud, 'Wittgenstein and logical necessity', in *Wittgenstein: The Philosophical Investigations*, George Pitcher, editor (New York, Doubleday, 1966), pp. 477-96, at pp. 493, 489. See also Wittgenstein, *Philosophical Investigations*, op. cit. n. 7, II:xii.
28 Wittgenstein, *ibid.*, I:337.
29 See Kripke, op. cit. n. 11, section 2.
30 Stroud, op. cit. n. 27, p. 492.
31 Wright, op. cit. n. 6, pp. 69, 70.
32 See, for example, Roger Trigg, *Reason and Commitment* (Cambridge, Cambridge University Press, 1973), pp. 66, 71, 123-4.
33 Wittgenstein, *Philosophical Investigations*, op. cit. n. 7, I:242.

34 Wittgenstein, *Remarks on the Foundations of Mathematics, op. cit.* n. 7, VI:39.
35 *Philosophical Investigations, op. cit.* n. 7, I:241.
36 *Remarks on the Foundations of Mathematics, op. cit.* n. 7, VI: 49. See also VI:30, VII:2, 43.
37 *Ibid.* VI:48; III:37. See also I:5, 136.
38 *Philosophical Investigations, op. cit.* n. 7, II:xi, p. 217.
39 See and compare John McDowell, 'On the sense and reference of a proper name', *Mind.* LXXXVI (1977), pp. 159-85, at pp. 168, 174-5, 177; and Kripke, *op. cit.* n. 11, p. 44.
40 Wittgenstein, *Philosophical Investigations, op. cit.* n. 7, I:201-2. Here and in what follows I am indebted to John McDowell's views in 'Non-cognitivism and rule-following', in *Wittgenstein: To Follow a Rule*, Steven H. Holtzman and Christopher M. Leich, editors (London, Routledge & Kegan Paul, 1981), pp. 141-62, and especially in 'Wittgenstein on following a rule', *op. cit.* n. 10. Compare Kripke, *op. cit.* n. 11, section 2.
41 Kripke, *ibid.*, pp. 66, 68-9.
42 Donald Davidson, 'On the very idea of a conceptual scheme', *American Philosophical Society Proceedings and Addresses* 47 (1973-1974), pp. 5-20, p. 19.
43 Wright, *op. cit.* n. 6, pp. 68, 72.
44 *Remarks on the Foundations of Mathematics, op. cit.* n. 7, VI:28.
45 *On Certainty, op. cit.* n. 7, section 630.
46 *Ibid.* 673.
47 See *Zettel*, G. E. M. Anscombe and G. H. von Wright, editors, G. E. M. Anscombe, translator (Oxford, Blackwell, 1967), I:354, 346. I am indebted here and in what follows to E. M. Fricker and indirectly to Gareth Evans for suggestions made in conversation about the usefulness of a distinction between sensory and articulated predicates in interpreting Wittgenstein. See her Oxford BPhil thesis, *Rules and Language: An Examination of Some of Wittgenstein's Arguments* (April 1979), p. 81ff. See also Wittgenstein's remarks at *Zettel* I:331, 332, 353, 362 and *Remarks on Colour*, G. E. M. Anscombe, editor, Linda McAlister and Margarete Schatte, translators (Oxford, Blackwell, 1977), III:73 and *passim.*
48 *Remarks on Colour, op. cit.* n. 47, I:66, III:154, III:42, III:88.
49 *Ibid.* I:14, III:127, III:86. Wittgenstein seems to think that green is a primary colour, rather than a mixture of blue and yellow.
50 *Zettel, op. cit.* n. 47, I:368. See also I:369, 266ff; compare I:257: Wittgenstein responds·to the question 'Would it be possible to discover a new colour?' by pointing out that '. . . a colour-blind man is in the same situation as we are, his colours form just as complete a system as ours do; he doesn't see any gaps where the remaining colours belong.'
51 *Remarks on Colour, op. cit.* n. 47, III:106.
52 *Philosophical Investigations, op. cit.* n. 7, II:xi, p. 226. See also

Zettel, op. cit. n. 47, I:393; *Remarks on the Foundations of Mathematics, op. cit.* n. 7, VII:43.

53 *Remarks on Colour, op. cit.* n. 47, III:293. Compare *Remarks on the Foundations of Mathematics, op. cit.* n. 7, I:5; see also III:75.

54 *Ibid.* I:116. See also Wittgenstein's comments in *Lectures and Conversations on Aesthetics, Psychology and Religious Belief*, compiled from notes taken by Yorick Smithies, Rush Rhees and James Taylor, Cyril Barrett, editor (Oxford, Blackwell, 1978), pp. 61–3; and Jonathan Lear, 'Leaving the world alone', *Journal of Philosophy* LXXIX (1982), pp. 382–403, at pp. 389–90. See also Edgley, *op. cit.* n. 14, pp. 79–82. For related remarks on the general sensory concepts of taste and of pain, see *Zettel, op. cit.* n. 47, I:366–7, 380–1. That the distinction between substantive and conceptual difference admits of degrees is implicit in Wittgenstein's remarks about gradual diachronic changes in language games. See *On Certainty, op. cit.* n. 7, sections 63, 256; *Remarks on the Foundations of Mathematics, op. cit.* n. 7, IV:30.

55 *Ibid.* VII:43.

56 *Philosophical Investigations, op. cit.* n. 7, I:164. See also *The Blue Book, op. cit.* n. 26, p. 17.

57 *Remarks on the Foundations of Mathematics, op. cit.* n. 7, VI:16; see also *Philosophical Investigations, op. cit.* n. 7, I:185.

58 *On Certainty, op. cit.* n. 7, sections 156 and 74.

59 Wittgenstein, *Lectures and Conversations, op. cit.* n. 54, p. 59. See also pp. 61–3, and *On Certainty, op. cit.* n. 7, section 255.

60 Gallie gives an artificial example involving the concept *champion*, and also the examples *democracy, the Christian life, art*; see W. B. Gallie, 'Essentially contested concepts', *Proceedings of the Aristotelian Society* (1955–1956), pp. 167–98. Wittgenstein gives as an example of such a concept that of the genuineness of an expression of feeling; see *Philosophical Investigations, op. cit.* n. 7, II:xi, p. 227.

61 Gallie, *op. cit.* n. 60, p. 175.

62 See *ibid.*, pp. 172, 176–7, 190.

63 *Philosophical Investigations, op. cit.* n. 7, I:217. See also McDowell, 'On the sense and reference of a proper name', *op. cit.* n. 39, p. 177.

64 Bernard Williams, 'Wittgenstein and idealism', *Moral Luck, op. cit.* n. 25, p. 160.

65 See and compare Dennett, *op. cit.*, n. 17, at p. 10. The examples are from: G. E. M. Anscombe, *Intention*, second edition (Oxford, Blackwell, 1976), pp. 70–1; Thomas Nagel, *The Possibility of Altruism* (Oxford, Clarendon Press, 1970), p. 45; and Derek Parfit, *Reasons and Persons* (Oxford, Oxford University Press, 1984), section 46, respectively.

66 See *Remarks on Colour, op. cit.* n. 47, III:293.

67 Lear, *op. cit.* n. 54, p. 385. Lear's interpretation of Wittgenstein is

in harmony with my objectivist interpretation; Lear also finds affinities between the positions of Wittgenstein and Davidson. See p. 392n.

68 Davidson, 'On the very idea of a conceptual scheme', *op. cit.* n. 42, p. 20. Compare: Quine, *op. cit.* n. 11, pp. 24–5; Putnam, *op. cit.* n. 4, p. 52.

69 See Williams, 'Wittgenstein and idealism', *Moral Luck*, *op. cit.* n. 25, pp. 146, 150, 161, 163 and *passim*; and Wittgenstein, *Tractatus Logico-Philosophicus*, D. F. Pears and B. F. McGuinness, translators (London, Routledge & Kegan Paul, 1961), 5.6–5.64.

70 Davidson, 'On the very idea of a conceptual scheme', *op. cit.* n. 42, pp. 19–20.

71 *Ibid.*, p. 20.

72 *On Certainty*, *op. cit.* n. 7, section 599.

V
TAKING MORALITY SERIOUSLY

Steven Lukes

'Protagoras, Hobbes, Hume and Warnock', writes John Mackie, 'are all at least broadly in agreement about the problem that morality is needed to solve: limited resources and limited sympathies together generate both competition leading to conflict and an absence of what would be mutually beneficial cooperation' (Mackie 1977: 111). Mackie endorses this view, meaning by 'morality' what he calls morality 'in the narrow sense', namely, 'a system of a particular sort of constraints on conduct — ones whose central task is to protect the interests of persons other than the agent and which present themselves to an agent as checks on his natural inclinations or spontaneous tendencies to act' (ibid.:106). In this paper, I shall seek to establish three conclusions: first, that Mackie's account of morality 'in the narrow sense' is useful and important, and denotes a central domain within morality more widely construed; second, that his account of the problem to which morality, thus conceived, is a solution is inadequate and misleading; and third, that it is importantly so.

MORALITY IN THE NARROW SENSE

The broad sense of morality with which the narrow sense contrasts is 'a general, all-inclusive theory of conduct: the morality to which someone subscribed would be whatever body of principles he allowed ultimately to guide or determine his choices of action' (ibid.: 106). So, in the narrow sense, 'moral considerations would be considerations from some limited range, and would not necessarily

98

include everything that a man allowed to determine what he did' (ibid.).

This contrast between senses of 'morality' is already useful, given the cacophony of senses in which the term is used, ranging from the 'moral majority' to the 'moral sciences'. But it does not, in itself, enable us to denote a specific object of reference as 'morality in the narrow sense'. What *is* the limited range of considerations that present themselves as constraints on conduct and protect interests in the manner indicated?

Mackie gives hints as to how to answer this question (Mackie 1977 and 1980) by focusing attention on rights and obligations, rules and prohibitions and, following Hume, on the notion of justice. We can consolidate these hints by drawing on some observations of H. L. A. Hart, John Stuart Mill and R. M. Hare. According to Hart, the German *'Recht'*, like the French *'droit'* and the Italian *'diritto'*, is a term used by continental jurists for which there is no direct English translation: these expressions

> seem to English jurists to hover uncertainly between law and morals, but they do in fact mark off an area of morality (the morality of law) which has special characteristics. It is occupied by the concepts of justice, fairness, rights and obligation (if the last is not used as it is by many moral philosophers as an obscuring general label to cover every action that morally we ought to do or forbear from doing). (Hart 1955: 177-8)

Hart adds that there are four factors that distinguish morality from law itself; namely, importance, immunity from deliberate change, the voluntary character of moral offences, and the distinctive form of moral pressure (Hart 1961).

It is doubtless this area of morality that Mill had in mind when he observed that justice is 'the chief part, and incomparably the most sacred and binding part, of all morality (Mill 1861: 315), meaning by 'justice' 'certain classes of moral rules' which protect rights that 'reside in persons' and which

> concern the essentials of human well-being more nearly, and are therefore of more absolute obligation, than any other rules for the guidance of life . . . The moral rules which forbid mankind to hurt one another (in which we must never forget to include wrongful interference with each other's freedom) are more vital to human

well-being than any other maxims, however important, which only
point out the best mode of managing some department of human
affairs. (ibid.: 316)

And consider finally R. M. Hare's suggestion that

within the general area of morality marked out by the use of 'ought'
and 'must' (which is not the whole of morality, because the word
'good' and the virtues have been left out of this picture), there is a
smaller field of obligation and rights, distinguished by being person-
related and by being, unlike 'must', overridable, but not so easily as
'ought'. (Hare 1981: 153)

And Hare, significantly, goes on to discuss, within the same chapter,
'the parallel problem of justice' (ibid.: 156), which he divides into
judicial and quasi-judicial justice on the one hand the distributive or
social and economic justice on the other — that is, 'justice in the distribution of the various benefits and harms which arise from membership
in a society and its economy, including small societies such as families
and partnerships and groups of friends' (ibid.: 161).

From these various suggestions we may conclude that the narrow
sense of morality serves to demarcate a distinct and central *domain* of
morality which has a certain distinctive form and function. It is the
domain of the Right rather than the Good, or at least it bears on the
Good only indirectly, by setting limits (which may be more or less
narrow) to what actions conceptions of the good may legitimately
advocate or encourage. It does not directly address the pursuit of virtue
or happiness or perfection, but purports to protect individuals' pursuit
of these, as they severally conceive them. It is the domain of principles
of justice, and of rights and obligations; these present themselves as
constraints on conduct, that are powerful but overridable, and serve to
protect vital interests of persons, touching on 'the essentials of their
well-being', including their freedom; and they have, taken together a
distinctive function or purpose in human life. It is to Mackie's account
of that function that we now turn.

THE OBJECT OF MORALITY

What, Mackie asks, gives morality in the narrow sense its point? His answer, not surprisingly, is Humean. He cites with approval Hume's statement that it is

> only from the selfishness and confin'd generosity of men, along with the scanty provision nature has made for his wants, that justice derives its origin. (Hume 1739: 495)

and comments, interpreting Hume, that

> If men had been overwhelmingly benevolent, if each had aimed only at the happiness of all, if everyone had loved his neighbour as himself, there would have been no need for the rules that constitute justice. (Mackie 1977: 110)

In this section, I shall seek to show that this view is radically mistaken, both with regard to justice in particular, and, in general, to the area of morality we have identified as morality in the narrow sense.

Mackie's developed Humean view is that morality in the narrow sense (which we shall henceforth call morality$_n$) is a device for solving a problem that he identifies as follows:

> We must think of a 'game' in which most, perhaps all, of the 'players' are largely selfish, or have limited sympathies, in a situation where scarce resources and the like tend to produce conflicts of interest; further, it is important for most of the 'players' that certain roughly specifiable evils (which, other things being equal, would result from the basic situation) should be prevented or reduced. (ibid.: 165)

Morality$_n$ provides 'acceptable principles of constraint on action the general encouragement of and widespread respect for which will do most to counter these evils, subject to the assumption that these constraints will not be respected by all the "players" all the time' (ibid.). The point of morality$_n$ is 'that it is necessary for the well-being of people in general that they should act to some extent in ways that they cannot see to be (egoistically) prudential and also in ways that in fact are not prudential.' The function of morality$_n$ is of 'checking what would be the natural result of prudence alone' (ibid.: 190).

In criticising this thesis of Mackie's, I shall argue (1) that it is unsatisfactory in itself, and (2) that it is an inadequate response to the question asked: that it takes far too narrow a view of the problem to which morality in the narrow sense is a solution.

(1) Consider the two key elements of the Hume-Mackie account of

the conditions calling forth morality$_n$: scarcity and limited sympathies.

What, in the first place, is scarcity? Hume and Mackie present it as a matter of nature's 'scanty provision' for man's wants and of 'limited resources'. But scarcity is a more complex notion than either of these formulations suggest. Consider the following four forms of scarcity: (i) insufficiency of production inputs (e.g. raw materials) relative to production requirements; (ii) insufficiency of produced goods relative to consumption requirements; (iii) limits upon the possibility of the joint realisation of individual goals, resulting from external conditions (e.g. limitations of space or time); and (iv) limits upon the possibility of the joint realisation of individual goals resulting from the nature of those goals (e.g. 'positional goods': we cannot all enjoy high status, or the quiet solitude of our neighbourhood park). Plainly these possibilities bring into view a range of determinants of scarcity, of which the niggardliness of nature and men's wants are only two (and these are themselves dependent variables, in turn determined by a range of social, cultural, scientific and technological factors). Scarcity (ii) can exist without scarcity (i): it may result entirely from the existing system of production and distribution. Scarcity (ii) can be absent despite 'limited resources'. And scarcity (iii) and (iv) may result from social, organisational and cultural factors and exist without scarcity (i) or (ii). All these forms of scarcity can generate interest conflicts. Furthermore, overcoming them all would involve an immense growth in the productive forces of society, changes in social organisation and appropriate preference changes, eliminating all non-compatible desires. I shall call this (unrealisable) state of affairs 'co-operative abundance'. The point being made here is that both the nature and the sources of scarcity are more complex and diverse than Hume and Mackie indicate.

Consider next what Hume calls 'selfishness and confin'd generosity' and Mackie 'egoism and self-referential altruism' (ibid.: 170) or 'limited sympathies'. Are these notions, as they say, perspicuous? I doubt it. For what counts, in any particular case, as 'egoism' or 'selfishness' depends on context and, in particular, on how the 'self' and its 'interests' are understood. Assume a world in which, over certain ranges of human interaction, zero-sum relation hold, such that if A gains B loses, and the self is seen as typically having interests which conflict with those of others, and with the public or common interest. Then, of course, 'egoism' and 'selfishness', or the pursuit of self-interest, will result in conflicts of interest. But imagine a world in which the Golden Rule always applied or the Buddhist notion of the self was widely shared. Then 'egoism' or 'selfishness' or 'self-interest' would result in, or at least be compatible with, social harmony, even under conditions of scarcity. In short, 'egoism' and 'selfishness', as we ordinarily understand them, presuppose, and are not themselves the source of, conflicting interests.

The same argument applies, *pari passu*, to 'confin'ed generosity' and 'self-referential altruism'. *Whether* the limits upon and self-referential character of altruistic sentiments result in conflicts of interest will depend on the social relations that prevail and on what pursuing the happiness or interests of those for whom one cares is taken to involve. From the mere fact that sympathies are limited nothing follows: only if specific ways of acting on them means acting against those beyond the limits do conflicts of interest result.

Mackie himself sees this when he asks: 'what action will be the most prudent or the most egoistically rational?' and answers that 'that depends partly on what sort of a person you are, and consequentially on what sort of a person you want to be' (ibid.: 192). If someone, he writes,

> from whatever causes, has at least fairly strong moral tendencies, the prudential course, for him, will almost certainly coincide with what he sees as the moral one, simply because he will have to live with his conscience. What *is* prudent is then not the same as what would be prudent if he did not have moral feelings. (ibid.: 192)

But Mackie's account of what is moral$_n$ relies on a contrast between constraints on an agent's conduct and 'his natural inclinations and spontaneous tendencies to act' (ibid.: 106). Yet what these are will depend on what sort of a person he is and whether they harm the interests of others will depend on this and on the sort of society in which he and they live. From all of which I conclude that the second element of the Hume-Mackie account — egoism and limited sympathies — presupposes rather than explains the conflicting interests it adduces morality to resolve.

(2) That the Hume-Mackie account of the conditions that call forth morality$_n$ is too narrow can be seen clearly if we ask whether the conditions so far (albeit unsatisfactorily) specified exhaustively explain the bases of interest conflicts in social life. Plainly, scarcity, in its several forms, combined with various familiar forms of egoism and limited sympathies among competing individuals and groups — such as 'possessive

individualism', acquisitiveness, status striving, wage bargaining, etc. – will generate conflicting claims and thus the need to adjudicate upon which claims are valid and of these which have priority.

There are, however, roots of interest conflict that lie deeper than this – that are less tied to a particular type of society and its social relations. Rawls gives a clue to what these might be in his account of the 'circumstances of justice': these are 'the normal conditions under which human co-operation is both possible and necessary' and they 'obtain whenever mutually disinterested persons put forward conflicting claims to the division of social advantages under conditions of moderate scarcity' (Rawls 1972: 128). Rawls's point here is (I take it) that the conflicting claims result not, or not only, from the attitudes and activities mentioned above but from the diversity of human ends: as he writes, 'the plurality of distinct persons with distinct systems of ends is an essential feature of human societies' (ibid.: 28-9). In other words, it is the conflict of interests resulting from different individuals' and groups' different and conflicting conceptions of the good, that in turn define those interests, that render adjudication and interest-protecting constraints necessary.

Notice that this condition is independent of the Hume-Mackie conditions (though of course it may co-exist with them). Hume mistakenly thought that if you increase 'to a sufficient degree the benevolence of men or the bounty of nature . . . you render justice useless by supplying its place with much nobler virtues, and more favourable blessings' (Hume 1739: 494-5). But even under conditions of co-operative abundance and altruism, there will, if conceptions of the good conflict, be a need for the fair allocation of benefits and burdens, for the assigning of obligations and the protection of rights; but we should then need them in the face of the benevolence rather than the selfishness of others. Altruists, sincerely and conscientiously pursuing their respective conceptions of the good, can certainly cause injustice and violate rights. For every conception of the good will favour certain social relationships and ways of defining individuals' interests – or, more precisely, certain ways of conceiving and ranking the various interests that individuals have. It will also disfavour others, and in a world in which no such conception is fully realised, and universally accepted, even the non-egoistic practitioners of one threaten the adherents of others: hence the need for justice, rights and obligations.

But what if divergent conceptions of the good, and of basic or vital interests, were to converge within a single moral and political consensus?

Here a fourth set of conditions for morality$_n$ come into view: lack of perfect rationality, information and understanding. Even under co-operative abundance, altruism, and the unification of interests within a common conception of the good, people may, after all, get it wrong: they may fail to act as they should toward others, because they do not know how to or make mistakes, with resulting misallocations of burdens and benefits, and damage to individuals' interests.

In seeking to supplement and deepen Mackie's account of the conditions of morality$_n$, I have so far been arguing very much in the spirit of his account, seeking to explain the point, function or object of morality$_n$ in terms of 'certain contingent features of the human condition' (Mackie 1977: 121). I shall now depart from that spirit and turn to fantasy, by asking whether *any* human society could dispense with morality$_n$: is its dispensability *conceivable*?

Joseph Raz has suggested that the co-ordinating, dispute-resolving and damage-remedying functions of law would be needed even in 'a society of angels' (Raz 1975: 159). Presumably by the same argument morality$_n$ would also be needed in such a society. On what grounds might one reject such a suggestion? Only on the ground that it takes too low a view of angels: that they would, in Hume's words, be endowed with 'much nobler virtues, and more favourable blessings', and in particular that the communal relations between them would be such as to render morality$_n$ unnecessary. But what could such communal relations be like?

Here there seem to be only two alternatives. On the one hand, such angels (or rather perhaps saints?) could agree upon and live by shared moral principles, in a kind of communal *Sittlichkeit*. Such principles would guide what would otherwise be conflictual into harmonious and mutually advantageous behaviour, by mediating and reconciling claims on common resources, enforcing respect for others' interests and views, settling disagreements of interpretation and fact, and so on. But what could such principles be but principles of morality$_n$?

The other alternative is that the angels would be free of conflicting self-interests. The relations between them would be relations between individuals without any sense of a self-interest conflicting with that of others, or with the public or collective interest. There is good reason to think that this was indeed Marx's conception of communism. For he always tended to see self-interest as tied to civil society and private property, and characteristic of 'egoistic man, of man separated from other men and from the community' (Marx and Engels 1843: 162) and he envisaged communism, not as the 'love-imbued opposite of selfishness' (Marx and Engels 1846: 41) but as the end of 'a cleavage between the particular and the common interest', as a state in which 'the contradiction between the interest of the separate individual or the individual family and the common interest of all individuals who have intercourse with one another' has been abolished (Marx and Engels 1845–6: 46–7).

It is difficult to get this image into clear focus, but it may help to imagine a range of possibilities from what we might call the minimum to the maximum picture. On the minimum picture, the diverse interests that individuals severally pursue are always overridden, when the need for choice arises, by the principle of preserving communal relations with others. The maintaining of the latter always takes priority over individuals' other desires and needs, wherever the two conflict. On the maximum picture, communal relations undercut rather than override individuals' conflicting interests: they enter into or help to constitute one's very conception of one's interests and one's self, and thus one's self-interest. The projects I value, the life-plans I pursue, the fulfilments I seek, and indeed my view of myself are what they are only because of the relations in which I stand to others; indeed, they cannot be conceived apart from such relations. My 'natural inclinations and spontaneous tendencies to act' and also my considered and reflective purposes and projects are always such as to maintain and enhance the communal relations in which I stand. My inclinations are 'naturally' communal, in this sense, but should they 'unnaturally' deviate, for whatever reason, reflection will make them so. I suppose that on the maximal maximum picture there just would be no such deviation. (There seems little doubt that Marx inclined towards some version of the maximum picture.)

Supposing such a community of angels or saints to exist, we must ask: what *are* its distinctive social relations? Are they face-to-face relations or do they hold between strangers, are they intimate or anonymous, are they relations of love, friendship, comradeship, neighbourliness or kinship, or of class, ethnicity, nationality, citizenship or common humanity, do they hold between producers, or between producers and consumers, or between citizens, are they relations of commitment and loyalty binding members to sub-communities or to the community as a whole? If the society in question is of any complexity, if indeed it is a *society*, then the only possible answer is: at least all of these. But then how are these various relations themselves related? Will not the interests dictated by these various social relations be likely to conflict with one another? If so, which should have priority and when? When, for example, should patriotism override friendship, or meeting the needs of one's family outweigh impersonal charity? How are we to balance the requirements of consumers and producers, of locality, citizenship and internationalism, and of all the diverse group-ings — ethnic, cultural, occupational, regional, and so on — into which our social or communal attachments inevitably divide us? Which of these sometimes conflicting requirements are more, and which less, funda-mental to what J. S. Mill called 'the essentials of human well-being'? How can the individual, on whom all these relations bear, and who must interpret their import, avoid hard choices between their various requirements? And how could such choices be avoided in any com-munity in which policy priorities have to be decided, public choices made and resources allocated? And how could such conflicts at the individual and at the collective level be resolved other than by appeal to agreed principles of justice and to rights and obligations? In short, do not even high-level, communally-related angels stand in need of morality$_n$?

From all of which I draw three conclusions. First, that Mackie's account of the object of morality$_n$ is, with respect to scarcity, too simple, and, with respect to egoism and limited sympathies, question-begging. Second, that it is far too narrow, ignoring, in particular, the significance of conflicting conceptions of the good and limited ration-ality, information and understanding. And third, that the conditions of morality$_n$ are nothing like as 'contingent' as Mackie suggests but appear to characterise all conceivable societies.

TAKING MORALITY SERIOUSLY

Why should the arguments just advanced matter? The reason is, I think, practical and, indeed, moral. It concerns the practical consequences of taking the Hume-Mackie view (though I hasten to add that the argu-ments stand or fall independently of such consequences; the conse-quences are not here intended as an argument against the view).

If morality$_n$ — the domain of justice, rights and obligations — is seen as a 'device' for solving the problem of limited resources and limited sympathies, the question immediately arises: what impact does seeing it in this way have upon how one sees the constraints it imposes? What difference would taking the Hume-Mackie view make to our moral beliefs and attitudes?

In answering this, we should note that an interesting parallel exists, in the form of indirect utilitarianism. This is the view that there are two levels of moral thinking: ordinary everyday thinking guided by ordinary morality (including rights, obligations, virtues, etc.) and higher-level critical thinking, which is utilitarian, reflecting on, guiding and testing judgments at the first level. Of this doctrine Mackie writes that the problem is

> the practical difficulty, for someone who is for part of the time a critical moral philosopher in this utilitarian style, to keep this from infecting his everyday moral thought and conduct. It cannot be easy for him to retain practical dispositions of honesty, justice and loyalty if in his heart of hearts he feels that these don't really matter, and sees them merely as devices to compensate for the inability of everyone, himself included, to calculate reliably and without bias in terms of aggregate utility. (Mackie 1980: 353)

I suggest that there is an analogous infection at work in the Hume-Mackie view (though, as with indirect utilitarianism, one far from its authors' intentions). For an adherent of that view must be aware that the domain of morality$_n$ is only needed to counteract certain unfortunate and contingent features of social life, which it might, after all, be better to attack directly, in the hope of eliminating them, or at least reducing their significance. Increase 'to a sufficient degree the benevolence of men or the bounty of nature' and you can 'render justice useless'. (This thought, of course, can only be strengthened by the arguments advanced in part (1) of the previous section: scarcity can be attacked at a number of points, and 'egoism' will seem more contingent than ever.)

Hence the inclination to see justice as a merely 'remedial virtue' (Sandel 1982: 31-2) and the tendency among both liberal-minded jurists and marxist critics, to see 'rights' as linked to the 'individualism' of capitalist societies (see Campbell 1983). Hence the altogether disastrous tendency of marxism, and certain other forms of socialist and communitarian thinking, to take a hostile view of 'justice', 'rights' and the morality of duty and to look forward to a withering away of this kind of morality – morality$_n$ – in a more communitarian society which has overcome, or greatly diminished, scarcity and egoism, and in which 'nobler virtues, and more favourable blessings' will prevail – a community beyond justice and rights.

If the arguments of this paper are cogent, all of this is a deep and dangerous mistake (not that John Mackie made it; but his view encourages it). If they hold, then morality, in the narrow sense, is a fundamentally important part of morality as a whole, deeply rooted in every possible form of social life and inseparable therefore from every attainable social ideal. To think otherwise is not to take morality seriously.

ACKNOWLEDGMENT

I am grateful to Ted Honderich and Jo Raz for comments that have helped improve this paper.

REFERENCES

Campbell, T. (1983), *The Left and Rights: A Conceptual Analysis of the Socialist Idea of Rights*, Routledge & Kegan Paul, London.

Hare, R.M. (1981), *Moral Thinking: Its Levels, Method and Point*, Oxford University Press, Oxford.

Hart, H.L.A. (1955), 'Are there any natural rights?', *Philosophical Review* vol. 64, pp. 175–91.

Hart, H.L.A. (1961), *The Concept of Law*, Clarendon Press, Oxford.

Hume, D. (1739), *A Treatise of Human Nature*, L. A. Selby-Bigge (ed.), Clarendon Press, Oxford, 1888.

Mackie, J.L. (1977), *Ethics: Inventing Right and Wrong*, Penguin, Harmondsworth.

Mackie, J.L. (1980), 'Can there be a right-based moral theory?' *Midwest Studies in Philosophy, Volume III, Studies in Ethical Theory, 1978*, University of Minnesota Press, Minneapolis.

Marx, K. (1843), 'On the Jewish question', Marx and Engels *Collected Works*, Lawrence & Wishart, London, 1975– , vol. III.

Marx, K. and Engels, F. (1845–6), *The German Ideology*, Marx and Engels, *Collected Works*, Lawrence & Wishart, London, 1975– , vol. V.

Marx, K. and Engels, F. (1846), 'Circular against Kriege', Marx and Engels, *Collected Works*, Lawrence & Wishart, London, 1975– , vol. VI.

Mill, J.S. (1861), *Utilitarianism*, Fontana Library, Collins, London, 1962.

Rawls, J. (1972), *A Theory of Justice*, Clarendon Press, Oxford.

Raz, J. (1975), *Practical Reason and Norms*, Hutchinson, London.

Sandel, M. (1982), *Liberalism and the Limits of Justice*, Cambridge University Press, Cambridge.

VI
VALUES AND SECONDARY QUALITIES

John McDowell

1 J. L. Mackie insists that ordinary evaluative thought presents itself as a matter of sensitivity to aspects of the world.[1] And this phenomenological thesis seems correct. When one or another variety of philosophical non-cognitivism claims to capture the truth about what the experience of value is like, or (in a familiar surrogate for phenomenology[2]) about what we mean by our evaluative language, the claim is never based on careful attention to the lived character of evaluative thought or discourse. The idea is, rather, that the very concept of the cognitive or factual rules out the possibility of an undiluted representation of how things are, enjoying, nevertheless, the internal relation to 'attitudes' or the will that would be needed for it to count as evaluative.[3] On this view the phenomenology of value would involve a mere incoherence, if it were as Mackie says – a possibility that then tends (naturally enough) not to be so much as entertained. But, as Mackie sees, there is no satisfactory justification for supposing that the factual is, by definition, attitudinatively and motivationally neutral. This clears away the only obstacle to accepting his phenomenological claim; and the upshot is that non-cognitivism must offer to correct the phenomenology of value, rather than to give an account of it.[4]

In Mackie's view the correction is called for. In this paper I want to suggest that he attributes an unmerited plausibility to this thesis, by giving a false picture of what one is committed to if one resists it.

2 Given that Mackie is right about the phenomenology of value, an attempt to accept the appearances makes it virtually irresistible to appeal to a perceptual model. Now Mackie holds that the model must

be perceptual awareness of *primary* qualities (see *HMT*, pp. 32, 60-1, 73-4). And this makes it comparatively easy to argue that the appearances are misleading. For it seems impossible — at least on reflection — to take seriously the idea of something that is like a primary quality in being simply *there*, independently of human sensibility, but is nevertheless intrinsically (not conditionally on contingencies about human sensibility) such as to elicit some 'attitude' or state of will from someone who becomes aware of it. Moreover, the primary-quality model turns the epistemology of value into mere mystification. The perceptual model is no more than a model: perception, strictly so called, does not mirror the role of reason in evaluative thinking, which seems to require us to regard the apprehension of value as an intellectual rather than a merely sensory matter. But if we are to take account of this, while preserving the model's picture of values as brutely and absolutely *there*, it seems that we need to postulate a faculty — 'intuition' — about which all that can be said is that it makes us aware of objective rational connections: the model itself ensures that there is nothing helpful to say about how such a faculty might work, or why its deliverances might deserve to count as knowledge.

But why is it supposed that the model must be awareness of primary qualities rather than secondary qualities? The answer is that Mackie, following Locke, takes secondary-quality perception, as conceived by a pre-philosophical consciousness, to involve a projective error: one analogous to the error he finds in ordinary evaluative thought. He holds that we are prone to conceive secondary-quality experience in a way that would be appropriate for experience of primary qualities. So a pre-philosophical secondary-quality model for awareness of value would in effect be, after all, a primary-quality model. And to accept a philosophically corrected secondary-quality model for the awareness of value would be simply to give up trying to go along with the appearances.

I believe, however, that this conception of secondary-quality experience is seriously mistaken.

3 A secondary quality is a property the ascription of which to an object is not adequately understood except as true, if it is true, in virtue of the object's disposition to present a certain sort of perceptual appearance: specifically, an appearance characterizable by using a word for the property itself to say how the object perceptually appears. Thus an object's being red is understood as obtaining in virtue of

111

the object's being such as (in certain circumstances) to look, precisely, red.

This account of secondary qualities is faithful to one key Lockean doctrine, namely the identification of secondary qualities with 'powers to produce various sensations in us'.[5] (The phrase 'perceptual appearance', with its gloss, goes beyond Locke's unspecific 'sensations', but harmlessly; it serves simply to restrict our attention, as Locke's word may not, to properties that are in a certain obvious sense perceptible.[6])

I have written of what property-ascriptions are understood to be true in virtue of, rather than of what they are true in virtue of. No doubt it is true that a given thing is red in virtue of some microscopic textural property of its surface; but a predication understood only in such terms — not in terms of how the object would look — would not be an ascription of the secondary quality of redness.[7]

Secondary-quality experience presents itself as perceptual awareness of properties genuinely possessed by the objects that confront one. And there is no general obstacle to taking that appearance at face value.[8] An object's being such as to look red is independent of its actually looking red to anyone on any particular occasion; so, notwithstanding the conceptual connection between being red and being experienced as red, an experience of something as red can count as a case of being presented with a property that is there anyway — there independently of the experience itself.[9] And there is no evident ground for accusing the appearance of being misleading. What would one expect it to be like to experience something's being such as to look red, if not to experience the thing in question (in the right circumstances) as looking, precisely, red?

On Mackie's account, by contrast, to take experiencing something as red at face value, as a non-misleading awareness of a property that really confronts one, is to attribute to the object a property which is 'thoroughly objective' (*PFL*, p. 18), in the sense that it does not need to be understood in terms of experiences that the object is disposed to give rise to; but which nevertheless resembles redness as it figures in our experience — this to ensure that the phenomenal character of the experience need not stand accused of misleadingness, as it would if the 'thoroughly objective' property of which it constituted an awareness were conceived as a microscopic textural basis for the object's disposition to look red. This use of the notion of resemblance corresponds to one key element in Locke's exposition of the concept of a primary quality.[10] In these Lockean terms Mackie's view amounts to accusing a naive perceptual consciousness of taking secondary qualities for primary qualities (see *PFL*, p. 16).

According to Mackie, this conception of primary qualities that resemble colours as we see them is coherent; that nothing is characterized by such qualities is established by merely empirical argument (see *PFL*, pp. 17-20). But is the idea coherent? This would require two things: first, that colours figure in perceptual experience neutrally, so to speak, rather than as essentially phenomenal qualities of objects, qualities that could not be adequately conceived except in terms of how their possessors would look; and, second, that we command a concept of resemblance that would enable us to construct notions of possible primary qualities out of the idea of resemblance to such neutral elements of experience. The first of these requirements is quite dubious. (I shall return to this.) But even if we try to let it pass, the second requirement seems impossible. Starting with, say, redness as it (putatively neutrally) figures in our experience, we are asked to form the notion of a feature of objects which resembles that, but which is adequately conceivable otherwise than in terms of how its possessors would look (since if it were adequately conceivable only in those terms it would simply be secondary). But the second part of these instructions leaves it wholly mysterious what to make of the first: it precludes the required resemblance being in phenomenal respects, but it is quite unclear what other sense we could make of the notion of resemblance to redness as it figures in our experience. (If we find no other, we have failed to let the first requirement pass; redness as it figures in our experience proves stubbornly phenomenal.)[11] I have indicated how we can make error-free sense of the thought that colours are authentic objects of perceptual awareness; in face of that, it seems a gratuitous slur on perceptual 'common sense' to accuse it of this wildly problematic understanding of itself.

Why is Mackie resolved, nevertheless, to convict 'common sense' of error? Secondary qualities are qualities not adequately conceivable except in terms of certain subjective states, and thus subjective themselves in a sense that that characterization defines. In the natural contrast, a primary quality would be objective in the sense that what it is for something to have it can be adequately understood otherwise than in terms of dispositions to give rise to subjective states. Now this contrast between objective and subjective is not a contrast between veridical and illusory experience. But it is easily confused with a different contrast, in which to call a putative object of awareness 'objective' is to say that it is there to be experienced, as opposed to being a mere figment of the subjective state that purports to be an experience of it. If secondary qualities were subjective in the sense that naturally contrasts with this, naive consciousness would indeed be wrong about them, and we would need something like Mackie's Lockean picture of the error it commits. What is acceptable, though, is only that secondary qualities are subjective in the first sense, and it would be simply wrong to suppose that this gives any support to the idea that they are subjective in the second.[12]

More specifically, Mackie seems insufficiently whole-hearted in an insight of his about perceptual experiences. In the case of 'realistic' depiction, it makes sense to think of veridicality as a matter of resemblance between aspects of a picture and aspects of what it depicts.[13] Mackie's insight is that the best hope of a philosophically hygienic interpretation for Locke's talk of 'ideas', in a perceptual context, is in terms of 'intentional objects': that is, aspects of representational content – aspects of how things seem to one in the enjoyment of a perceptual experience. (See *PFL*, pp. 47–50.) Now it is an illusion to suppose, as Mackie does, that this warrants thinking of the relation between a quality and an 'idea' of it on the model of the relation between a property of a picture's subject and an aspect of the picture. Explaining 'ideas' as 'intentional objects' should direct our attention to the relation between how things are and how an experience represents them as being – in fact identity, not resemblance, if the representation is veridical.[14] Mackie's Lockean appeal to resemblance fits something quite different: a relation borne to aspects of how things are by intrinsic aspects of a bearer of representational content – not how things are represented to be, but features of an item that does the representing, with particular aspects of its content carried by particular aspects of what it is intrinsically (non-representationally) like.[15] Perceptual experiences have representational content; but nothing in Mackie's defence of the 'intentional objects' gloss on 'ideas' would force us to suppose that they have it in that sort of way.[16]

The temptation to which Mackie succumbs, to suppose that intrinsic features of experience function as vehicles for particular aspects of representational content, is indifferent to any distinction between primary and secondary qualities in the representational significance that these features supposedly carry. What it is for a colour to figure in experience and what it is for a shape to figure in experience would be alike, on this view, in so far as both are a matter of an experience's having a certain intrinsic feature. If one wants, within this framework, to preserve Locke's intuition that primary-quality experience is distinctive in potentially disclosing the objective properties of things, one will be naturally led to Locke's use of the notion of resemblance. But no notion of resemblance could get us from an essentially experiential state of affairs to the concept of a feature of objects intelligible otherwise than in terms of how its possessors would strike us. (A version of this point told against Mackie's idea of possible primary qualities answering to 'colours as we see them'; it tells equally against the Lockean conception of shapes.)

If one gives up the Lockean use of resemblance, but retains the idea that primary and secondary qualities are experientially on a par, one will be led to suppose that the properties attributed to objects in the 'manifest image' are all equally phenomenal – intelligible, that is, only in terms of how their possessors are disposed to appear. Properties that are objective, in the contrasting sense, can then figure only in the 'scientific image'.[17] On these lines one altogether loses hold of Locke's intuition that primary qualities are distinctive in being both objective and perceptible.[18]

If we want to preserve the intuition, as I believe we should, then we need to exorcize the idea that what it is for a quality to figure in experience is for an experience to have a certain intrinsic feature: in fact I believe that we need to reject these supposed vehicles of content altogether. Then we can say that colours and shapes figure in experience, not as the representational significance carried by features that are – being intrinsic features of experience – indifferently subjective (which makes it hard to see how a difference in respect of objectivity could show up in their representational significance); but simply as properties that objects are represented as having, distinctively phenomenal in the one case and not so in the other. (Without the supposed intrinsic features, we should be immune to the illusion that experiences cannot represent objects as having properties that are not phenomenal – properties that are adequately conceivable otherwise than in terms of dispositions to produce suitable experiences.[19]) What Locke unfelicitously tried to yoke together, with his picture of real resemblances of our 'ideas', can now divide into two notions that we must insist on keeping separate: first, the possible veridicality of experience (the objectivity of its object, in the second of the two senses I distinguished), in respect of which primary and secondary qualities are on all fours; and, second, the not essentially phenomenal character of some properties that experience represents objects as having (their objectivity in the first sense), which marks off the primary perceptible qualities from the secondary ones.

In order to deny that a quality's figuring in experience consists in an experience's having a certain intrinsic feature, we do not need to reject the intrinsic features altogether; it would suffice to insist that a quality's figuring in experience consists in an experience's having a certain intrinsic feature *together with* the quality's being the representational significance carried by that feature. But I do not believe that this yields a position in which acceptance of the supposed vehicles of content coheres with a satisfactory account of perception. This position would have it that the fact that an experience represents things as being one way rather than another is strictly additional to the experience's intrinsic nature, and so extrinsic to the experience itself (it seems natural to say 'read into it'). There is a phenomenological falsification here. (This brings out a third role for Locke's resemblance, namely to obviate the threat of such a falsification by constituting a sort of intrinsic representationality: Locke's 'ideas' carry the representational significance they do by virtue of what they are like, and this can be glossed both as 'how they are intrinsically' and as 'what they resemble'.) In any case, given that we cannot project ourselves from features of experience to non-phenomenal properties of objects by means of an appeal to resemblance, it is doubtful that the metaphor of representational significance being 'read into' intrinsic features can be spelled out in such a way as to avoid the second horn of our dilemma. How could representational significance be 'read into' intrinsic features of experience in such a way that what was signified did not need to be understood in terms of them? How could a not intrinsically representational feature of experience become imbued with objective significance in such a way that an experience could count, by virtue of having that feature, as a direct awareness of a not essentially phenomenal property of objects?[20]

How things strike someone as being is, in a clear sense, a subjective matter: there is no conceiving it in abstraction from the subject of the experience. Now a motive for insisting on the supposed vehicles of aspects of content might lie in an aspiration, familiar in philosophy, to bring subjectivity within the compass of a fundamentally objective conception of reality.[21] If aspects of content are not carried by elements in an intrinsic structure, their subjectivity is irreducible. By contrast, one might hope to objectivize any 'essential subjectivity' that needs to be attributed to not intrinsically representational features of experience, by exploiting a picture involving special access on a subject's part to something conceived in a broadly objective way – its presence in the world not conceived as constituted by the subject's special access to it.[22] Given this move, it becomes natural to suppose that the phenomenal character of the 'manifest image' can be explained in terms of a certain familiar picture: one in which a confronted 'external' reality, conceived as having only an objective nature, is processed through a structured 'subjectivity', conceived in this objectivistic manner. This picture seems to capture the essence of Mackie's approach to the secondary qualities.[23] What I have tried to suggest is that the picture is suspect in threatening to cut us off from the *primary* (not essentially phenomenal) qualities of the objects that we perceive: either (with the appeal to resemblance) making it impossible, after all, to keep an essentially phenomenal character out of our conception of the qualities in question, or else making them merely hypothetical, not accessible to perception. If we are to achieve a satisfactory understanding of experience's openness to objective reality, we must put a more radical construction on experience's essential subjectivity. And this removes an insidious obstacle – one whose foundation is summarily captured in Mackie's idea that it is not simply wrong to count 'colours as we see them' as items in our minds (see the diagram at *PFL*, p. 17) – that stands in the way of understanding how secondary-quality experience can be awareness, with nothing misleading about its phenomenal character, of properties genuinely possessed by elements in a not exclusively phenomenal reality.

4 The empirical ground that Mackie thinks we have for not postulating 'thoroughly objective features which resemble our ideas of secondary qualities' (*PFL*, pp. 18-19) is that attributing such features to objects is surplus to the requirements of explaining our experience of secondary qualities (see *PFL*, pp. 17-18). If it would be incoherent to attribute such features to objects, as I believe, this empirical argument falls away as unnecessary. But it is worth considering how an argument from explanatory superfluity might fare against the less extravagant construal I have suggested for the thought that secondary qualities genuinely characterize objects: not because the question is difficult or contentious, but because of the light it casts on how an explanatory test for reality – which is commonly thought to undermine the claims of values – should be applied.

A '*virtus dormitiva*' objection would tell against the idea that one might mount a satisfying explanation of an object's looking red on its being such as to look red. The weight of the explanation would fall through the disposition to its structural ground.[24] Still, however optimistic we are about the prospects for explaining colour experience on the basis of surface textures,[25] it would be obviously wrong to suppose that someone who gave such an explanation could in consistency deny that the object was such as to look red. The right explanatory test is not whether something pulls its own weight in the favoured explanation (it may fail to do so without thereby being explained away), but whether the explainer can consistently deny its reality.[26]

Given Mackie's view about secondary qualities, the thought that values fail an explanatory test for reality is implicit in a parallel that he commonly draws between them (see, for instance, *HMT*, pp. 51-2; *E*, pp. 19-20). It is nearer the surface in his 'argument from queerness' (*E*, pp. 38-42), and explicit in his citing 'patterns of objectification' to explain the distinctive phenomenology of value experience (*E*, pp. 42-6).[27] Now it is, if anything, even more obvious with values than with essentially phenomenal qualities that they cannot be credited with causal efficacy: values would not pull their weight in any explanation of value experience even remotely analogous to the standard explanations of primary-quality experience. But reflection on the case of secondary qualities has already opened a gap between that admission and any concession that values are not genuine aspects of reality. And the point is reinforced by a crucial disanalogy between values and secondary qualities. To press the analogy is to stress that evaluative 'attitudes', or states of will, are like (say) colour experience in being unintelligible except as modifications of a sensibility like ours. The idea of value experience involves taking admiration, say, to represent its object as having a property which (although there in the object) is essentially subjective in much the same way as the property that an object is represented as having by an experience of redness – that is, understood adequately only in terms of the appropriate modification of human (or similar) sensibility. The disanalogy, now, is that a virtue (say) is conceived to be not merely such as to elicit the appropriate 'attitude' (as a colour is merely such as to cause the appropriate experiences), but rather such as to *merit* it. And this makes it doubtful whether merely causal explanations of value experience are relevant to the explanatory test, even to the extent that the question to ask is whether someone could consistently give such explanations while denying that the values involved are real. It looks as if we should be raising that question about explanations of a different kind.

For simplicity's sake, I shall elaborate this point in connection with something that is not a value, though it shares the crucial feature: namely danger or the fearful. On the face of it, this might seem a promising subject for a projectivist treatment (a treatment that appeals to what Hume called the mind's 'propensity to spread itself on external objects').[28] At any rate the response that, according to such a treatment, is projected into the world can be characterized, without phenomenological falsification, otherwise than in terms of seeming to find the supposed product of projection already there.[29] And it would be obviously grotesque to fancy that a case of fear might be explained as the upshot of a mechanical (or perhaps para-mechanical) process initiated by an instance of 'objective fearfulness'. But if what we are engaged in is an 'attempt to understand ourselves',[30] then merely causal explanations of responses like fear will not be satisfying anyway.[31] What we want here is a style of explanation that makes sense of what is explained (in so far as sense can be made of it). This means that a technique for giving satisfying explanations of cases of fear — which would perhaps amount to a satisfactory explanatory theory of danger, though the label is possibly too grand — must allow for the possibility of criticism; we make sense of fear by seeing it as a response to objects that *merit* such a response, or as the intelligibly defective product of a propensity towards responses that would be intelligible in that way.[32] For an object to merit fear just is for it to be fearful. So explanations of fear that manifest our capacity to understand ourselves in this region of our lives will simply not cohere with the claim that reality contains nothing in the way of fearfulness.[33] Any such claim would undermine the intelligibility that the explanations confer on our responses.

The shared crucial feature suggests that this disarming of a supposed explanatory argument for unreality should carry over to the case of values. There is, of course, a striking disanalogy in the contentiousness that is typical of values; but I think it would be a mistake to suppose that this spoils the point. In so far as we succeed in achieving the sort of understanding of our responses that is in question, we do so on the basis of preparedness to attribute, to at least some possible objects of the responses, properties that would validate the responses. What the disanalogy makes especially clear is that the explanations that preclude our denying the reality of the special properties that are putatively discernible from some (broadly) evaluative point of view are themselves constructed from that point of view. (We already had this in the case of the fearful, but the point is brought home when the validation of the

119

responses is controversial.) However, the critical dimension of the explanations that we want means that there is no question of just any actual response pulling itself up by its own bootstraps into counting as an undistorted perception of the relevant special aspect of reality.[34] Indeed, awareness that values are contentious tells against an unreflective contentment with the current state of one's critical outlook, and in favour of a readiness to suppose that there may be something to be learned from people with whom one's first inclination is to disagree. The aspiration to understand oneself is an aspiration to change one's responses, if that is necessary for them to become intelligible otherwise than as defective. But although a sensible person will never be confident that his evaluative outlook is incapable of improvement, that need not stop him supposing, of some of his evaluative responses, that their objects really do merit them. He will be able to back up this supposition with explanations that show how the responses are well-placed; the explanations will share the contentiousness of the values whose reality they certify, but that should not stop him accepting the explanations any more than (what nobody thinks) it should stop him endorsing the values.[35] There is perhaps an air of bootstrapping about this. But if we restrict ourselves to explanations from a more external standpoint, at which values are not in our field of view, we deprive ourselves of a kind of intelligibility that we aspire to; and projectivists have given no reason whatever to suppose that there would be anything better about whatever different kind of self-understanding the restriction would permit.

5 It will be obvious how these considerations undermine the damaging effect of the primary-quality model. Shifting to a secondary-quality analogy renders irrelevant any worry about how something that is brutely *there* could nevertheless stand in an internal relation to some exercise of human sensibility. Values are not brutely there – not there independently of our sensibility – any more than colours are: though, as with colours, this does not stop us supposing that they are there independently of any particular apparent experience of them. As for the epistemology of value, the epistemology of danger is a good model. (Fearfulness is not a secondary quality, although the model is available only after the primary-quality model has been dislodged. A secondary-quality analogy for value experience gives out at certain points, no less than the primary-quality analogy that Mackie attacks.) To drop the primary-quality model in this case is to give up the idea that fearfulness itself, were it real, would need to be intelligible from a standpoint

independent of the propensity to fear; the same must go for the relations of rational consequentiality in which fearfulness stands to more straightforward properties of things.[36] Explanations of fear of the sort I envisaged would not only establish, from a different standpoint, that some of its objects are really fearful, but also make plain, case by case, what it is about them that makes them so; this should leave it quite unmysterious how a fear response rationally grounded in awareness (unproblematic, at least for present purposes) of these 'fearful-making characteristics' can be counted as being, or yielding, knowledge that one is confronted by an instance of real fearfulness.[37]

Simon Blackburn has written, on behalf of a projectivist sentimentalism in ethics, that 'we profit . . . by realizing that a training of the feelings rather than a cultivation of a mysterious ability to spot the immutable fitnesses of things is the foundation of how to live'.[38] This picture of what an opponent of projectivism must hold is of a piece with Mackie's primary-quality model; it simply fails to fit the position I have described.[39] Perhaps with Aristotle's notion of practical wisdom in mind, one might ask why a training of the feelings (as long as the notion of feeling is comprehensive enough) cannot *be* the cultivation of an ability — utterly unmysterious just because of its connections with feelings — to spot (if you like) the fitnesses of things; even 'immutable' may be all right, so long as it is not understood (as I take it Blackburn intends) to suggest a 'platonistic' conception of the fitnesses of things, which would reimport the characteristic ideas of the primary-quality model.[40]

Mackie's response to this suggestion used to be, in effect, that it simply conceded his point.[41] Can a projectivist claim that the position I have outlined is at best a notational variant, perhaps an inferior notational variant, of his own position?

It would be inferior if, in eschewing the projectivist metaphysical framework, it obscured some important truth. But what truth would this be? It will not do at this point to answer 'The truth of projectivism'. I have disarmed the explanatory argument for the projectivist's thin conception of genuine reality. What remains is rhetoric expressing what amounts to a now unargued primary-quality model for genuine reality.[42] The picture that this suggests for value experience — objective (value-free) reality processed through a moulded subjectivity — is no less questionable than the picture of secondary-quality experience on which, in Mackie at any rate, it is explicitly modelled. In fact I should be inclined to argue that it is projectivism that is inferior. Deprived of the specious explanatory argument, projectivism has nothing to sustain its thin conception of reality (that on to which the projections are effected) but a contentiously substantial version of the correspondence theory of truth, with the associated picture of genuinely true judgment as something to which the judger makes no contribution at all.[43]

I do not want to argue this now. The point I want to make is that even if projectivism were not actually worse, metaphysically speaking, than the alternative I have described, it would be wrong to regard the issue between them as nothing but a question of metaphysical preference.[44] In the projectivist picture, having one's ethical or aesthetic responses rationally suited to their objects would be a matter of having the relevant processing mechanism functioning acceptably. Now projectivism can of course perfectly well accommodate the idea of assessing one's processing mechanism. But it pictures the mechanism as something that one can contemplate as an object in itself. It would be appropriate to say 'something one can step back from', were it not for the fact that one needs to use the mechanism itself in assessing it; at any rate one is supposed to be able to step back from any naively realistic acceptance of the values that the first-level employment of the mechanism has one attribute to items in the world. How, then, are we to understand this pictured availability of the processing mechanism as an object for contemplation, separated off from the world of value? Is there any alternative to thinking of it as capable of being captured, at least in theory, by a set of principles for superimposing values on to a value-free reality? The upshot is that the search for an evaluative outlook that one can endorse as rational becomes, virtually irresistibly, a search for such a set of principles: a search for a *theory* of beauty or goodness. One comes to count 'intuitions' respectable only in so far as they can be validated by an approximation to that ideal.[45] (This is the shape that the attempt to objectivize subjectivity takes here.) I have a hunch that such efforts are misguided; not that we should rest content with an 'anything goes' irrationalism, but that we need a conception of rationality in evaluation that will cohere with the possibility that particular cases may stubbornly resist capture in any general net. Such a conception is straightforwardly available within the alternative to projectivism that I have described. I allowed that being able to explain cases of fear in the right way might amount to having a theory of danger, but there is no need to generalize that feature of the case; the explanatory capacity that certifies the special objects of an evaluative outlook as real, and certifies its responses to them as rational, would need to be exactly as creative and case-specific as the capacity to discern those objects itself. (It would be the same capacity: the picture of 'stepping back' does not fit here.)[46] I take it that my hunch poses a question of moral and aesthetic taste, which — like other questions of taste — should be capable of being argued about. The trouble with projectivism is that it threatens to bypass that argument, on the basis of a metaphysical picture whose purported justification falls well short of making it compulsory. We should not let the question seem to be settled by what stands revealed, in the absence of compelling argument, as a prejudice claiming the honour due to metaphysical good taste.

ACKNOWLEDGMENT

This paper grew out of my contributions to a seminar on J. L. Mackie's *Ethics: Inventing Right and Wrong* (Penguin, Harmondsworth, 1977: I refer to this as *E*) which I had the privilege of sharing with Mackie and R. M. Hare in 1978. I do not believe that John Mackie would have found it strange that I should pay tribute to a sadly missed colleague by continuing a strenuous disagreement with him.

NOTES

1 See *E*, pp. 31-5. I shall also abbreviate references to the following other books by Mackie: *Problems from Locke* (Clarendon Press, Oxford, 1976: hereafter *PFL*); and *Hume's Moral Theory* (Routledge & Kegan Paul, London, 1980; hereafter *HMT*).

2 An inferior surrogate: it leads us to exaggerate the extent to which expressions of our sensitivity to values are signalled by the use of a special vocabulary. See my 'Aesthetic value, objectivity, and the fabric of the world', in Eva Schaper, ed., *Pleasure, Preference, and Value* (Cambridge University Press, Cambridge, 1983), pp. 1-16, at pp. 1-2.

3 I am trying here to soften a sharpness of focus that Mackie introduces by stressing the notion of prescriptivity. Mackie's singleness of vision here has the perhaps unfortunate effect of discouraging a distinction such as David Wiggins has drawn between 'valuations' and 'directives or deliberative (or practical) judgements' (see 'Truth, invention, and the meaning of life', *Proceedings of the British Academy* LXII (1976), pp. 331-78, at pp. 338-9). My topic here is really the former of these. (It may be that the distinction does not matter in the way that Wiggins suggests: see n. 35 below.)

4 I do not believe that the 'quasi-realism' that Simon Blackburn has elaborated is a real alternative to this. (See p. 358 of his 'Truth, realism, and the regulation of theory', in Peter A. French, Theodore E. Uehling, Jr., and Howard Wettstein, eds, *Midwest Studies in Philosophy V: Studies in Epistemology* (University of Minnesota Press, Minneapolis, 1980), pp. 353-71.) In so far as the quasi-realist holds that the values, in his thought and speech about which he imitates the practices supposedly characteristic of realism, are *really* products of projecting 'attitudes' into the world, he must have a conception of genuine reality — that which the values lack and the things on to which they are projected have. And the phenomenological claim ought to be that *that* is what the appearances entice us to attribute to values.

5 *An Essay concerning Human Understanding*, II.viii.10.

6 Being stung by a nettle is an actualization of a power in the nettle that conforms to Locke's description, but it seems wrong to regard it as a perception of that power; the experience lacks an intrinsically representational character which that would require. (It is implausible that looking red is intelligible independently of being red; combined with the account of secondary qualities that I am giving, this sets up a circle. But it is quite unclear that we ought to have the sort of analytic or definitional aspirations that would make the circle problematic. See Colin McGinn, *The Subjective View* (Clarendon Press, Oxford, 1983), pp. 6-8.)

7 See McGinn, op. cit., pp. 12-14.

8 Of course there is room for the concept of illusion, not only because the senses can malfunction but also becuse of the need for a modifier like my '(in certain circumstances)', in an account of what it is for something to have a secondary quality. (The latter has no counterpart with primary qualities.)

9 See the discussion of (one interpretation of the notion of) objectivity at pp. 77-8 of Gareth Evans, 'Things without the mind', in Zak van Straaten, ed., *Philosophical Subjects: Essays presented to P. F. Strawson* (Clarendon Press, Oxford, 1980), pp. 76-116. Throughout the present section I am heavily indebted to this most important paper.

10 See *Essay*, II.viii.15.

11 Cf. pp. 56-7 of P. F. Strawson, 'Perception and its objects', in G. F. Macdonald, ed., *Perception and Identity: Essays presented to A. J. Ayer* (Macmillan, London, 1979), pp. 41-60.

12 This is a different way of formulating a point made by McGinn, op. cit., p. 121. Mackie's phrase 'the fabric of the world' belongs with the second sense of 'objective', but I think his arguments really address only the first. *Pace* p. 103 of A. W. Price, 'Varieties of objectivity and values', *Proceedings of the Aristotelian Society* LXXXII (1982-3), 103-19, I do not think the phrase can be passed over as unhelpful, in favour of what the arguments do succeed in

establishing, without missing something that Mackie wanted to say. (A gloss on 'objective' as 'there to be experienced' does not figure in Price's inventory, p. 104. It seems to be the obvious response to his challenge at pp. 118-19.)

13 I do not say it is correct: scepticism about this is very much in point. (See Nelson Goodman, *Languages of Art* (Oxford University Press, London, 1969), chapter I.)

14 When resemblance is in play, it functions as a palliative to lack of veridicality, not as what veridicality consists in.

15 Intrinsic features of experience, functioning as vehicles for aspects of content, seem to be taken for granted in Mackie's discussion of Molyneux's problem (*PFL*, pp. 28-32). The slide from talk of content to talk that fits only bearers of content seems to happen also in Mackie's discussion of truth, in *Truth, Probability, and Paradox* (Clarendon Press, Oxford, 1973), with the idea that a formulation like 'A true statement is one such that the way things are is the way it represents things as being' makes truth consist in a relation of correspondence (rather than identity) between how things are and how things are represented as being; pp. 56-7 come too late to undo the damage done by the earlier talk of 'comparison', e.g. at pp. 50, 51. (A subject matter for the talk that fits bearers is unproblematically available in this case; but Mackie does not mean to be discussing truth as a property of sentences or utterances.)

16 Indeed, this goes against the spirit of a passage about the word 'content' at *PFL*, p. 48. Mackie's failure to profit by his insight emerges particularly strikingly in his remarkable claim (*PFL*, p. 50) that the 'intentional object' conception of the content of experience yields an account of perception that is within the target area of 'the stock objections against an argument from an effect to a supposed cause of a type which is never directly observed'. (Part of the trouble here is a misconception of direct realism as a surely forlorn attempt to make perceptual knowledge unproblematic: *PFL*, p. 43.)

17 The phrases 'manifest image' and 'scientific image' are due to Wilfrid Sellars; see 'Philosophy and the scientific image of man', in *Science, Perception and Reality* (Routledge & Kegan Paul, London, 1963).

18 This is the position of Strawson, op. cit. (and see also his 'Reply to Evans' in van Straaten, ed., op. cit., pp. 273-82). I am suggesting a diagnosis, to back up McGinn's complaint, op. cit., p. 124n.

19 Notice Strawson's sleight of hand with phrases like 'shapes-as-seen', at p. 280 of 'Reply to Evans'. Strawson's understanding of what Evans is trying to say fails altogether to accommodate Evans's remark ('Things without the mind', p. 96) that 'to deny that . . . primary properties are *sensory* is not at all to deny that they are *sensible* or *observable*'. Shapes as seen are *shapes* — that is,

non-sensory properties; it is one thing to deny, as Evans does, that experience can furnish us with the concepts of such properties, but quite another to deny that experience can disclose instantiations of them to us.

20 Features of physiologically specified states are not to the point here. Such features are not apparent in experience; whereas the supposed features that I am concerned with would have to be aspects of what experience is like for us, in order to function intelligibly as carriers for aspects of the content that experience presents to us. There may be an inclination to ask why it should be any harder for a feature of experience to acquire an objective significance than it is for a word to do so. But the case of language affords no counterpart to the fact that the objective significance in the case we are concerned with is a matter of how things (e.g.) *look* to be; the special problem is how to stop that 'look' having the effect that a supposed intrinsic feature of experience get taken up into its own representational significance, thus ensuring that the significance is phenomenal and not primary.

21 See Thomas Nagel, 'Subjective and objective', in *Mortal Questions* (Cambridge University Press, Cambridge, 1979), pp. 196–213.

22 Cf. Bernard Williams, *Descartes: The Project of Pure Enquiry* (Penguin, Harmondsworth, 1978), p. 295.

23 Although McGinn, op. cit., is not taken in by the idea that 'external' reality has only objective characteristics, I am not sure that he sufficiently avoids the picture that underlies that idea: see pp. 106–9. (This connects with a suspicion that at pp. 9–10 he partly succumbs to a temptation to objectivize the subjective properties of objects that he countenances: it is not as clear as he seems to suppose that, say, redness can be, so to speak, abstracted from the way things strike *us* by an appeal to relativity. His worry at pp. 132–6, that secondary-quality experience may after all be phenomenologically misleading, seems to betray the influence of the idea of content-bearing intrinsic features of experience.)

24 See McGinn, op. cit., p. 14.

25 There are difficulties over how complete such explanations could aspire to be: see Price, op. cit., pp. 114–15, and my 'Aesthetic value, objectivity, and the fabric of the world', op. cit., pp. 10–12.

26 Cf. pp. 206–8, especially p. 208, of David Wiggins, 'What would be a substantial theory of truth?', in van Straaten, ed., op. cit., pp. 189–221. The test of whether the explanations in question are consistent with rejecting the item in contention is something that Wiggins once mooted, in the course of a continuing attempt to improve that formulation: I am indebted to discussion with him.

27 See also Simon Blackburn, 'Rule-following and moral realism', in Steven Holtzman and Christopher Leich, eds, *Wittgenstein: To Follow a Rule* (Routledge & Kegan Paul, London, 1981),

pp. 163–87; and the first chapter of Gilbert Harman, *The Nature of Morality* (Oxford University Press, New York, 1977).

28 *A Treatise of Human Nature*, I.iii.14. 'Projectivist' is Blackburn's useful label: see 'Rule-following and moral realism', op. cit., and 'Opinions and chances', in D. H. Mellor, ed., *Prospects for Pragmatism* (Cambridge University Press, Cambridge, 1980), pp. 175–96.

29 At pp. 180–1 of 'Opinions and chances', Blackburn suggests that a projectivist need not mind whether or not this is so; but I think he trades on a slide between 'can . . . only be understood in terms of' and 'our best vocabulary for identifying' (which allows that there may be an admittedly inferior alternative).

30 The phrase is from p. 165 of Blackburn, 'Rule-following and moral realism'.

31 I do not mean that satisfying explanations will not be causal. But they will not be *merely* causal.

32 I am assuming that we are not in the presence of a theory according to which no responses of the kind in question *could* be well-placed. That would have a quite unintended effect. (See *E*, p. 16.) Notice that it will not meet my point to suggest that calling a response 'well-placed' is to be understood only quasi-realistically. Explanatory indispensability is supposed to be the test for the *genuine* reality supposedly lacked by what warrants only quasi-realistic treatment.

33 Cf. Blackburn, 'Rule-following and moral realism', op. cit., p. 164.

34 This will be so even in a case in which there are no materials for constructing standards of criticism except actual responses: something that is not so with fearfulness, although given a not implausible holism it will be so with values.

35 I can see no reason why we should not regard the contentiousness as ineliminable. The effect of this would be to detach the explanatory test of reality from a requirement of convergence (cf. the passage by Wiggins cited in n. 26 above). As far as I can see, this separation would be a good thing. It would enable resistance to projectivism to free itself, with a good conscience, of some unnecessary worries about relativism. It might also discourage a misconception of the appeal to Wittgenstein that comes naturally to such a position. (Blackburn, 'Rule-following and moral realism', pp. 170–4, reads into my 'Non-cognitivism and rule-following', in Holtzman and Leich, eds, op. cit., pp. 141–62, an interpretation of Wittgenstein as, in effect, making truth a matter of consensus, and has no difficulty in arguing that this will not make room for hard cases; but the interpretation is not mine.) With the requirement of convergence dropped, or at least radically relativized to a point of view, the question of the claim to truth of directives may come closer to the question of the truth status of evaluations than Wiggins suggests, at least in 'Truth, invention, and the meaning of life', op. cit.

36 Mackie's question (*E*, p. 41) 'Just what *in the world* is signified by this "because"?' involves a tendentious notion of 'the world'.

37 See Price, op. cit., pp. 106–7, 115.

38 'Rule-following and moral realism', p. 186.

39 Blackburn's realist evades the explanatory burdens that sentimentalism discharges, by making the world rich (cf. p. 181) and then picturing it as simply setting its print on us. Cf. *E*, p. 22: 'If there were something in the fabric of the world that validated certain kinds of concern, then it would be possible to acquire these merely by finding something out, by letting one's thinking be controlled by how things were'. This saddles an opponent of projectivism with a picture of awareness of value as an exercise of pure receptivity, preventing him from deriving any profit from an analogy with secondary-quality perception.

40 On 'platonism', see my 'Non-cognitivism and rule-following', op. cit., at pp. 156–7. On Aristotle, see M. F. Burnyeat, 'Aristotle on learning to be good', in Amelie O. Rorty, ed., *Essays on Aristotle's Ethics* (University of California Press, Berkeley, Los Angeles, London, 1980), pp. 69–92.

41 Price, op. cit. p. 107, cites Mackie's response to one of my contributions to the 1978 seminar (see Acknowledgment above).

42 We must not let the confusion between the two notions of objectivity distinguished in §3 above seem to support this conception of reality.

43 Blackburn uses the correspondence theorist's pictures for rhetorical effect, but he is properly sceptical about whether this sort of realism makes sense (see 'Truth, realism, and the regulation of theory', op. cit.). His idea is that the explanatory argument makes a counterpart to its metaphysical favouritism safely available to a projectivist about values in particular. Deprived of the explanatory argument, this projectivism should simply wither away. (See 'Rule-following and moral realism', p. 165. Of course I am not saying that the thin conception of reality that Blackburn's projectivism needs is unattainable, in the sense of being unformulable. What we lack is reasons of a respectable kind to recognize it as a complete conception *of reality*.)

44 Something like this seems to be suggested by Price, op. cit., pp. 107–8.

45 It is hard to see how a rational *inventing* of values could take a more piecemeal form.

46 Why do I suggest that a particularistic conception of evaluative rationality is unavailable to a projectivist? (See Blackburn, 'Rule-following and moral realism', pp. 167–70.) In the terms of that discussion, the point is that (with no good explanatory argument for his metaphysical favouritism) a projectivist has no alternative to being 'a *real* realist' about the world on which he thinks values are superimposed. He cannot stop this from generating a quite

un-Wittgensteinian picture of what *really* going on in the same way would be; which means that *he* cannot appeal to Wittgenstein in order to avert, as Blackburn puts it, 'the threat which shapelessness poses to a respectable notion of consistency' (p. 169). So, at any rate, I meant to argue in my 'Non-cognitivism and rule-following', to which Blackburn's paper is a reply. Blackburn thinks his projectivism is untouched by the argument, because he thinks he can sustain its metaphysical favouritism without appealing to *'real* realism', on the basis of the explanatory argument. But I have argued that this is an illusion. (At p. 181, Blackburn writes: 'Of course, it is true that our reactions are "simply felt" and, in a sense, not rationally explicable.' He thinks he can comfortably say this because our conception of reason will go along with the quasi-realist truth that his projectivism confers on some evaluations. But how can one restrain the metaphysical favouritism that a projectivist must show from generating some such thought as 'This is not *real* reason'? If that is allowed to happen, a remark like the one I have quoted will merely threaten — like an ordinary nihilism — to dislodge us from our ethical and aesthetic convictions.)

VII
RIGHTS AND CAPABILITIES
Amartya Sen

1 OVERLOOKING

In his *Principles of Psychology*, William James has remarked: 'The art of being wise is the art of knowing what to overlook.' I like the remark not just because it wisely overlooks so many other aspects of wisdom, but also because assessing what is overlooked does indeed seem to be quite a good way of judging what is being asserted. For example, the various approaches to moral judgments can plausibly be examined in terms of what the approaches respectively leave out. The dog that does not bark provides the clue.

Take utilitarianism. In insisting on justification of actions, rules, institutions, etc., in terms of their effects on human happiness and suffering, the Benthamite tradition overlooks the claims of such hallowed sentiments as national glory and pride. This overlooking clearly must have introduced a breath of fresh air in the debates on public policy in Bentham's time. Indeed, the need for that air is not altogether lost in the present-day world either, not even in the more sophisticated countries, as the nature of public reaction to the recent Falklands crisis clearly demonstrated in Britain. Bentham's insistence on judging choices in terms of effects on human beings has become neither obsolete, nor irrelevant, in the modern world.[1]

On the other hand the list of 'overlooked' items under the utilitarian approach is by no means confined only to such objects as national pride or glory, and blind prejudice or bloated sanctimony. Indeed, it is not quite correct to say that utilitarianism judges choices in terms of their effects on human beings, since it in fact judges them by the effects

130

exclusively on one limited aspect of human beings, to wit, their utilities — just their pleasures and pains and over-all desires.[2] It has been argued, with a good deal of justice, that utilitarianism is not really interested in persons as such, and that a person is viewed by a utilitarian as nothing other than the *place* in which that valuable thing called happiness takes place. It does not ultimately matter how this happiness happens, what causes it, what goes with it, and whether it is shared by many or grabbed by a few. All that really matters is the total amount of this 'marvellous' thing: happiness or desire-fulfilment.

In fact, utilitarianism is unable to distinguish even between different types of pleasures and pains, or different types of desires, when the valuation is performed. This was, of course, one of John Stuart Mill's difficulties, though like his other complaints against utilitarianism, this too figured in the unlikely form of an indirect defence of the utilitarian outlook. In fact, utilitarianism has to face the problem of heterogeneity of utilities even in the distinction between pleasure and pain, since pain can hardly be seen as negative pleasure. Dr Johnson's well-known remark: 'Marriage has many pains, but celibacy has no pleasures',[3] would have — I imagine — prompted the purest utilitarian to check whether the *net* sum was positive or negative without wasting further time.

The limitation of utilitarianism arising from its overlooking everything other than total utility — aggregated over different types of utilities and different persons — has been much discussed in the recent literature.[4] There is, however, one particular aspect of this limitation which has received much less attention than, I believe, is due. The most blatant forms of inequalities and exploitations survive in the world through making allies out of the deprived and the exploited. The underdog learns to bear the burden so well that he or she overlooks the burden itself. Discontent is replaced by acceptance, hopeless rebellion by conformist quiet, and — most relevantly in the present context — suffering and anger by cheerful endurance. As people learn to adjust to the existing horrors by the sheer necessity of uneventful survival, the horrors look less terrible in the metric of utilities.[5]

Let me illustrate the point with an example. In 1944 — the year after the Great Bengal Famine — a survey was carried out by the All-India Institute of Hygiene and Public Health in Singur — near Calcutta.[6] Among the categories of people surveyed in this immediate post-famine year there were many widows and widowers. I should add that the condition of women in India outside elite groups — and of widows in

131

particular — is generally recognized to be nothing short of scandalous, and the position of women in terms of nutrition tends to be particularly bad. But how did the different groups respond to the questionnaire? As many as 48.5 per cent of widow*ers* — men that is — confided that they were 'ill' or in 'indifferent' health. The proportion of widows, on the other hand, in that dual category was just 2.5 per cent. The picture becomes even more interesting if we look at the answers to the question as to whether one was in indifferent health, leaving out the question about being definitely ill, for which of course there are more objective standards. In the more subjective category of being in 'indifferent' health, we find 45.6 per cent of the widowers. And what about the widows? It is reported that the answer is 0 per cent! Quiet acceptance of deprivation and bad fate affects the scale of dissatisfaction generated, and the utilitarian calculus gives sanctity to that distortion. This is especially so in *interpersonal* comparisons. If one has to get away from this mental-reaction view of deprivation that utilitarianism has made common, then one must look at deprivation in terms of some other metric. I shall presently argue that the metric of capabilities to function is a sensible one to choose, using information regarding who can in fact *do* what, and not just the way people *desire or react to* their ability or disability to do these things. But I have other approaches to consider before I get there.

2   RIGHTS AND ENTITLEMENTS

It has been argued that a rights-based moral approach has many advantages.[7] In particular, it may be able to do a better job of dealing with deprivation than the utility-based approaches can. A person has some moral rights, and to be denied them is to be deprived of something valuable. But this starting point may be seen as begging a question: *why* do people have rights? Indeed, *do* they have moral rights? Whether this is at all a plausible point to begin has been forcefully disputed in recent years, despite the long history of morally appealing to natural rights, or human rights, or some other similar concept.

   I raise this question here not because I intend to discuss it, but because I don't. The question of foundation is a very difficult one to resolve, and it is not very clear what would count as providing an adequate foundation of a substantive moral theory. There is, in fact, some evidence of arbitrary distinction when it comes to evaluation of particular moral theories. Some who find no difficulty at all in intrinsically valuing 'utility', or 'interests' of individuals, or some idea of 'equal treatment', find it intolerably arbitrary to begin with an assertion of rights. But any moral theory would have to begin with some primitive diagnosis of value (even if it is a procedural one in terms of some mythical primordial state), and the real question is whether the acknowledgment of rights cannot play that primitive role. The question is not meant as a rhetorical one. I accept fully that one has to dig for foundation,[8] but there is a substantial issue involved in deciding where to stop digging.

The issue also depends on what kind of activity we take moral evaluation to be.[9] I shall not have the opportunity of pursuing these deeper questions in this paper.

Rights can take very many different forms. In terms of actual legal rights against the state, they sometimes take the form of a substantive claim to, say, minimal health care, unemployment benefit, poverty relief, etc. But such specific legal rights are typically not justified in terms of their intrinsic importance, but on some instrumental grounds, e.g., the belief that they lead to a happier community. I shall have more to say on this question presently. But I first take up the approach that is more common in moral theories of rights and which takes a strongly *procedural* form.

In this form, rights do not specify directly what a person may or may not have, but specify the rules that have to be followed to make his or her actual holdings and actions legitimate. For example, the rights may take the form of specifying rules of ownership and transfer, and the results of these rules are accepted precisely because they have resulted from obeying the right rules, not because the results judged as outcomes are in themselves good, which they may or may not be. In his justly famous book, *Anarchy, State and Utopia*,[10] Robert Nozick argued against any 'patterning' of outcomes. Such 'patterning' would — as it were — over-determine the system, since the rules that are accepted would lead to some outcomes and not others, and respecting these procedures does require the acceptance of whatever outcomes happen to emerge.

I believe this consequence-independent way of seeing rights is fundamentally defective.[11] Take a theory of entitlements based on a set of rights of 'ownership, transfer and rectification'. In this system a set of holdings of different people are judged to be just (or not just) by looking at past history, and not by checking the consequences of that set of holdings. But what if the consequences are recognizably terrible? I shall be self-indulgent enough at this point to refer to some empirical findings in a work on famines I did recently. In a book called *Poverty and Famines: An Essay on Entitlement and Deprivation*,[12] I have presented evidence to indicate that in many large famines in the recent past, in which millions of people have died, there was no over-all decline in food availability at all, and the famines occurred precisely because of shifts in entitlements resulting from exercises of rights that are perfectly legitimate. The legitimacy referred to here is, of course, of the legal type rather than that of being supported by a given moral system, but as it happens the moral system of ownership, transfer and rectification outlined by Nozick is, in many respects, quite close to such a legal system of property rights and market exchange.

I do not wish to spend any time in discussing whether or not famines can plausibly occur with a system of rights of the kind morally defended in various ethical theories, including Nozick's. I believe the answer is straightforwardly yes, since for many people the only resource that they legitimately possess, viz., their labour-power, may well turn out to be unsaleable in the market, giving the persons no command over food. The question I am asking is this: if results such as starvation and famines were to occur, would the distribution of holdings still be morally acceptable despite their disastrous consequences? There is something deeply implausible in the affirmative answer. Why should it be the case that rules of ownership, etc., should have such absolute priority over life-and-death questions?

It is, of course, possible to claim that only in these extreme cases should the entitlements based on rights of ownership and transfer be compromised, but not otherwise. Indeed, Nozick keeps the question open as to whether 'catastrophic moral horrors' can provide a ground for justly violating rights. But once it is admitted that consequences can be important in judging what rights we do or do not morally have, surely the door is quite open for taking a less narrow view of rights, rejecting assessment by procedures only. The bad consequences may of course, be less disastrous in some other cases, but the extent of violation of procedural rights to avoid the bad consequences could be weaker *too*. Once trade-offs based on consequential evaluation are accepted, there is no obvious stopping place for a theory that was set up on a purely procedural approach.

Many authors in recent years have argued against what is often called 'consequentialism' — judging choices (say between actions, or

134

between rules, or between institutions) exclusively in terms of consequent states of affairs. I believe some of these attacks may exaggerate difficulties with consequentialism since they do not take full note of the extent of freedom that consequentialism permits if the states of affairs are seen more completely than many traditional theories allow, e.g. if non-utility features in the states of affairs are taken seriously (against the tradition of utilitarian concern with utility information only).[13] Nevertheless, it is not implausible to argue that even with as rich a view of states of affairs as is possible, consequentialism will still leave something to be desired. But that debate, viz., 'consequentialism or not', must not be confused with the debate 'consequence-sensitivity or not'. A substantive moral theory can be non-consequentialist but consequence-sensitive. Consequent states of affairs may not be the *only* things that matter, but they can nevertheless *matter*. Since is is implausible − indeed I believe incredible − to claim that consequences in the form of life or death, starvation or nourishment, indeed pleasure or pain, are intrinsically matters of moral indifference, or have only very weak intrinsic moral relevance, it is not easy to see why history-based rules of procedure should be so invulnerable to the facts of their consequences.

The procedural view of rights have typically taken what may be called a 'negative' form, corresponding somewhat to the well-known distinction between negative and positive freedoms. This affinity might at first sight appear to be a bit puzzling. If we are asserting the moral legitimacy of certain procedures, e.g. of ownership and exchange, why is it not just as much a positive assertion that we do have these rights, as it is a negative assertion that others must not stop us from enjoying these rights? But the negative assertion in this view has a practical content that the positive assertion lacks. The rights in question are not concerned with my actual capability of doing this or that, but my freedom to do them without let or hindrance. It binds others negatively − they must not interfere − but they are under no obligation to help me to exercise these rights.

This begs a difficult − and a very old − question. Why is it important that I do not be stopped from doing something and − at the same time − unimportant whether or not I can in fact do that thing? I shall have something to say on that presently, but before that I ask a more limited question. Suppose we are concerned only with negative freedom, to wit, that people *should not be stopped by others* from doing what they have a right to do (e.g. to move about freely). Should we see the ability to exercise these negative rights as good things that should be supported, or do we take the constraint view of negative freedom and just assert that one should not oneself interfere in these rights of others? If the former, i.e. if the violation of negative freedoms counts as a bad consequence which is to be avoided, consequential reasoning can justify — indeed require — many *positive* actions in pursuit of *negative* freedom, e.g. that one should stop A from stopping B from moving about freely.

Indeed, *valuing* negative freedom *must* have some positive implications. If I see that negative freedom is valuable, and I hear that you are about to be molested by someone, and I can stop him or her from doing that, then I should certainly be under some obligation to consider doing that stopping. It is not adequate for me to resist molesting you; it is necessary that I value the things I can *do* to stop others from molesting you. I would fail to *value negative freedom* if I were to refuse to consider what I could do in defence of negative freedom.

In fact, the positive implications of negative freedom can go further. Suppose I can stop A from molesting B by using C's telephone, in his absence, and suppose I also know that C would not have permitted me to use his telephone for this purpose had he been around. Should I violate C's negative freedom not to have me enter his room and use his personal telephone against his wishes, to stop the violation of the negative freedom of B not to be beaten up by A? I would say — unless there is something important not captured by the description of the story — the answer must be yes. But that implies that it must be sometimes right to violate deliberately someone's negative freedom to bring about the prevention of a more serious violation of the negative freedom of someone else.

There is no tension in all this if we are allowed to assess or qualify rights — including negative freedoms — using consequence-sensitive analysis. The benefits in the form of stopping serious violations of negative freedoms can be seen as outweighing the costs in the form of less serious violations of negative freedom. Such a 'cost-benefit analysis' may not be decisive except for the full consequentialist, but even non-consequentialists could accept a good deal of consequence-sensitivity in an otherwise deontological perspective. But consequence-sensitive evaluation with trade-offs is, of course, precisely what the constraint view of rights and negative freedom rules out. That view seems to me to be deeply defective. If freedom is important, it may *well be* valuable. If freedom *is* valuable, it may have some consequential relevance to the choice of actions. The old idea that vigilance — eternal or not — may indeed be important for liberty is not so easily dismissible.[14]

Thus, even if negative freedoms were all we valued, there would still be a strong case for having consequence-sensitive evaluation of negative freedoms, and for accepting contingently some *positive* obligation to protect negative freedoms. But — to move on — why should our concern stop only at protecting negative freedoms rather than be involved with what people can actually do? Should one be under an obligation to save the person who has been *pushed* into the river but not the person who has *fallen* into it? In deciding whether one is under an obligation to help a starving person, should one say 'yes' if the person has been robbed (with his negative freedom being violated), but remain free to say 'no' if he has been fired from his job, or has lost his land to the moneylender, or has suffered from flooding or drought (without any violation of negative freedom)?

I shall not pursue this question further here. But I would like to investigate some interesting questions that arise once positive freedoms are accepted as valuable and when some obligation to support such freedoms is given an important place in our moral thinking. How should these freedoms be characterized? Should they be seen as inputs to other —more fundamental — goals, e.g. the creation of a better society from the utilitarian point of view? Should they be seen as collateral benefits arising from the application of some deeper theory of justice, e.g. John Rawls's difference principle involving a just distribution of what he calls primary goods? I will, in fact, dispute these possible diagnoses, but before that I should try to outline a characterization of positive freedoms in the form of capabilities of persons.

3   CAPABILITIES

Consider a good, e.g. rice. The utilitarian will be concerned with the fact that the good in question creates utility through its consumption. And indeed, so it does. But that is not the only thing it does. It can also give the person nutrition. *Owning* some rice gives the person the *capability* of meeting some of his or her nutritional requirements.

In modern consumer theory in economics, the nature of the goods has been seen in terms of their 'characteristics', and authors such as Terence Gorman and Kelvin Lancaster have done much to explore the view of goods as bundles of characteristics.[15] Rice has nutrition-giving characteristics, but other characteristics as well, e.g. satisfying hunger, providing stimulation, meeting social conventions, offering the opportunity of getting together, etc.[16] Not all of these characteristics are easy to pursue through the use of market data, and in that context economic analysis has tended to concentrate on a more restricted view of characteristics. But in this paper I am not really concerned with characteristics as such, but wish to go beyond that to what I have been calling capabilities. A characteristic — as used in consumer theory— is a feature of a good, whereas a capability is a feature of a person in relation to goods. Having some rice gives me the capability of functioning in a particular way, e.g. without nutritional deficiencies of particular types. The capability to function is the thing that comes closest to the notion of positive freedom, and if freedom is valued then capability itself can serve as an object of value and moral importance.

Four different notions need distinction in this context. There is the notion of a *good* (in this case, rice); that of a *characteristic* of a good (e.g. giving calories and nutrition); that of *functioning* of a person (in this case, living without calorie deficiency); that of *utility* (in this case, the pleasure or desire-fulfilment from the functioning in question, or from some other functioning related to the characteristics of rice). The entitlement theorists such as Nozick would be concerned with none of these directly, but would accept whatever holdings of goods of different persons follow from rules that are seen as legitimate or just. Utilitarianism — or more generally any utility-based moral theory — would concentrate on the last item of the four, and this is related to the view that the only thing of intrinsic value is utility. Egalitarians concerned with income distribution will come close to worrying about the distribution of goods, and will focus on the first item. The Rawlsian focus on primary goods (including incomes) in the context of the difference principle again relates to the category of goods in this four-fold classification, though — as I shall argue presently — there are also other elements in the Rawlsian perspective.

Focusing on the third item — the functioning of a person — has advantages that are both unique and important.[17] In fact, the natural interpretation of the traditional view of positive freedoms is in terms of capabilities to function. They specify what a person can or cannot do, *or* can or cannot be. These freedoms are not primarily concerned with what goods or income or resources people have. Nor with precisely how much pleasure or desire-fulfilment people get out of these activities (or from the ability to do these activities). The category of capabilities is the natural candidate for reflecting the idea of freedom to do. This is not to say that there are no ambiguities in this correspondence. Indeed, there are ambiguities, and I will discuss some of these later, but nevertheless the category of capabilities does come close to being able to reflect freedom in the positive sense.

The distinctions involved in the four-fold classification are obvious enough, but they are sometimes confused, and perhaps the contrast between characteristics and functioning is worth a further remark. Characteristics represent, of course, an abstraction from goods, but they relate to goods rather than to persons. Functionings are, however, personal features; they tell us what a person is doing. Capability to function reflects what a person *can* do. Of course, characteristics of goods owned by a person do *relate* to the capabilities of persons, because a person achieves these capabilities through the use of those goods, among other things, but still capabilities of persons are quite different from the characteristics of goods possessed. Valuing one has *implications* on favouring the other, but valuing one is *not the same thing* as valuing the other.

If, for example, we value a person's ability to function without nutritional deficiency, we would tend to favour, up to a point, arrangements in which the person in question has more food with those nutritional characteristics, but that is not the same thing as valuing the possession of that food as such. If, say, some disease makes the person unable to achieve the capability of avoiding nutritional deficiency even with an amount of the food that would suffice for others, then the fact that he does possess that amount of the food (or has the resources to possess it) and command its characteristics, would not outweigh the loss of capability. If we value capabilities, then that is what we do value, and the possession of goods with the corresponding characteristics is instrumentally and contingently valued only to the extent that it helps in the achievement of the thing that we do value, viz., capabilities.

All this would not be worth spelling out in such painful detail but for the fact that despite the obvious relevance of capabilities of persons, various moral explorers have decided to pitch their tents on grounds other than capabilities. I turn now to an examination of some of those other positions.

4   UTILITY

The class of 'welfarist' moral theories includes utilitarianism. But what distinguished the class is not the fact that utilities are summed up to reflect the goodness of a state of affairs, but that utilities are regarded as adequate information for judging states of affairs. Furthermore – in the case of moral theories that are *both* welfarist and consequentialist – all choices of actions, rules, motives, institutions, etc., can also be judged in terms of the utility information only, regarding the consequent states of affairs. An example of a moral theory that is welfarist (i.e. utility-based, in this sense), without being utilitarian, is the theory that has been much explored in welfare economics under the influence of Rawls's writings and which is called, by stretching a point, 'Rawlsian'. This takes the form of judging the goodness of a state of affairs in terms of the utility level of the worst-off individual in that society in that state, and economists such as Phelps and Atkinson, among others,[18] have done much to explore the implications of such an approach.

There are two distinct reasons why any welfarist theory must be inadequate in dealing with freedom. First, freedom is concerned with what one *can* do, and not just with what one does do. Second, freedom is concerned with what one can *do*, and not just with what utility that doing leads to. Taking the latter question first, a welfarist distributional system determines what one should get on the basis of the psychological reactions in the form of pleasures and pains, or anticipations in the form of desires. Utilitarians reward *high marginal utility*, i.e. high psychological response to rewards; the so-called 'Rawlsians' of the welfarist variety, on the other hand, respond to *low total utility*, i.e. low over-all psychological state of happiness. These different uses of utility information may take us in different directions, but all welfarist theories agree that if two persons have identical utility features then they must have the same claims to a share of a given total. But suppose one of them is really much more deprived in terms of what he can do, e.g. he is blind or disabled in some other way, and his utility features match that of the other only because he has a much more cheerful and resilient temperament. The fact of his disadvantage should then play no part in the welfarist calculus, but it remains true to say that he has less capabilities since he cannot do many things that the other can do. Is the fact of this disadvantaged person's cheerfulness, or easier desire-fulfilment, adequate ground for him to be given no special resource to help combat that disadvantage? Does a cheerful blind person because of his buoyancy forgo the help that he could otherwise claim from the society? We need not drown the information about a person's disadvantages in the loud noise of utilities, as welfarists would do. A person, as we argued before, is more than the location of utilities, and it does matter what kind of a deal he is getting.

The other issue concerns the special attention that freedom has to pay to the *possibilities* open to a person as opposed to the particular one he or she happens to choose. It could be the case that an illiterate person, had he been literate, would have still chosen not to read anything, and it certainly could be the case that his or her utility would not have been any different had he been literate. For the welfarist such an illiterate person need not be seen as deprived, but from the point of view of freedom, notwithstanding the congruence on the utility space, the positions of the literate and the illiterate persons are not the same. One can do many things that the other cannot, and this fact is not rendered irrelevant by the other fact that they happen to choose to do the same things and get the same utility in the case under discussion.

This last point should not be taken to imply that it is being asserted that it does not morally matter at all whether a person himself values some capability or not, and whether he chooses to use that capability. Far from it. This is partly because freedom is not the only moral consideration that a freedom-inclusive moral system might support. Even if something is irrelevant to freedom, it could be morally important in such a plural system because of the other value elements in that system. But more immediately, freedom itself is not insensitive to what a person values. The index of capabilities can be sensitive to the strength of desires without converting everything into the metric of desires. The welfarist picture drops out everything other than desires. A non-welfarist overall index of capabilities may not drop out desires and may well be sensitive to the strength of desires *without ignoring* other influences on the indexing.[19]

5   PRIMARY GOODS

I turn now to the Rawlsian approach as reflected in his difference principle. In this view a person's advantage is judged by an index of primary goods, including income. This differs from the welfarist approach in refusing to accept the hegemony of the metric of desires or pleasures. While this is achieved at the cost of having to devise an alternative system of weighting of different primary goods, the task of weighting is – explicitly or implicitly – an essential one in any moral theory of this kind. But it is important to check first whether the holding of primary goods is a good guide to a person's advantage.

On the reasoning presented earlier, if what we value is freedom, then primary goods can be valued only instrumentally *and* very contingently. If someone has a physical handicap, it is quite possible that income may do less for him or her than it does for another, and other primary goods – similarly – may have variable importance. These are not just special cases, as Rawls has been somewhat inclined to think.[20] Depending on our size and body metabolism, our need for food varies between community and community, and within a community, between person to person, and the resulting difference can be enormous in the context of a poor country. When it comes to rich countries, the income requirements of various social goals such as taking part in the life of the community or having self-respect may vary depending on a variety of circumstances. The correspondence between 'primary goods' and what may be called 'primary capabilities' is not that of a tight mapping that operates independently of persons or communities.[21]

There are, however, good reasons to think that Rawls himself – contrary to what his own theory formally states – is really after something like capabilities. He motivates the focus on primary goods by discussing what the primary goods enable people to do. It is only because of his assumption – often implicit – that the same mapping of primary goods to capabilities holds for all, that he can sensibly concentrate on primary goods rather than on the corresponding capabilities. Once that untenable assumption about the same mapping is dropped, the natural response should be to come back to the motivating concern with capabilities.[22]

Rawls's ambiguity on this subject is caught very well by his vacillation between taking 'self-respect' as a primary good, on the one hand, and 'the social bases of self-respect', or simply 'the bases of self-respect', as the primary good dealing with this feature. Sometimes he moves from one to the other within one page.[23] Self-respect is, of course, just an outcome, and by extension it can refer to the ability to achieve this particular functioning of a person. On the other hand, social *bases* of self-respect – like income – are only means to the end of that functioning. Rawls is more consistent in his list of primary goods when he talks about the 'social bases' or 'bases' of self-respect, along with other primary goods such as 'rights, liberties and opportunities, income and wealth'. But he seems, in fact, to be closer to his real concern when he talks about the 'primary good of self-respect'.

6   RESOURCES

I turn now to a different — though not unrelated — ground on which to base moral analysis, to wit, the resources of persons. The case for equality of resources has been persuasively developed recently by Ronald Dworkin.[24] Much of his argument is concerned with what equality of resource might really mean, and Dworkin argues that the idea involves both the operation of an economic (in fact competitive) market and the assumption — strongly counterfactual — of the existence of some insurance markets covering differences of abilities and productive power to make the equality of resources a persuasive moral criterion.

In this context Dworkin considers the focus on capabilities advocated by this author in an earlier paper (my Tanner Lecture, 'Equality of what?').[25] He notes that 'people's powers are indeed resources, because these are used, together with material resources, in making something valuable out of one's life'.[26] This comes close to taking explicit note of capabilities in defining the resources themselves, and it could be argued that this way of seeing resources would lead to a congruence of the requirements of equality of capabilities and that of equality of resources. This raises an interesting issue, but as it happens, while Dworkin sees the taking of counterfactual insurance against handicaps as part and parcel of his characterization of the good society, he argues against bringing in handicaps into the idea of equality of resources as such. This is partly because these personal resources are not transferable, but also because of two 'practical and theoretical inadequacies'. First, Dworkin argues that for effective use of the idea of compensating for mental or physical handicaps, we require 'some standard of "normal" powers to serve as the benchmark for compensation', and this does not exist. Second, he notes that 'no amount of initial compensation could make someone born blind or mentally incompetent equal in physical or mental resources with someone taken to be 'normal' in these ways'.[27]

The first of these arguments seems to suffer from the unjustified belief that the equality of capabilities — and the equality of resources derived from that — cannot make sense without some idea of normal levels of capabilities. Why so? The case for equality of capabilities is no more dependent on the idea of 'normal capabilities' than the case for equality of resources of other kinds is dependent on the idea of 'normal resources' such as 'normal income'. The latter would be absurd, since the notion of normal income varies from society to society. The former is absurd for much the same reason. But neither compromises the possibility and indeed the importance of thinking in terms of equality of either kind. The notion of normality is not central to *comparing* capabilities, and to *ranking* them as 'more' or 'less' in interpersonal contrasts. Indeed, the idea of normality is quite unnecessary for such binary comparisons.

The second argument – related to the impossibility of full compensation of the handicapped person such as the blind – rests on the implicit beliefs that one cannot talk about the value of equality, if it is not feasible, and one cannot recommend a move towards equality if absolute equality cannot be achieved. Both presumptions are open to questioning. Many ideals are known to be unachievable without being useless for that reason. Indeed, very few egalitarians of any kind – Babeuf or Marx not excluded – had thought that absolute equality of the kind they advocated would be really achievable.

Further, since equality of capabilities in the aggregate sense is based on some kind of an over-all *index* of capabilities, it may indeed be possible to achieve full equality even without giving sight to the blind, or making the deaf hear all. Finally, even when full equality is not achievable, a move towards it may be possible. 'More equality' is not an empty slogan, and the best need not be made the enemy of the good.

But Dworkin is certainly right that personal physical and mental qualities are not resources in the sense in which ordinary material resources are, and they cannot be 'manipulated or transferred' in the way material resources can be. More importantly, there does not seem to be any real advantage in translating the valuation of capabilities into an equivalent notion of the valuation of resources and getting an idea of equality of resources that is thoroughly parasitical on the idea of equality of capabilities. But in all these recognitions, there is no argument for rejecting the value of capabilities as such, nor the moral claim of equality of capabilities to be the right general concept of equality, and Dworkin presents no such argument. Thus, in an important way, the rather limited notion of equality of resources, which overlooks the interpersonal differences in the mapping from resources to capabilities, remains undefended.

Indeed, to see the interpersonal variations of the mapping from resources to capabilities as due only to handicaps of some people is to underestimate the general nature of the problem. As was already mentioned, depending on our body size, metabolism, temperament, social conditions, etc., the translation of resources into the ability to do things does vary substantially from person to person and from community to community, and to ignore that is to miss out on an important general dimension of moral concern.

7   CONCLUDING REMARKS

In this paper I have outlined and defended an interpretation of positive freedoms. The interpretation sees freedoms in the form of particular capabilities. While a moral argument need not require that the various capabilities be converted into an aggregate measure, some arguments will need this, and that requires the use of some procedure of indexation. The problem is similar to that of constructing an index of primary goods . as needed by John Rawls, but it is in some ways easier to handle.

Capabilities are — as I have argued — directly valuable in a way that the possession of primary goods cannot be, since they evidently are means to some more human ends. Judgments of relative importance are, thus, less contingent and less remote in the case of capabilities as opposed to primary goods. Nevertheless, there are difficulties in such indexation. I have not discussed that issue in this paper, though I have tried to do this elsewhere.[28]

I have argued against the utilitarian — and more generally welfarist — moral focus as well as against the focus of Rawlsian difference principle and Dworkin's notion of equality of resources. The Rawlsian and Dworkinian notions are moves in the right direction, but they seem to me to be generally deficient as moral criteria, and in particular take inadequate note of the ideas behind positive freedom.

I have also argued against the consequence-insensitive ways of characterizing moral rights and entitlements, as put forward by Robert Nozick and others. Valuing negative freedoms in the form of constraints on action is, I have tried to show, a fundamentally defective moral perspective. If, on the other hand, preserving negative freedom is seen as valuable, then some positive action recommendations follow from this consequentially. In addition to arguing that negative freedoms have positive implications, I have also argued against confining attention to negative freedoms only.

Concern with positive freedoms leads directly to valuing people's capabilities and instrumentally to valuing things that enhance these capabilities. The notion of capabilities relates closely to the functioning of a person. This has to be contrasted with the ownership of goods, the characteristics of goods owned, and the utilities generated.

ACKNOWLEDGMENTS

This paper draws much on my James Lecture at the New York Institute for the Humanities in November 1982 and my Boutwood Lectures at Corpus Christi College, Cambridge, in November 1983. For helpful comments on an earlier draft I am most grateful to John Bennett, John Broome, Ronald Dworkin, Isaac Levi and Tom Nagel. I also had the privilege of having several interesting and illuminating discussions with John Mackie on the subject matter of this paper during 1980-1.

NOTES

1 Samuel Brittan has made this point forcefully in 'Two cheers for utilitarianism', in his *The Role and Limits of Government: Essays in Political Economy* (London: Temple Smith, 1983).

2 See especially John Rawls, *A Theory of Justice* (Cambridge, Mass.: Harvard University Press, and Oxford: Clarendon Press, 1971), and 'Social unity and primary goods', in Amartya Sen and Bernard Williams (eds), *Utilitarianism and Beyond* (Cambridge: Cambridge University Press, 1982).

3 *Rasselas*, Chapter 26.

4 For a recent collection of papers presenting arguments on different sides and of different types, see Sen and Williams (eds), *Utilitarianism and Beyond*. The editors' own assessment is presented there in the 'Introduction' to the volume. See also J. J. C. Smart and B. A. O. Williams, *Utilitarianism: For and Against* (Cambridge: Cambridge University Press, 1973), and A. K. Sen, 'Utilitarianism and welfarism', *Journal of Philosophy*, 76 (1979).

5 I have tried to discuss this problem, in the specific context of sex discrimination in the distribution of food and medical facilities, in my 'Family and food: sex-bias in poverty' in *Resources, Values and Development* (Oxford: Blackwell, and Cambridge, Mass.: Harvard University Press, 1984). The general question of adjustment of wants and desires in the light of feasibilities has been well discussed by Jon Elster, 'Sour grapes — utilitarianism and the genesis of wants', in Sen and Williams (eds), *Utilitarianism and Beyond*.

6 See R. B. Lal and S. C. Seal, *General Health Survey, Singur Health Centre, 1944* (Calcutta, All-India Institute of Hygiene and Public Health, 1949).

7 See particularly John Mackie, 'Can there be a right-based moral theory', *Midwest Studies in Philosophy*, 3 (1978).

8 See T. N. Scanlon, 'Contractualism and utilitarianism', in Sen and Williams (eds), *Utilitarianism and Beyond*.

9 See Thomas Nagel, 'The limits of objectivity', in S. McMurrin (ed.), *Tanner Lectures on Human Values* (Cambridge: Cambridge University Press, 1980).

10 R. Nozick, *Anarchy, State and Utopia* (New York: Basic Books, and Oxford: Basil Blackwell, 1974).

11 See my 'Rights and agency', *Philosophy and Public Affairs*, 11 (1982).

12 *Poverty and Famines: An Essay on Entitlement and Deprivation* (Oxford: Clarendon Press, and New York: Oxford University Press, 1981).

13 I have tried to discuss this question in my 'Rights and agency', *Philosophy and Public Affairs*, 11 (1982), and 'Evaluator relativity and consequential evaluation', *Philosophy and Public Affairs*, 12 (1983).

14 On this see my 'Liberty as control: an appraisal', *Midwest Studies in Philosophy*, 7 (1982), and 'Liberty and social choice', *Journal of Philosophy*, 80 (1983).

15 W. M. Gorman, 'The demand for related goods', *Journal Paper J3129*, Iowa Experiment Station, Ames, Iowa, 1956; K. J. Lancaster, 'A new approach to consumer theory', *Journal of Political Economy*, 74 (1966).

16 See Mary Douglas and B. Isherwood, *The World of Goods* (New York: Basic Books, 1979). See also T. Scitovsky, *The Joyless Economy* (Oxford: Oxford University Press, 1976).

17 See my 'Equality of what?' in S. McMurrin (ed.), *Tanner Lectures on Human Values* (Cambridge: Cambridge University Press, and Salt Lake City: University of Utah Press, 1980); reprinted in my *Choice, Welfare and Measurement* (Oxford: Basil Blackwell, and Cambridge, Mass.: MIT Press, 1982). In the latter volume, see also 'Introduction', pp. 30–1.

18 See E. S. Phelps (ed.), *Economic Justice* (Harmondsworth: Penguin, 1973); A. B. Atkinson, *Social Justice and Public Policy* (Brighton: Wheatsheaf, 1983).

19 The problems of indexing capabilities, I have discussed elsewhere, in my 1982 Hennipman Lecture, given at Amsterdam University; *Commodities and Capabilities*, to be published by North-Holland.

20 J. Rawls, 'A Kantian concept of equality', *Cambridge Review*, February 1975.

21 See my 'Equality of what?'. These issues are central to comparisons of standard of living. I have tried to go into this question, among

others, in 'The living standard', *Oxford Economic Papers*, 36 (1984).

22 See my 'Equality of what?'. Incidentally, in that paper, I had in fact, unwittingly, somewhat misstated Rawls's own position and this has been clarified in my *Choice, Welfare and Measurement* (1982), pp. 365–6. Also see Rawls's response to this point in his recent paper 'Social unity and primary goods', in Sen and Williams (eds), *Utilitarianism and Beyond*, pp. 168–9.

23 Rawls, *A Theory of Justice*, p. 62.

24 Ronald Dworkin, 'Equality of resources', *Philosophy and Public Affairs*, 10 (1981).

25 See note 17 above.

26 Dworkin, *op. cit.*, p. 300.

27 *Ibid.*, p. 300.

28 In my Hennipman Lecture (1982), *Commodities and Capabilities* (North-Holland, forthcoming).

VIII
CLAIMS OF NEED

David Wiggins

It has been felt for a long time that there must be some intimate connection between people's needs and the abstract rights they have. H. L. A. Hart was giving voice to a strong and widespread intuition when he wrote:

> A concept of legal rights limited to those cases where the law . . .
> respects the choice of individuals would be too narrow. For there
> is a form of the moral criticism of law which . . . is inspired by regard
> for the needs of individuals for certain fundamental freedoms
> and protections or benefits. Criticism of the law for its failure to pro-
> vide for such individual needs is distinct from, and sometimes at war
> with, the criticism with which Bentham was perhaps too exclusively
> concerned, that the law often fails to maximize aggregate utility.[1]

In practice however the connection between needs and rights has proved elusive. It ought not of course to have been expected that a linkage of this kind would be simple or hard and fast, or provide the single most important clue to everything that still puzzles us in the idea of justice. But if the connection is not only complicated but also important, and if some connection is there to be discovered among the sentiments that actually sustain our various ideas about justice, it will be a great shame if its failure to be simple or hard and fast continues to stand in the way of the attempt to understand the special force and political impact of a claim of serious need.

J. L. Mackie never, so far as I know, made any special study of the idea of a need. But I think that, towards the end of his life, in the succession of papers that began with 'Can there be a rights-based moral

149

theory?', was continued in 'Rights, utility and universalization',[2] and was then so abruptly cut short by his sudden death, he suggested a framework in which, without presupposing the welfare state, one can try to reason positively about the kind of entitlement that needing creates. I hope that Mackie would not have disapproved of what is attempted in §13 following, and that he would have found a discussion of the main contentions advanced there an enjoyable change from the meta-ethical disputations on which we carelessly expended so many of the (it proved) not numerous opportunities we had after I became his colleague to talk together about philosophy.

In advance, however, of any questions of justice and entitlement, where I have been happy to adopt something rather similar to Mackie's approach, it will be necessary to attend for its own sake and at some length to the question of what needing is – a precaution disregarded almost equally by champions and critics of the idea that there is something serious to be made of this notion in political philosophy. One can hardly explain the special force of a claim when one will not first determine what exactly one who makes it says, or in what context it seems particularly natural to make it, or what conceptions and misconceptions these contexts especially lend themselves to.

1. Those who complain that the question what it is to need something is relatively neglected in our tradition are sometimes directed to the writings of Hegel and Marx. But there one is likely to be disappointed. It is true that each of these writers makes heartening acknowledgment of the familiarity and importance of the concept of need, and true again that in Marx one will encounter the famous or infamous formula 'From each according to his ability; to each according to his need'.[3] (Although Marx did not in fact invent this principle.[4]) But neither Marx nor Hegel says what a need is, or indicates what it really turns on whether in a given case this or that is needed by someone. In Hegel, there is a strong tendency for needs to be simply run together with desires: needs are first placed with desires on the side of subjectivity, in opposition to the objects of needs and desires and the reality that resists them (as in the description of the evolution of self-consciousness in the *Phenomenology of Spirit*); and then they are put with desires again, on the social level, in the totality comprehending *all* interests and motivations that constitutes civil society as a 'system of needs' (as in the *Philosophy of Right*). Marx can be read as innocent of this conflation: but what we encounter in his case is the philosophically

debilitating refusal to say anything that will substantially forejudge the public criterion of need that it is supposed history will supply or to anticipate in any other way the needs that some future 'consciousness exceeding its bounds' will acknowledge as properly expressive of 'human essence'.

Analytical philosophers are not as constrained here as it seems Marx was. But in our kind of philosophy, sensitive though it always is to questions of the form *what is it to ϕ?*, the idea of needing something suffers from guilt by association. Either the idea smells of *dirigisme*, state interference in the processes of production, and distaste for 'consumer preference';[5] or else it revives bad memories of the 'means test' and numerous earlier attempts to restrict the number of indigent persons entitled to the outdoor relief provided by the Poor Law of 1601 and its more recent counterparts (social security etc.); or else the idea somehow contrives to arouse both sorts of association. What is more, those who have wanted to give the idea an extended trial have been dismayed to find, seeing the question of social justice in the way they were apt to see it, that, if anything, *need* aggravated instead of simplifying the problem.

2. However inhibiting these doubts and suspicions have been in philosophy itself, it is a surprising and most important fact that they operate only at the level of theory. In practice – and to an extent that could not be predicted or even suspected on the basis of an examination of present-day political theory –, the political cum administrative process as we know it in Europe and North America could scarcely continue (could scarcely even conclude an argument) without constant recourse to the idea:[6]

> 'The outstanding object of the Beveridge Plan is to provide as far as possible a unified system of income maintenance to cover needs arising from a variety of causes.' (G. D. H. Cole, pamphlet explaining the Beveridge Plan)
> 'Scientists are almost unanimous that in spite of the development of *in vitro* methods of testing and experiment, and in spite of advances in tissue culture techniques, we still need to perform experiments on live animals.'
> 'The United Kingdom Atomic Energy Authority . . . has told the Government that it thinks that a fast reactor needs to be built and it is naturally keen to move on from the experience gained on the two small-scale plants it has operated at Dounreay in Scotland and

to the logical next stage of development.' (*The Times*, 18 March 1981)

'The minister decided not to reopen the inquiry, and in his decision he said that he had taken into account the general changes relating to design flow standards and traffic forecasts since the inquiry, and he was satisfied that they did not affect the evidence on which the inspector made his recommendation. He was convinced the schemes were needed and the road should be constructed.' (*The Times*, Law Report, 10 December 1977)

An economist once said to me 'What do you mean by a need? Is a need just something you want, but aren't prepared to pay for?'. This was in a certain way insightful (cp. §24 foll.). as well as witty. But the literal inaccuracy of the suggestion will appear plainly to anyone who makes the experiment of reformulating 'needs' claims like those cited above by replacing 'need' by 'want', 'desire', 'prefer', or their nominal derivatives. No matter how one does this, the result lacks not simply the rhetorical force of the original, but all its meaning, coherence and argumentative point. And this is something that we have to explain, rather than rail against the idea of need and accuse it of trying to force our hand or of aiding and abetting some illicit transition from a statement of what is to a statement of what must be.[7] Indeed I should say that, given the special force carried by 'need', we ought to try to grasp some special content that the word possesses in virtue of which that force accrues to it. It would be a sort of word magic if so striking a difference as that between 'want' and 'need' could arise except from a difference of substance.

3. The last contention might be defended on general grounds relating to meaning and force. But where someone is seriously tempted by the idea that needs are a certain class of strong desires or preferences, or strong unconscious desires or preferences,[8] more particular considerations can be adduced. If I want to have x and $x = y$, then I do not necessarily want to have y. If I want to eat that oyster and that oyster is the oyster that will consign me to oblivion, it doesn't follow that I want to eat the oyster that will consign me to oblivion. But with needs it is different. I can only need to have x if anything identical with x is something that I need. Unlike 'desire' or 'want' then, 'need' is not apparently an intentional verb. What I need depends not on thought or the workings of my mind (or not only on these) but on the way the world is. Again, if one wants something because it is F, one believes or

suspects that it is F. But if one needs something because it is F, it must really be F, whether or not one believes that it is.[9]

4. The apparent distinctiveness of needing being registered in this way, we may now move one step closer to a positive elucidation. Something that has been insisted upon in most analytical accounts of needing[10] is that needing is by its nature needing for a purpose, and that statements of need which do not mention relevant purposes are elliptical – some will say dishonestly elliptical – for sentences that do mention them.[11]

One thing seems right with this claim, and another seems wrong.

The thing that seems right concerns what may be called purely instrumental needing. Someone may say 'I now need to have £200 to buy a suit', or, speaking elliptically, 'I need £200'. If he can't get the suit he has in mind for less than £200, then it is true, on an instrumental reading of his claim, that he needs £200. What has to hold for this to be the case is something of the form:

It is necessary (relative to time t and relative to the t circumstances c) that if (.... at t'') then ($-$ at t').

In the present case, the antecedent of the conditional relates to the man's having the suit and the consequent to his having £200.[12]

So far so good. If something like this is right, then it makes excellent sense of the claim that certain uses of 'I need to have x' are elliptical (e.g. the claim 'I need £200' as made by this man): and one whole class of non-elliptical *need* sentences receives a plausible treatment. But there is something else the elucidation fails to make sense of. This is the fact that, if we have already been through everything this man can say about his need, then we can properly and pointedly respond to his claim with: 'You need £200 to buy that suit, but you don't need £200 – because you don't need to buy that suit'. The ellipse theory suggests that he ought then to insist that there is an end of his for which the suit is necessary. But it is plain that without deliberate misunderstanding of what we are now saying, he cannot make this retort. If he did respond in this way, then it would be open to us, meaning our remark to him in the only way we could mean it, to say that he was simply missing the point. What he has to show, if he wants to make more than the instrumental claim, is that he *cannot get on without that suit*, that *his life will be blighted without it*, or some such thing.

What is suggested by the existence of this extra, however problematical requirement? It suggests that, although there is an instrumental sense of 'need' where we can ask for some purpose to be specified in a non-elliptical version of the 'needs' claim and there are no limits on what purpose this is, there is another sense of 'need' by which the purpose is already fixed, and fixed in virtue of the meaning of the word. What is more, this must be the sense of the word employed by the majority of scientists, the UKAEA, the Minister, and the other makers of needs claims quoted in §2 above.[13] These men are representing, and the meanings of their words commit them to representing, that we simply can't get on without more roads, more reactors, or more animal experiments or whatever. ('We have no real alternative.') They might be wrong. There might be minor obscurity in what exactly is intended by this. But what is controversial in what is said is not the necessity for the avoidance of harm to human beings — it is precisely the fact that such avoidance is not as such a controversial purpose that lends needs claims their *prima facie* special practical and argumentative force — , but the claim that our prior adherence to this end *commits us* (leaves us with no alternative but) to have more roads, more fast reactors, more animal experiments or whatever.

5. We have then to assign at least two senses to 'need' if we are to assign the right significance to the sorts of thing people use the word to say and to understand the special argumentative force of needs claims. But of course there is a connection between the purely instrumental and the not purely instrumental sense, or what we may call (simply for the sake of a name, not to exclude the relativities to be set out in §6) the absolute or categorical sense of the word. Thus:

I need [absolutely] to have x
    if and only if
I need [instrumentally] to have x if I am to avoid harm
    if and only if
It is necessary, things being what they actually are, that if I avoid then I have x.

What distinguishes the second sense of 'need', so defined by reference to the first, is that it is in virtue of what is carried along by this sense itself of the word 'need', not in virtue of context (whatever part context plays in determining that this is the sense intended), that appeal is made to the necessary conditions of harm's being avoided. If so, the identity of the antecedent '. . . . .' of the conditional 'Necessarily, since circumstances are what they are, if . . . . ., then ———' is fixed by the presence of the word 'need' taken in this absolute sense.[14] It must follow that there is then no question of ellipse in this case. (One does not have to supply again what is already there.)[15]

Given this account of the word's content, it becomes unsurprising that 'need' taken in the absolute sense should have the special point and force it appears to have both in the individual case and in the case of the community needing something. (I postpone *sine die* the neither easy nor impossible task of explicating the relation of these two cases of needing.) It is also to be expected that 'need' should be normative or evaluative, and normative or evaluative in virtue of its content.

6. Normativeness apart, there are at least three distinct ways in which needs-statements of the simple singular variety we have elucidated must appear to be *relative* (notwithstanding the one respect, see §5, in which they are absolute).

First, the suggested elucidation in terms of harm exposes a certain parameter that is always there to be discovered within claims of absolute needing. This is the idea of well-being or flourishing, by reference to which we make judgments of harm.

What follows from this first relativity? Relativeness to something else is no obstacle in itself to the most extreme or perfect kind of objectivity. Indeed making such relativities fully explicit sometimes has the effect of revealing the subject matter in question as a candidate for unqualified or absolute truth.[16]

The first relativity is only a matter of *need*'s involving a relation. The second and quite different way in which need-sentences are relative qualifies any hopes that might be inspired by my account of the first. – What constitutes suffering or wretchedness or harm is an essentially contestable matter, and is to some extent relative to a culture, even to some extent relative to people's conceptions of suffering, wretchedness and harm. Obviously there is much more to be said about that (even if it is doubtful how much of it involves the idea of 'relative deprivation' – a relativity we have ventured to omit altogether from the argument); but instead let us hurry on, simply insisting that, even when the instability is conceded of some of the opinions that have been reached within our culture about absolute needs, some needs claims are so far from being indeterminate or seriously contestable that they are more or less decidable. But we shall return briefly to this point after making mention of a third relativity.

The third relativity is relativity to the particular circumstances of the time or times (see note 12) associated with the need and the background of (no doubt normative) assumptions associated with those circumstances.

When we make a claim of the form *Necessarily at t if such and such then so and so*, where t is a moment for which this *necessarily* is temporally indexed, we thereby confine our consideration to all alternative futures from t onwards, and what we are saying is equivalent to the claim that every alternative in which such and such holds is one in which so and so holds. If pure historical necessity at t were our concern, $\Box_t$, then a future would count as an alternative for times $\geqslant t$ just if it could coherently be described, and every correct description of it was compatible with the conjunction of (i) the state of the world that actually obtained at t and (ii) all true laws of nature. Thus $\Box_t$ (p) is true if and only if p is true in every alternative world whose history is indistinguishable from the history of the actual world up to the moment t, natural laws being counted as part of the history of the world and fixed as of t.[17] Where needing is concerned, however, the definition of alternativeness must it seems be modified to restrict the class of alternative futures to futures $\geqslant t$ that (i) are economically or technologically realistically conceivable, and (ii) do not involve us in morally (or otherwise) unacceptable acts[18] or interventions in the arrangements of particular human lives or society or whatever, and (iii) can be envisaged without our envisaging ourselves tolerating what we do not have to tolerate.

This relativity to circumstance imports one more feature that deserves special comment. The fixed antecedent of the whole conditional that is governed by the modal operator 'necessarily relative to the circumstances c obtaining at t' speaks of avoidance to harm. This is not in itself obscure, but it will not give quite the sense we require to cover all the kinds of absolute (more than merely instrumental) needing that usage allows, unless some associated standard is thought of as supplied for harm to be judged according to the context, the standard creating the presumption that it is itself suggested by *some however minimal level of flourishing that is actually attainable here*. Avoidance of harm can then be understood always by reference to a norm of flourishing that is relative to c, and this in its turn can import the entailment or implicature that, if z non-instrumentally needs x at t under circumstances c, then there *exists* some alternative future in which z does flourish to some however minimal extent.[19] (When I am utterly doomed however the future is realistically envisaged, then I *begin* to lose even my needs.)

For non-instrumental needing, this third species of relativity furnishes more of what was already furnished by the second. It is not just that the idea of harm, or the norm of flourishing by reference to which harm is judged, is historically conditioned and essentially contestable. It is also circumstantially conditioned *as of some time t* what futures are to count as realistic, acceptable alternatives, how long a forward view we have to take of flourishing in considering harm, and what the relevant standard of harm ought to be with respect to the time-span that is agreed to be the right one to apply in the given case. It may even be contestable — before we consider how much the present constrains the future — what exactly the circumstances are that prevail at *t*. Here the second and third sorts of relativity interact.

There is plenty here for an objectivist to face up to. And yet in spite of the real and manifold contestability of most of these things, some will be tempted to conclude that the agreement that can be reached about the truth or falsity of a wide variety of needs claims (when they are seriously and correctly construed as making the contextually much constrained but very strong claims they do make) is far more striking than the disagreement some others will arouse. The temptation exists, though I shall not try to evaluate it here, to claim that objectivity is a matter of degree and that some significant degree of it can coexist with even the second of the three kinds of relativity we have distinguished.

7. The thought we have now arrived at is that a person needs *x* [absolutely] if and only if, whatever morally and socially acceptable variation it is (economically, technologically, politically, historically . . . etc.) possible to envisage within the relevant time-span, he will be harmed if he goes without *x*. A proper development of it which enabled us to try to measure the relative public weights of various claims of need would have to make room for certain obvious and essential refinements. And it would have to prepare the ground for these by distinguishing certain distinct questions.

There is the question of the *badness* of needs. How much harm or suffering would be occasioned by going without the thing in question? And there is a consequential question of *urgency*: given that some not inconsiderable harm or suffering would be occasioned by going without the thing in question, how soon must this thing be supplied? And then there is the question of *basicness*, the *entrenchment*, and the *substitutability* of needs. Being technical terms, however, these categorizations all require more elaborate introduction.

When we attempt to survey the class of alternative possible futures and then, restricting this to envisageable acceptable futures, we ask whether every future in which person z is not harmed is one in which he has x, we shall often discover that it is a matter of degree how difficult it is to identify and envisage some alternative realistically, or how morally acceptable it is. Often we shall then have to resolve such difficulties by imposing a threshold on what departures from the familiar we are to regard as realistically envisageable, or as practical politics. The lower the threshold is placed the more futures then count as real alternatives and the harder it may then become for a need statement to count as true. Seeing the effects of this placement of the threshold and being reluctant to deny that z really needs x at all, we shall often have to choose between (i) raising the threshold of acceptability cum envisageability again; (ii) lowering (relaxing) the standard by which harm is judged, allowing more things to count as harm (here, as with option (i), owing reasons for this decision to anyone who asks for them); and (iii) keeping this lower threshold of realistic envisageability, together with the more exigent truth-condition it imports, but disjoining having x with having some slightly inferior substitute for x.

In the light of all this, it will be a useful stipulation to say that y's need for x is *entrenched* if the question of whether y can remain unharmed without having x is rather insensitive to the placing of the aforementioned threshold of realistic envisageability and/or acceptability of alternative futures. When we are concerned with the problem of arbitration between needs claims or arbitration between needs claims and other claims, it will then be useful to distinguish between entrenchment with respect to the shorter term (where extant arrangements create definite requirements that cannot be escaped immediately but may be in due course escaped) and entrenchment with respect to the longer term. Although some disruptions of the established order that would enable y to escape all harm without having x cannot be envisaged happening as it were overnight, however desirable they may be, yet often they are readily described, and can be realistically envisaged as taking place gradually.

Developing one special case of entrenchment, one might then stipulate that y's need for x is *basic* just if what excludes futures in which y remains unharmed despite his not having x are laws of nature, unalterable and invariable environmental facts, or facts about human constitution.[20] And within the basic, one might try to discriminate between that which is owed to something un-negotiable in the ideas of flourishing and harm and that which is owed to unchangeable tendencies of things to turn out in one rather than another specifiable kind of way.

Finally, we may find it useful to be able to say that y's need for x is *substitutable with respect to x* if some slight lowering of the standard by which y's harm is judged permits us to weaken claims of need by disjoining y's having x with his having u or w or whatever.

It should be obvious that these labels correspond to overlapping but independent categorizations. A need for x can be not very bad but basic, for instance; or bad and also urgent yet substitutable with respect to x; or bad in the extreme and highly entrenched in so far as it is urgent, but, in so far as it is not urgent, relatively superficially entrenched in the mid term and not entrenched at all in the long term. It should be equally obvious how important it is to be clear whether the need we are talking about stems from a judgment about a particular man, or about all men in specified kinds of circumstances, or (making the truth-condition most exigent of all) all men under all actual variations of circumstance.

8. How then are needs and desires and needs and interests related? Perhaps we had better see needs themselves (contrast things needed) as *states of dependency (in respect of not being harmed)*, which have as their proper object things x needed, or more strictly *having* or *using* ... x. In that case our categorization in §7 is a categorization of states of dependency. Such states can often be expressed by desire or striving (or avoidance or whatever); and often the propositional object of the desire or striving will be the same as that which we find in some correct statement of the need. But even in this special case I should take some persuading that the desire ought to be simply identified with the need. A more plausible identification is between someone's having a certain need and his having a certain interest. If a man needs x, then he has an interest in x's being or becoming available to him. And if (say) a man very badly needs at t to have x at t, and the need is significantly entrenched as of t and scarcely substitutable at all, then his having x may be said to represent a *vital interest* of his. (Strictly, his having the need for x is the same as his having a vital interest in·having x.) This is a good ruling, I believe, but only if we use the word 'interest' to mean what it means in English, where its connection with 'want' or 'desire' is

complicated and indirect (cp. White, op. cit. p. 120), and if the proposed equivalence is without prejudice to any general alignment between needs and interests.

So far then so good. Inasmuch as the idea of need has begun to appear at least clarifiable and intelligibly related to familiar notions, its champions will now hasten to point out what an important part it played in the motivation of the later nineteenth- and twentieth-century humanitarian efforts that have transformed the living conditions of so many twentieth-century city-dwellers. Certainly nobody can safely criticize the improvements that have been brought about without taking precautions not to be misunderstood.

But it is important that there is another side to this picture. Detractors of the *need* concept will point out that, among those who know the failures as well as the successes of modern planning, the regulations and minimum standards that claims about what people need have inspired national and municipal governments to lay down and impose with the effect of law are now widely blamed for urban blight, the bleak monotonous environment, the graceless stereotyped architecture, and even the economic inertia of that which has come to replace the city of slums and smoking factories. Over and over again, they may say, rigid housing standards, building regulations, public health regulations, or zoning restrictions, all founded in the idea of human need, and many of them supposed to afford particular protection to the poorest and wretchedest members of society, have combined in a singular and unforeseen way to their conspicuous disadvantage. In operation, these standards and restrictions have first reduced the housing stock actually available at any time for human habitation, thus raising rents and house-prices against those least able to afford them; then conspired to inhibit all individual efforts at piecemeal improvement in neighbourhoods that will probably be condemned in their entirety; and finally they have narrowed the choice, where new building is concerned, to the meanest and least flexible kinds of treatment, excluding from consideration almost all that we are wont to admire when we encounter them in the architecture and town-planning of the past. Thus a quarter of alleys, tenements and terraces that long ago replaced a semi-rural slum of huts and hovels built on small plots is not itself replaced gradually, or at a pace that corresponds to what can be practically envisaged or anticipated by anyone with a direct interest there, but − such is the power of an idea like *need* − is demolished and swept away in its entirety. Inhabitants and local industries are dispersed. And then, after long dereliction, to a lengthening list of statutory specifications, on a shrinking budget (itself ill-defended from corruption), the towers or blocks we now see in the East End of London (or Liverpool, or Glasgow or, more benignly, Sheffield) are built upon the wide communal space that has been razed clear, connected only by windswept walkways or (where new, higher capacity roads dictate this) pedestrian underpasses, in an environment that repels all human attempts to come to terms with it and almost paralyses practical thinking. It can still be hoped that trees or grass will catch root somewhere and grow where they can. But otherwise, and at least in part as a result of an official determination of need, a whole quarter is sterilized against all beneficial adaptation, initiative or change. And, except in the rare cases where industry and business reestablish themselves there in strength, it will be beyond the powers of most of the tenants of the place to escape from the client condition to which they have been reduced.

9. Anyone who wants to take needs seriously would not be well advised to deny that such occurrences are in practice familiar or to seek to defend them. He would do better to answer the question how such things can ever have happened where human need really was the dominant motivation. For the indictment he faces is a serious one, and attributions of need are deeply implicated in the charge. He may of course declare that so many misapprehensions and oversights lie buried in the dense history of shortage, emergency and unreasoning optimism that makes up the record of the early post-Second World War reconstruction — and its more recent history is overlaid by so much unconscious or conscious corruption,[21] dogmatism and megalomania (all sustained by the in practice nearly limitless ambiguity of the expression 'the public interest') — that the critic cannot really claim to have disentangled one key error or master confusion that explains everything that he correctly laments here. There is some justice in that. But, given the original motivation and the need-oriented thoughts that were entertained in good faith by statesmen, public officials and the experts they relied upon, a more substantial defence is required. Unless we can find some serious misconception of need among the ideas that motivated these men, can, as I suspect, identify some definite coarseness in their appreciation of it, the case for superseding the idea of need altogether in political philosophy will be extremely hard to rebut. (Indeed I expect that, however simplistically, some new Tory thinkers will already have blamed the dismal scenes just described on the very attempt to give the

idea of need any positive place in politics beyond the residual role of determining minimum levels of social security.)

The first thing I should myself say in defence of the idea is that, as we have elucidated statements about what is needed by a given person or set of persons, they commit us, not only to answers for certain general questions about harm, what can be tolerated or not, and what sort of thing can and cannot be realistically envisaged, but also to something highly particular and special to the given circumstances of whoever they are who, allegedly, will not (here and now, placed just as they are placed) escape harm without the thing stated to be needed. This combination of particular and general is one of the most important and intriguing features of particular non-instrumental needs. And it is open to question whether it has been properly grasped by those who have been happy to think in terms of codes of minimum standards. Certainly, the rigid standard is in constant danger of institutionalizing the neglect of such differences. It threatens the distinction between particular needs that are *bad* or amount to the vital interest of certain people at a certain time and what it is even harder to identify and formulate, viz. needs that are *basic* or *deeply entrenched* and can be *generalized* to arrive at practical precepts that it is safe and sensible to act upon over indefinitely many cases in indefinitely many kinds of circumstances.[22]

In the second place, if the relativities set out in §6 were imperfectly understood by those charged with the task of reconstruction, it was not likely that there would be much understanding of the interaction of the second and third kinds. Many claims of needing depend crucially for their acceptance or rejection on our being ready to try to find the practically envisageable standard of flourishing or well-being by reference to which harm, or the lesser or greater harm, can be judged, and questions of substitutivity resolved, in a way that respects real political possibility. Of course every necessary condition of a possible state of affairs of not being harmed is consistent with every other necessary condition (whenever harm is not inevitable). But if, in pride or in a spirit of would-be revolution that will in fact come to nothing, or for whatever other reason, statesmen or managers pitch the standard too high (and in effect this has already happened in any case where the replacement of what is condemned will *in fact* represent no real improvement), or if they fail to be realistic about what futures are envisageable, then, in the limited space which is all there really is here, one condition will be met at the expense of another condition. (Even at the expense of a condition that is more important and is necessary for what may be an even more minimal state of not being harmed.) If the standard is set impossibly high in one sphere of concern,[23] and we fail at the same time to respect (if only by *not* doing things) the totality of the needs of this or that man or men and the needs of other men as well (and if we do not recognize that we don't know too much about any of these things), then something like this is bound to happen. The more resources that are then diverted to the task of meeting the standard that has been set, the worse this tendency is likely to become, and the greater the danger that one specific requirement will eventually crowd out other less specific, less behaviourally transparent, but perhaps equally or even more important requirements (especially requirements such as choice and independence); or the greater the danger that what is provided may suit some people and not suit others – an outcome that is not inconsistent with the objectivity of value, but reflects the settled tendency for values to compete with one another, and for the lives of different men to represent widely different responses to irreducibly distinct value claims. (A different emphasis or value focus.)

10. If we have enough faith in this defence to persist in the wish to take needs with a seriousness at all proportionate to the frequency with which they are actually invoked in political and administrative argument (cp. §2), then it now seems that, having now grasped the complexity and stringency of the truth-condition, we shall have to start to see any statement of the form 'y needs x [absolutely]' as tantamount to a challenge to imagine an alternative future in which y escapes harm or damage without having x, or where y's vital interests are better adjusted to others' vital interests than they would be if x were what he had. We must proceed like this not because to be concerned with needs is to take up an attitude of stinginess or meanness (if it connotes any particular attitude, the attitude is much closer to the concern for *all* rights, 'counter-rights', cp. §18 below, and right-like claims), but because, if we do not, some vital needs and interests may not be properly determined, or may go unheeded. It is without prejudice one way or the other to the satisfaction of desires for things that are not needed.

Now sometimes (as we have noticed) this sort of challenge to the imagination will not lead to outright rejection of a statement, but to a weakening of the specification of the thing said to be needed: 'He will get by if he has x or w or z'. This is a very familiar move, and the elucidation of needing given here explains why that is. Overspecificity in a 'needs' sentence makes it false.[24] But what our elucidation equally predicts is that often the thing that survives the weakening (introduction of disjunctions etc.) will still be a very strong statement — most especially where the particular judgment of z's non-instrumental need results from a process in which the actuality of z's concrete situation and the constraints that this puts upon the future are fully apprehended, taking into account the real, however hypothetical, intentions of all relevant other persons or groups of persons, and where the process clarifies both the worst and the best that can befall z and z's vital interests. (Perhaps prompting us to climb down from 'z needs x', where x is the best but most expensive remedy, well out of z's reach unless he forgoes everything else, to 'what z really needs, [given the circumstances] is y', where absence of y will blight even that minimal level of well-being that is the best real possibility for z.) Certainly we shall be left with more than a tiny handful of needs statements. And there will be no more postponement of the question whether vital needs are better or worse satisfied now than they once were, why they are worse satisfied (wherever they are), and whether they can be better satisfied.

11. It is sometimes held that it is the role of government to make itself as responsive as possible in as many ways as possible to as many of its subjects' desires as possible. But obviously the more strongly someone inclines to the opposing view that what prudence and justice demand is that public policy be selective in what it attempts and be primarily based upon needs, the more important he must think it is for governments, in so far as they are directly or indirectly involved in some matter, not to specify needs incorrectly, and to be careful to take the greatest advantage of all alternative ways of satisfying them and/or letting them go on being satisfied (however they already were satisfied). For such a policy, the more plastic needs must make accommodation for the less plastic, and (what is different) the less bad must give way to the worse. A proper balance must be found between present needs and future needs. And *ceteris paribus*, desires as such must cede rank to what emerge from careful scrutiny as bad, entrenched, non-substitutable needs. Nobody's bad, entrenched, non-substitutable need, or as one might say (exploiting the ambiguity in the adjective that was surely made for just this purpose) nobody's *vital interest*, must be sacrificed by society to the mere desire of anybody else, or of any however large group of other people. — Or as we have this contention in Del Vecchio's

formulation of what is called, in his classic study of the history of the idea of justice, *providential*, *assisting* or *social* justice:

> It is a requirement of justice, that, before being assigned to any other purpose whatever, all the means which the state has legally at its disposal should be assigned by it to the protection of the life and physical and moral integrity of its members,. especially of those who are not in a position to provide for this by their own means or by means of persons particularly obliged thereto.[25]

Del Vecchio is no friend of *need*. I have singled him out here as one who is explicitly hostile in principle to this way of making claims upon society.[26] But what we may now suspect is that the indispensable role of the concept of need is precisely to assist us in singling or marking out those very interests that have to be the *special* concern of social justice, both where the state has to intervene on their behalf and also in the cases where it is the business of the state to insist on some pause or hesitation, e.g. in connection with grand projects (private or public) that will serve the actual or hypothetical desires of millions but sacrifice to them the present or future vital interests of other identifiable or un-identifiable people.[27]

If this suspicion can be shown to be well-founded, it will certainly put in a new light the ineliminable vagueness, contestability, or non-effectiveness for which the idea of need is so often criticized. The true situation may really be that these charges against it are an indirect tribute to the idea's actual importance and indispensability to us. For it may be that, *pace* some liberal and conservative critics, one aspect of its indispensability concerns the defence it can afford to the individual, in a community that has found a way of adjusting its institutions to its sentiments, against the arbitrary use of state power. (Cp. §21 below.)

12. Having thus arrived at the frontier of political philosophy and canvassed — so far without much attempt at precision or argument — a priority principle about true needs that is either a specifically political principle (a principle of social justice) or nothing (not a principle of individual morality as such), I want to pause for the space of one section and try to see more clearly where we have come from, before moving further forward.

We have taken Anscombe's and Feinberg's part against White, Barry and Flew (see notes 9, 10, 11) in seeking to identify an absolute sense of 'need'. We have been with White, however, in insisting that *need* is a modal notion. And here again, we are not the first to take up such a position.

Aristotle is not usually credited with having any view of what a need is; but in his philosophical lexicon at *Metaphysics V* he has the following entry for 'necessary':

1015ª20: We call NECESSARY (a) that without which, as a joint-cause, it is not possible to live, as for instance breathing and nourishment are necessary for an animal, because it is incapable of existing without them: and (b) anything without which it is not possible for good to exist or come to be, or for bad to be discarded or got rid of, as for instance drinking medicine is necessary so as not to be ill, and sailing to Aegina so as to get money. (trans. Kirwan)

For good reasons (especially the importance of the chapter's being seen as Aristotle's single entry for several senses of the Greek word for 'necessary'), the word ἀναγκαῖον has never been translated here as 'needed'. But, in another way, it is a shame that it was not. In the presence of an Aristotelian elucidation, the reductive, rationalized strong desires conception of need might not have passed so long without serious challenge.

Aristotle's (a)-paraphrase appears too restrictive to exhaust what we have called the absolute sense. (The case for some relaxation of the condition is, of course, of long standing. Cp. Adam Smith, *Wealth of Nations* [V.2.2], 'By necessities I understand not only the commodities which are indispensably necessary for the support of life, but whatever the custom of the country renders it indecent for creditable people even of the lowest rank to be without'.) And Aristotle's (b)-paraphrase is in danger of causing us to classify certain absolute occurrences of 'need' (needing to drink medicine for instance) with other occurrences of the word that it may be better to treat as elliptical and purely instrumental (e.g. needing to sail to Aegina). These two faults, if they are faults, are better corrected in the 'harm' formulation of Feinberg, we have come to think, than by substituting 'flourishing' for 'living' in Aristotle's (a)-paraphrase. — One is bound to think that they are better corrected by the 'harm' formula if one is reluctant to be led by the tautology that flourishing is a necessary condition of flourishing to say that human beings *need to flourish*, but one does not mind being led by the same form of argument to the conclusion that human beings need to avoid harm. — But the value of Aristotle's contribution to this subject is not obscured by the necessity to negotiate for these amendments.

It resides in his having signalled (even if only to those already open to the thought) that *need* is a modal concept of a special kind[28] which imports the linked ideas of a situation and a non-negotiable (or in-the-circumstances-non-negotiable) good that *together* leave no real alternative but to . . . .

13. Even those who urge us to dispense with this idea concede the *prima facie* compelling character of a true unexaggerated statement of need. Hence, I suppose, their animus against the idea. But what sort of claim is made upon society by such a statement? And is this really a claim of justice, or sometimes a claim of justice and sometimes an appeal to something beyond or beside justice? Or what is it? The rest of the paper will be devoted to these questions.

14. It is a marked tendency in most of the writers in whom one can discover an interest in the force of claims of need to subsume them for all purposes of justice under the general category of equality-claims (claims to equality of treatment, or claims about the intolerability of certain *in*equalities).[29] Many liberal conservatives, as well as seeing the concern with needs as such as symptomatic of an ill-conceived, busybody or interventionist attitude to public policy, distrust the idea of a need precisely because they view it as indissolubly linked with conceptions of equality that they find deeply suspect. And the same linkage between needs and equality claims would appear to be assumed by radical or anti-conservative writers. Indeed, in so far as there are differences of opinion between radicals in the matter of needing, the significant divergence seems to turn on the question whether they see the idea of need as a positive help[30] or as a hindrance in the justification and further elucidation of the idea of equality.[31]

There is nothing, I think, to be gained by denying how natural and appropriate it is, where a writer already has a strong, positive argument in support of the idea of men's having a title and an equal title to all advantages that are generally desired and are in fact conducive to well-being (*a fortiori* where he has an argument in support of the idea of men's having a title to an equal share in such advantages),[32] for him to call on the concept of need to help him articulate his proposal. (A redistribution of everything in accordance with need is no doubt a more efficient approach to equality of welfare than, say, assigning everyone an equal share of goods.) The thing that does deserve to be denied is that need-claims are essentially, or by their nature, claims to be treated in accordance with the precepts of the distinctive sorts of social justice that are advocated by egalitarians. There are several ways of seeing that, as such, they are not. I shall offer two considerations. Neither proves. Each points I hope at something the reader is already able to see.

The first consideration I advance is this. Claims of vital need can be satisfied (or satisfied to a great extent at least) in a society where there is considerable inequality of wealth and even some appreciable inequality of economic opportunity[33] (especially — however big an *if* this may be — if economic inequalities are prevented from undermining legal rights and effective equality before the law). When one looks at how matters stand within such a society, and what it will involve on the levels of thought and action and refraining from action (cp. §§6-10) to maintain this happy state of affairs, nothing appears rationally inevitable in the progression from taking claims of need as seriously as this society does to taking similarly seriously everyone's claim to a level of well-being effectively equal to that of anyone else.[34]

In the second place, needs claims and claims to equal treatment are sustained by and appeal to interestingly different sentiments. The matter is clearest perhaps where disappointment is in question. Under these conditions, claims to equal treatment typically proceed out of feelings of being affronted, insulted, belittled or (more generally) left out, or slightingly used; and they may, in their debased or pathological form, lapse into simple envy. What these claims call out for is for those who advance them to be treated with the respect due to a human being who is accepted, simply *qua* human being, as an equal participant with an equal stake in a common venture or a particular society.[35] Claims of need on the other hand, even when tinged with moral indignation, may be pressed from a simple passion to subsist (or for one's dependents to subsist) under tolerable conditions — a passion that lapses in its extreme or pathological form not into envy necessarily, but into self-pity or helplessness or self-absorption. When claims of need go unheeded, what is disappointed is the expectation that it would be taken into account that the claimant's very survival or most minimal well-being was at issue. The appeal here depends of course on recognition of the claimant as a participant in human society; but that which sustains the appeal of the claimant and lends it strength may have to comprise, among other things, simple compassion or sympathy (on the part of the recognizer of the claim, and the expectation of this on the part of the claimant), or a particularized form of what Hume called the 'resentment of the misery of mankind' — a much more powerful sentiment, as

Schopenhauer and others have truly observed, than benevolence as such, however particularized. It is true of course that, in so far as claims of equality and claims of need are accepted as claims of justice, the acceptance must involve the recognition of the claimant as party to a whole network of intersubjectively established interrelations between selves which create actual duties and entitlements.[36] But for purposes of any special entitlement or expectation that is conferred by need, this system does not have to legitimize any expectation of substantive equality of title to all advantages. (Except where it legitimizes the expectation that equal *needs* for ϕ will import equal titles to ϕ-derived benefit wherever rights are themselves formulated in terms of needing as such: but that is not the title to economic equality *per se*, or in general.) We do not have to speak here of the claimant's *equal stake*, for instance.

15. What then, if it is *sui generis*, and not to be reduced to the claim that some inequality ought to be removed, is the distinctive political force of a statement of a serious need? The positive answer to be offered to that question will depend on our dividing it in a way corresponding to three phases or levels, and on our beginning by excogitating the prerequisites of something's counting as a possible social morality in order to identify the role that such a thing must give (at phase or level one) to the idea of a right. Some needs will then appear as special candidates to make abstract claim-rights (claim-rights that ought to be recognized and realized concretely); and some others that do not attain to this status will appear as candidates to represent *counter-rights* – or, more strictly speaking (since these claims are normally only right-*like*, though none the worse for this), abstract *counter-claims*. But these counter-claims will lie well within the province of justice, however strictly it is conceived, and will rest upon the same sort of foundation as abstract rights rest upon.

There are two necessary preliminaries to giving this answer, however. First, although need statements, when they weigh with us at all, do always weigh at least in part *as* statements of need, yet we must note that their public force is highly variable, even when their truth is not being questioned. Certainly this force is not always proportional to the need's admitted seriousness. Any account of these matters must explain or allow for this variability, and leave room for the influence or countervailing influence of factors other than need itself. Second, it is still worth insisting, against one kind of positivist, that the moral force of a claim of need cannot be identified with its being acknowledged to have this force, or with society's acting upon it or having regard to it — just as the social morality that a claim of need depends on for its force ought to be clearly distinguished both from the actual norms of reciprocity and cooperation that the morality makes possible and from the extant laws and social institutions that regulate these norms. (How can such a morality coincide with any of these things if it can sometimes muster criticisms of existing social arrangements, and can also serve to *sustain* mores, institutions and laws, weakly or strongly even as it subjects them to scrutiny?)

These preliminaries being completed, the first part of my answer to our question is that, in the case of some needs-statements, they report a need for something whose being needed is one part of what precisely creates the abstract right or entitlement to it. For I suggest that, for purposes of a social morality *S* that is actually lived and succeeds in proposing to agents shared concerns that they can make their own, there is an *abstract right or entitlement to x under conditions C* just where *x is something the denial or removal of which under conditions C is seen*[37] *as giving the person denied or deprived part or all of a reason, and a reason that is avowable and publicly sustainable within S, to reconsider his adherence to the norms of reciprocity and cooperation sustained by S.* This is to say that, if in such a case the victim who is deprived of *x* disappoints us in some spoken or previously unspoken expectation of cooperation, then that counts as something morally intelligible within the shared sensibility that depends on this expectation.[38]

To grasp the full import of this condition for the existence of a right it will assist to state the assumption it rests upon. This is the assumption that unless there existed *some* condition under which withdrawal of consensus was found intelligible and natural *even within S* — i.e. some condition under which *S* at least permitted a man party to *S* to think of himself as having been unjustly (even unjustifiably) sacrificed — , then *S* could scarcely count as a social morality at all. For a social morality, as conceived for these purposes, is not just any old set of abstract principles. It is something that exists only as realized or embodied (or as capable of being realized or embodied) in a shared sensibility, and in the historically given *mores* and institutions that are themselves perpetuated by it. It is only by virtue of participating in this sort of thing, and seeing one another as participating in it, that ordinary men as actually constituted are able to embrace common concerns and common goals that can take on a life of their own and be perceived as enshrining values that enjoy what Hume sometimes called 'moral beauty'. A social morality cannot of course give any particular person a guaranteed title to wealth, health, happiness, or security from ordinary misfortune. But equally it must not be such as to threaten anyone who is to be bound by it that it will bring upon him or any other individual participant, as if gratuitously, the misfortune of having his vital interests simply sacrificed for the sake of some larger public good.[39] What sustains and regulates or adjusts a social morality and what rebuts objections to it, must be something intelligible to all its individual participants, in human (never mind archangelic or ideal observer) terms.[40] It must engage with the passions of those who are to live by it, or at the very least not *dis*engage with those passions.

16. Obviously it is only a small step from requiring that a social morality lack this licence to requiring, more positively and definitely: (i) that it should place explicit limitations on the social goals it promotes or tolerates, on the burdens individuals can normally be asked to endure in the common pursuit of this or that kind of public goal, and on the scope and ambit of any modes of aggregative reasoning it countenances; (ii) that it should sustain rights under a rule of law, securing individuals from arbitrary arrest, imprisonment or punishment, and assuring them of other civic and legal protections; and (iii) that it should uphold the right to make certain sorts of agreement with other individuals, to buy the necessities of life, sell the product of one's labour, and be not dispossessed of that which one has appropriated or mixed one's labour with in definite ways seen as worthy of being accorded legal recognition.

Items that find a place in this enumeration do not find it simply because they are needed. But, as Hart anticipated, the idea of need plays its own distinctive and recognizable role in helping to generate and constrain the enumeration. What is more, its presence helps I think to render the idea of an abstract claim-right unmysterious. Certainly the derivation is not obliged to represent itself as *a priori* or *pre-moral* or as resting upon natural law (a concept it needs neither to invoke nor to denounce). In a very general way it is *a posteriori*. I know that the *a posteriority* of the question what social moralities have to be like to be possible will appear to many philosophers of some temperaments to disqualify the entire approach. But surely *a posteriority* is what we ought to have predicted if we expect morality to have the hold upon motive and action that Hume has so persuasively suggested that it must, and if it is to have this hold intelligibly, by virtue of the content of the judgments it delivers, and by virtue of the values and concerns that it proposes to agents being able to become for them ends in themselves, furnishing them with what they can see as reasons for being concerned or affected in certain particular ways.[41]

This whole view of rights may provoke the accusation that I say there is a right wherever there is an opportunity for blackmail, or that I submit morality itself to what Nietzsche called 'the trading mentality', and might equally well with almost equal moral ugliness, have called 'the contracting mentality'. But wherever else this accusation may be appropriate, it does not belong here. The view of rights that I am defending is consistent with a morality's *not* being something whose force, nature or content is supplied from any kind of prudence. Not only have I respected the fact that we do not opt or contract into a social morality. No weight at all has had to be attached to the possibility (which I discount) of reconstructing the reasons we would or might, as pre-socially conceived, have had for so opting or contracting. A social morality, as conceived here, is not even something which *it is as if* we have opted or contracted into.[42] It is simply the sort of thing that we find ourselves in the midst of, and that by virtue of being what it is, having the content it does have and deserving to command the consensus of those who live within it, does not afford what it would be constrained to regard as decently avowable reasons to *opt out of it*. It is neither here nor there if there are all sorts of *other* moralities that pass this test and that we might have found ourselves in the midst of. Our attachment does not depend on that's not being so, or on our satisfying ourselves that there is no other social morality that might have offered someone in our position a better package of rights.

17. (i) (ii) (iii) are great goods, and consideration of what it takes to ensure their persistence in the real world will doubtless lend colour to the independent demand for certain much more specifically political rights, as well as for publicly provided systems of education, legal aid and basic health care. These are intelligible extensions, of which I shall say more later, in what it is still just possible to recognize as the same spirit. But I should say that these things were at most one step beyond the rights whose non-realization gives men good reason for disaffection from society, because (i) (ii) (iii) and these natural extensions are simply the preconditions of a man's securing his own material survival in his

own way, or in the best way relative to his circumstances, by his own efforts. A man who demands such rights as these asks for scarcely any strictly first order goods — only for the wherewith to get his own, within a community that recognizes him as a participant with this right and that he in his turn recognizes as conferring, guaranteeing and limiting that right and as presupposed, in some condition or other, to any life that he can fully value. Still less does he ask for an equal title to an equal share of first order goods.

However familiar or unfamiliar our general method of justification may have appeared, the embryo rights that it generates are familiar enough. What will be noted, however, is that, although some needs have now turned up as generating rights, we still have no general vindication of the force of serious needs claims as such. It is true of course that some who set store by rights are apt to insist on more numerous and stronger rights than any afforded under (i), (ii) and (iii), and it is also true and important that, in practice, many extant social moralities will recognize, and impress upon the institutions and laws that they sustain, more rights than the abstract rights one can demonstrate by the general method we have sketched.[43] (In their special circumstances, they may have to. See below § 19 foll.) But that is not enough for our purposes. For, having rejected the idea of a social contract, and what one is *owed* for one's accord in the same, because we rejected the idea of a reconstruction of any however hypothetical, prudence-based reasons for opting into morality, we dare not see first order benefits that go too far beyond (i) (ii) (iii), or all needs simply as such, under the aspect of moral rights or abstract entitlements — lest they appear under the guise of a sort of *quid pro quo* for the retention of participative adherence or consensus. No idea could more quickly subvert a social morality, or more effectively despoil the achievement that it represents. (Cp. Schopenhauer, *On the Foundation of Morality*, §7, 'My egoism decides for justice and philanthropy not because it desires to practise these virtues but because it wants to experience them'.)

There is a second reason not to find rights, or what have sometimes been called 'claim-rights in the making' or 'manifesto rights', wherever there happen to be some serious needs, and this reason will hold good even for cases where needs are far harder to ignore than some unproblematical, acknowledged rights are. If we hold on to the conception of rights introduced in §15, then it will be natural to suppose that a categorical abstract claim-right only exists where there could in principle be some institutional obligation on someone or something to arrange for men to have the chance to take official or legal action against some specific defendant or legal entity in order to require some specific performance of him or it.[44] But however we rearrange society and its processes there will always be claims of dire need that fail this test. If we use the idea of right to prevent these from falling into oblivion, then we risk having to do without any criterion at all for right-hood and losing all sharpness in the idea of a right.[45]

There will be a temptation at this point to try to find room for needs in our picture by seeing needs that are not good candidates to be simple rights as having a force somehow comparable to a claim-right, and as requiring that whoever has this or that serious need should be recognized as owed *special consideration* when the mass of claims that bear upon any particular matter is reviewed. But, although this is correct enough for certain kinds of claims of needing, it is too vague (even by the relaxed standards appropriate in this area), and, what is far worse, it still leaves everything unexplained. Why *should* these kinds of needing deserve special public consideration?

The general form of the answer that I shall offer to this question, in the second phase of the explanation, is that serious non-instrumental needs that do not constitute rights or entitlements can sometimes stand in a certain counterpoise relation, first with straightforward rights actually recognized, and then (in a potentially contrasting way) with the ends of concerted public action.

18. (i) (ii) (iii) of §16 start life as scarcely more than the preconditions of men's securing their own survival in their own way, or in the best way relative to their circumstances. But they have a tendency to outgrow their beginnings. And on our *a posteriori* consensual approach, the strength and status of class (iii) rights and entitlements to property, inheritance etc. is not fixed exactly or for all places and times. What *is* determined about them — given the finitude of the world's natural resources, the long-term impossibility of each man's appropriation from natural resources leaving behind as much and as good for the next, and the accumulation of power that has inevitably accrued in a finite social space to those who stand at the end of long chains of inheritance of property and influence — is only that the stronger the support and confirmation that a given social morality provides for entrenched entitlements, and the greater the legal and political protection accordingly extended to those exercising a large number of class (iii) rights, the greater will be society's moral duty to respect in all its legal and

political deliberation the needs and vital interests of the human beings there will always be who have not got themselves into a position to acquire or exercise very many such rights and entitlements. – And the readier society must be, having marked out property and other entitlements, to diminish the extent to which such entrenched rights can countervail against true claims of vital need that must otherwise go unsatisfied. Surely needs must offset property rights *at least* to the extent that the appropriations and transfers of the centuries render ineffective all present efforts to command the resources that one requires to live by one's own efforts.[46] But one ought to go further. The stronger the property rights that are politically recognized and legally enforced, and the greater the efficacity of the social morality in protecting these rights, the more self-conscious society must become (at least under the conditions we are now used to in all the more populated, civilized and economically exploited parts of the earth) about the *inflexibility* and *possible failure* of the systems of entitlement relations that govern possession and use,[47] and the readier it must be to give practical expression to this self-consciousness, by (say) strengthening the position of the weak (e.g. in the regulation of commerce to eliminate monopoly or other abuse), or by projects intended to minister directly to the vital interests that will otherwise go unsatisfied. Society must cultivate this self-consciousness on pain of being seen as precisely worsening the plight of those who have least and who might otherwise have combined to take by force what they needed for self-sufficiency,[48] – or on pain of finding itself forced to subdue these people by methods that will in the end subvert morality itself.

19. It would be a great mistake to suppose that the public perception of the failure of entitlement relations is wedded even historically (let alone philosophically, see §15) to the ideal of equality (in the sense of everyone's having an equal title to all advantages), or that the failure is new and somehow the problem child of the welfare state as such. Classical and medieval anticipations aside, even nineteenth-century capitalism hard-headedly recognized what was nothing other than a failure of entitlement relations when it saw a problem in the housing of the poor (the employed and industrious poor especially).[49] It is true that *de facto*, and perhaps inevitably, philanthropy entered in here. (If justice is really blind, then philanthropy must do some of its seeing for it.) But even if it takes emergency to make us attend to what is intolerable in certain failures of entitlement, e.g. in famine as Amartya Sen has

anatomized that, we must still distinguish that mixed sort of disaster from natural disasters like flooding, earthquake or hurricane. Society intervenes here too, but only in the cause of philanthropy. Whereas in the case of simple starvation or lack of shelter, the duty to ask whether these are failures of entitlement, and to be prepared to abridge or modify various type (iii) rights if necessary, is a requirement of justice, and will remain so even if we cannot describe it illuminatingly in terms of any specific rights. Of course, in the context of a given system of law and administration that has grown sensitive to counterclaims, it can come about that citizens acquire certain legal rights to certain sorts of benefits, in money or in kind, e.g. health-care, or subsidized housing or even subsidized transport. And, as we have seen, there can be backing in moral justice for these rights, as conditionally considered, at least in the presence of certain now familiar social conditions arising from distortions of various heterogeneous kinds. But this backing can scarcely comprise categorical abstract rights to such goods or services.

20. With counterclaims and everything they involve, one enters immediately into an area of conflict, of revolution even. So it is unsurprising that it is hard to say anything, however theoretical, to satisfy all parties to the conflict. One half of the difficulty is that rights like those of class (iii) give rise to entirely legitimate expectations about the character and extent of the interventions against historical contingency and luck that society will undertake in the name of justice. Not only are rights like those falling in class (iii) founded in a human need. It is also a deep human need to be *able* to frame such long-term expectations of tenure and security. To remove the possibility of these is to abandon one of the most distinctive advantages of the very civilization that almost everyone who looks to politics for the redress of injustice aspires to enjoy. The other half of the difficulty is of course that the situation of those whom a certain system of rights impedes from living by their own efforts will in certain cases be simply desperate.

Sticking to what our approach here suggests ought to be least controversial, I would urge (1) that the clearest case, both for rights falling within the kinds (i), (ii), (iii) and for counterclaims, reposes upon vital needs that men will not otherwise be able to satisfy by their own efforts; (2) that, however strong the case in need for however stringent an abridgment of rights of acquisition or tenure, the correction or redistribution ought to be gradual and non-retrospective (lest social justice invade and annihilate the very idea of a right). Again (3), when

the satisfaction of counter-claims makes it necessary to abridge rights or
raise taxes above levels which were justified by the expenses of providing
and protecting rights and benefits falling within categories (i), (ii), (iii),
this should be done in a manner that is (a) perspicuous in intention; (b)
generally consistent (more consistent perhaps than are certain new
methods of taxing payments at source) with a man's original title to
what he earns;[50] (c) such as to force upon us the question whether
enough (or too much) is being attempted, and whether in the right
way.[51] Otherwise we lose sight of the terms of the original conflict, and
blur the distinction between that issue and other issues that arise at a
later phase of the evolution of social justice (viz. phase three, see below,
§24). Finally (4), it ought, I think, to be uncontroversial that the more
complicated and diverse the admissible counter-claims that can appear
under the aspect of claims in justice, and the more complicated and
diverse the response to them that is attempted in society's name, the
more likely this response is to get muddled up with public projects
whose rationale is not counter-claim based at all; and the more necessary
it is to renew and consolidate the original thinking that gave rise to
rights of the classes (i), (ii), (iii) — lest the original rationale for admitting rights and counterclaims be undermined and society overrun even
the minimum space about individual persons and their vital interests
that is so eloquently pleaded for by liberal writers like J. S. Mill and
Isaiah Berlin.

21. Perhaps the principle we require for the limitation and restriction
of collective reasoning conducted in pursuit of public goods should be
roughly this. Even if society makes one man poorer to make another
man less poor than he was (in kind or money), it is *pro tanto* unjust if
society intervenes against contingency or changes its policy or con-
founds men's sensible expectations in a way that sacrifices anyone's
vital interests to the mere desires of however many others; and it is *pro
tanto* unjust if, among vital interest actually affected by any such intervention by society, the greater vital need of anyone is sacrificed to the
lesser vital needs of however many others.

Such a principle — which must be founded, as always, in the connection between justice, consensus and citizens' sense of the legitimacy of
government — is still in the spirit of the arguments of §§18-19. A
society that allows type (iii) rights to outgrow their proper rationale
does precisely threaten vital interests. And the same applies to a society
that is uncritical of the counter-claims it finds valid. But it is not only

the rich and the fortunate who need to be protected by such a principle when rights are abridged, and it is not only the question of counter-claims that gives rise to the need for it. Almost invariably, actual societies' perception of the duty of governments to intervene in the name of counter-claims has coincided with (or even been preceded by) a perception of quite different reasons for public intervention, e.g. the necessity to solve coordination problems or provide benefits that coordination problems prevent the market from providing. It is hard to show any objection in principle to this, even where the resulting projects are not vital needs-based. But all experience suggests that, as society's public actions become more heterogeneous, and as lower incomes begin to be heavily taxed, and public projects impinge more and more severely upon the environment, displacing citizens for public works such as schools, hospitals, parks and public road building (the last having an understandable tendency always to seek out the areas of lowest rateable value), those who stand in the direst need of the Principle of Limitation are almost never the rich or the fortunate. And the more that it then begins to seem proper for the State to undertake, the smaller the probability that all consensually requisite protection of the individual's private sphere will be available already, in the shape of effective, recognized legal and/or constitutional rights and remedies, like those falling in our classes (i), (ii), (iii), that can be opposed to the actual or prospective, direct or indirect effects of public action.

22. In the face of this sort of problem, some have suggested that accepted methods such as cost benefit analysis be more widely used and simultaneously strengthened to reflect the observed fact that the most a person will pay for a benefit he has not got, or to avert an evil he already suffers, is a smaller amount than the smallest amount he would accept to be deprived of the benefit or be forced to put up with the evil; or that it be modified again to give a special weighting to burdens and benefits that will accrue from a scheme to the poorer sections of the community.[52] But this palliative scarcely goes to the middle of the difficulty, which is that a sufficient number of mere desires can always swamp any however heavily weighted need; and that a sufficient number of needs of the less vital variety can always outweigh any however heavily weighted vital need.[53]

Others have considered that what was required was an extension of the common law rights of individuals. But in practice this would almost certainly have been ineffective in some cases and too effective in others — if it means that certain sorts of public project, even projects justified by the direst need, could always be obstructed (e.g. by the refusal or threatened refusal by the victims of a public project to accept proffered compensation as adequate).[54] I do not of course deny that there may be a case for some strengthening in the common law. But as a general response, this sort of approach does not address the real problem. *What* new common law rights are to be created, and on what principle? And how can these ever be arranged to anticipate the indefinite number of possible future injustices that will be committed against identifiable and non-identifiable people in the name of public interest?[55]

Another slightly different approach has proposed the institution of a procedural-cum-constitutional right to have one's needs or vital interests taken as vital interest when public schemes are mooted, this right being backed by the legal power to force relevant officials either to prove at a hearing that these interests have been taken into account and treated in accord with some relevant principle or to abandon their project. But, however impressive this may sound, it would be curiously ineffective in the absence of any agreed principles about how vital interests that are not legal rights are to be treated, as well as suffering from the same difficulties as the common law approach with unidentified or unidentifiable victims.

So the direction in which one is finally inclined is along the path that leads not through rights as such but directly back to what now appears as nothing less than a necessity of political culture, namely the explicit acknowledgment as a constituent principle of justice (along with whatever other principles we can muster) of some principle like the one I stated in §21. (Cp. again also §11.) Administrative and legal details are important but secondary. What matters first is that something like the Principle of Limitation should be confirmed in the status of a principle of fairness, and should come to be taken so much for granted as a principle of fairness that it is impossible for administrative practice and political decision-making to proceed in apparent defiance of the principle. In the presence of the expectation of this, it will be largely a matter of legal tradition whether or not citizens have the envisaged procedural-constitutional rights or how else the operation of the principle is guaranteed.[56] In the absence of the expectation that vital needs will rank in this way, the long-term prospects are not very good, in the world as it is now, for government with the full consent of the governed. There will be things that stick in the throat when we seek to justify what government is forced to say and do to those who take exception to its encroachments.

23. If the Limitation Principle is an attempt to spell out, in terms of a vagueness suited to the subject matter, one of the prerequisites for the adherents of a workable social morality to lack avowable reasons to abdicate from it, then in all modern societies that are governed by consent, men's moral consciousness ought to concur in the Limitation Principle. But perhaps one should not expect to find any very direct practical or phenomenological test for the correctness of the argument that I have offered for it. For we must be prepared to accept that different societies may differ considerably in the interpretation they put on 'vital' as it figures in 'vital interest or need'. (Cp. §6.) One would predict that these and other differences in interpretation and emphasis will combine with divergent conceptions of the interventive role of government to issue in many important variations in the practice and sentiments of justice. The existence of these variations is perfectly consistent with the correctness of the Limitation Principle, whose operation is in any case highly sensitive, even at a particular time in a particular context, to where exactly the frontier of vital interests is seen as lying. Where a need is (as correctly formulated) vital and is specially protected as such by the principle, then it limits the space within which it is just for society to seek to maximize aggregated social advantage. If on the other hand the need falls short of that threshold, then it takes its chance with other needs, and there are conditions under which it may be sacrificed, and sacrificed without injustice, to the aggregated weight of other interests.

This discontinuity may seem strange. But reflection suggests that things have to be like this. There are some things we cannot justly do to a man, however much other men may benefit.[57] (Almost nobody thinks that it can be just say to kill one innocent man, simply in order that millions will benefit.) The only question is how far this special protection extends beyond life itself. And of course there must be *some* cut-off. Otherwise we could scarcely ever reason aggregatively without incurring the charge of being to some extent unjust to someone.

What one ought to hope then is not that we can dispense with the threshold just mentioned, but that, given a place, a time, a climate of opinion and a set of expectations, the placing of the threshold will not be arbitrary but at worst essentially contestable. One might also expect that, as a society grows richer — and as it enlarges its sympathies to treat as if they were counter-claims in justice the claims of those who are prevented by natural handicap rather than by the power or prior appropriations of others from living through their own efforts –, men will construe 'vital interests' more generously. Perhaps in feeling they do. In practice, however – even if the human sentiments are prepared in principle for this, and also prepared to understand the Limitation Principle thus generously interpreted as playing the excluding role I have proposed for it – , the bureaucratic consciousness construes 'vital interests' extremely narrowly, so narrowly sometimes as to include little more than the bare prerequisites of life.[58]

The long-term dangers of this narrow construal are the same, I believe, as the dangers of an outright rejection of the principle. But the chief reason for the narrow interpretation is not, I think, any particular wickedness of bureaucrats, but the intense competition that they are apt to find themselves witnessing at close quarters (or involved in, as the recipients of lobbying, special pleading, pressure from newspapers about particular cases etc.) between considerations like the Limitation Principle (understood as a principle of justice but not properly understood as a principle of limitation, and almost always under-represented because very few projects endanger the vital interests of a larger number of people than the number they benefit) and very different kinds of need-based claims, claims having their rationale (which should not be lightly assumed to be a rationale in justice) at what is logically (if not historically) a third phase, after the two phases I have described in the preceding sections.

24. A society reaches the third phase, by my count, when government not only sees itself as the guardian of rights (the first phase) and counter-claims (the second phase), but also confirms itself in its role as the agent of coordination and the indispensable minister (at least in certain particular spheres) to human needs that will otherwise go unsatisfied. (And desires too, no doubt; though, as we noticed at the beginning, once taken on board, these are usually accorded the official title of needs.) Here the numbers who benefit from any project and the quantity of need that can be satisfied by a given resource are felt to be a strong consideration – and, given the shortage of resources, rightly so. For what the administrator is now involved with is aggregative or agglomerative reasoning – he is maximizing something – , and what presumably matters most *within the proper sphere of such reasoning* is accurate measurement and prediction of consequences, and the will to

jump off the treadmill whenever necessary for the imaginative exploration of alternatives that will bring greater total satisfaction and avoid the projection into the future of situations already giving rise to dissatisfaction and the mounting consumption of resources.[59]

Once a society is launched into phase three (and launched there for reasons having nothing specially to do with justice) and has instituted corresponding rules and practices, it moves into a whole new range of possible unfairness. And protestation at unfairness is likely to become unprecedently shrill and rancorous, giving even an obsession with the older and more important part of justice the unjustified reputation of enviousness and stridency. 'If z with need x had such and such done for him, why is nothing done for me with my need x?' What every administration that has entered the third phase requires is a range of defensible answers to such questions. It seems it must always be able to reply either 'Yes, we will!' or 'z's need is greater', or 'Your need is more expensive to satisfy'. Whatever it gives to anyone placed in such and such a way, it must also give to anyone else so placed; and (following what, given only finite resources, comes down to the same policy) it must be careful never to give anyone anything before it has looked to the ends of the earth to ensure that there are not too many who will be able to represent that they have the very same entitlement.

25. There is no going back from phase three. We are too used to the benefits we attribute to it. And our feelings are commendably (however confusedly) fixed upon at least one small but conspicuous concomitant of it, namely our new willingness to intervene against contingency to help remedy certain entitlement failures that are in no way society's fault or strict responsibility. We did not have to feel this, but we do in fact. What was claimed about the distinction between claims of need and claims of the intolerability of inequality still holds good; but that distinction leaves room for an idea (not itself lacking some lien with consensus) that there can be such a thing as too great a gap between people's life-chances.[60]

But if there is no going back, and phase three is where we resolve to take our stand, the time has arrived to try to understand much better the essential instability of the conception of social justice that we have got ourselves — which we can scarcely do if we will never try to decipher the palimpsest of divergent ideas that it comprises.

In the first place *need* itself now figures not only on the side of *justice as limitative, protective and remedial*, but also on the frequently conflicting side of *justice as the keeper and distributor of public largesse*. In the conversation with the economist that I reported at §2, we could barely understand one another because he was preoccupied with the second of these roles and I was so preoccupied with the first. Had we realized this, and had I then expressed my concurrence in his belief that claims of need are often found in the company of abuse and special pleading, we could have got a little further and might even have found ourselves discussing vital interests, the limits of compensation and the problem of bequeathing our descendants a world with at least as many tolerable niches for individual human existence as the one we inherited. Few questions are more urgent. But no progress at all can be made on them without some public understanding of the distinction of these two ways in which need claims are made, some sense of the putative priority in justice itself of phase one and phase two considerations over phase three considerations.

In the second place, we must learn to acquiesce in a tension there must always be *within* our way of thinking of justice as keeper and distributor of whatever wealth is to be deemed public.

Consider the two following principles of justice:

(U) *Ceteris paribus* it is unjust not to have equal regard to equal needs, and subject to possibility and cost, it is just to satisfy equal needs equally.

(E) *Ceteris paribus* it is unjust to accord different weight to people in respect of their needs; and, subject to possibility and cost, it is just to satisfy people equally in respect of their need.

Each will seem compelling, especially in the absence of the suggestion that the other is compelling.

(U) looks like just the kind of principle the hard pressed bureaucrat or manager requires. What he is there for is to rid the world of all of the various kinds of unsatisfied need, starting presumably with the worst among unsatisfied needs. At any stage he reaches in the process[61] he must identify all outstanding needs that are as bad as or worse than (equal to or greater than) those so far attended to, and attend to them — *subject* of course *to cost*. But what effectively can that mean? The answer that suggests itself is: Consider the resources available, and do the most you can with them by way of need satisfaction. And of course the next thought is: Needs do after all shade off into desires, so it would be less arbitrary to do the best one can with the resources available to satisfy all unsatisfied needs and desires. And then having reached that point — that is, act utilitarianism with respect to public policy — even the Limitation Principle must begin to seem anomalous, or ripe to be swallowed by the new doctrine. Indeed, the Limitation Principle, in so far as it suggests any policy at variance with what is suggested by the diminishing marginal usefulness to individuals of public largesse, will now seem simply irrational. It can only appear to stand in the way of the war against unsatisfied needs and desires.

But the principle (E) can initiate its own progression. Surely when we treat people differently, there must be a reason to treat them differently. And what better reason to treat them differently than that one of them has more unsatisfied needs? So we must proportion the largesse people receive to how much they stand in want of. — Or rather we must do this subject to the cost. We cannot spend a million pounds on making one paraplegic's life just appreciably less bad simply because his suffering is greater than that of others who also have serious needs, or in spite of the fact that the same money would have given these others a very great deal of what they need. So, as we said, it is all subject to cost. But what effectively can that mean? The manager will want a rule. And if he must have a rule, then perhaps the only possible rule is to allocate the same to each person for his needs (or, since they shade off, for his needs and desires) for him to do the best he can with. — Or rather, remembering the starting point and the concern at the fact that some had more unsatisfied need and others less, the rule must be to allocate public resources in such a way that the total that each person eventually enjoys (of public and private resources taken together) is equal to that which anyone else eventually enjoys. And having got to that point, or to some further sophistication of it — that is to a public philosophy of pure equality — it must seem anomalous and absurd to recognize a separate Limitation Principle. Since we are doing the best we can for each, everybody's vital interests will be intact if anyone's are. The distributive principle (E) simply swallows the limitative protective principle.

26. (U) and (E) so developed stand in stark opposition with one another. Each initiates a progression or simplification that seems within its own terms of reference irresistible. But each then loses touch with the original impulse that placed it there. (U) prepares us in principle to sacrifice individuals without limit, as Mackie would put it. (E) serves up a notion of equality of resources that is so abstract that it can scarcely

184

impinge at all upon the sentiments that made needs seem important in the first place.

If the idea of living with this conflict and tolerating the essential contestability of the frontier that contains it seems unbearable, then, having deciphered the palimpsest I spoke of, we could, I suppose try to retrace the marks we have made and contemplate the restoration (by deletion of the most recent) of the simpler moral universe in which there is scarcely any public largesse and in which rights and counter-claims make up the whole of justice. It seems certain that it could induce a sense of proportion to think through the moral advantages of this. But this is not to say that it is really possible to get back to that point.

A much more characteristic response on the part of philosophers and political scientists is to tinker and try to find a principle that mediates or compromises somehow between (U) and (E). And there is no end I am sure to the ingenuity that can be brought to bear on the task of qualifying and adjusting the arguments that lead (U) and (E) from the state of tension into the state of outright practical incompossibility. But perhaps it would be better to learn to live with (U), (E) and the Limitation Principle as marking three separate, mutually irreducible sorts of claim upon us, and to prevent the deafening noise of the con-flict between (U) and (E) from drowning the pleas of all other demands of justice. It would be better to refrain from assimilating limitative protective justice to distributive justice, and to refrain from taking pro-tective justice (properly understood as protective and not as presup-posing largesse) to be in any conflict at all with aggregative public rationality. (Surely they are not in conflict with it. One simply defines the other's proper theatre of operation, however essentially contestably.)

Why then might the prospect of living with this seem unbearable – or any more unnerving than the prospect of riding a bicycle? I suspect that it will seem unbearable only if we see it as the task of a theory of justice to hit on suitable principles or axioms that generate a description or blueprint for a just state or society, e.g. in the manner Plato adopts in the *Republic*, relying upon the non-self-sufficiency of men and the supposed truism that each kind of man should do what he does best, or in the manner of John Rawls, who arrives at a just order of things by working out what departures from strict equality would have been written into a social contract drawn up under ideal conditions, in ignorance of social reality as we have it and of the positions of particular people therein. In the thought-experimentation that is characteristic of these approaches, nothing is left to chance, and nothing is *prima facie* anybody's (even if the thing in question would never have existed at all but for him) until it is *assigned* to him as his share. — Though of course the exactitude of the theoretical calculations that the procedure purports in some variants to make possible is diminished out of recognition when we reach the problem of social criticism and attempt the concrete comparison of actual with hypothetically just holdings, a baffling and multiple counterfactual problem.

So long as one is committed to this approach, one will think one has to try to construct a sort of *model* of justice. Our own attempt has been quite different — indeed almost opposite in intention. We have started out with the historical contingency that men live in societies, societies being things that we discover in existence possessing whatever nature they do possess, completing and conditioning the lives of men in all sorts of different ways and manifesting different degrees of cohesion and consensus. And we have then speculated on what it now takes for societies that exist by consensus to perpetuate themselves, on terms and by means that their participants can avow to themselves without having to unlearn their instinctive capacity to recognize other men as conscious subjects and objects of reciprocity and interpretation[62] — and what it takes for them to continue to do so even as the awareness grows among these societies' subjects of their own power. In this consensual, evolutionary approach, the philosophy of justice does not have to invent and hold up for comparison some contractualist (or whatever) *ideal polity* with which reality can be confronted for purposes of adjustment and criticism. It has to try to draw upon the various potentially divergent ideas and feelings we already have in order to describe how and to what extent historical contingency, and whatever other goals besides justice men and societies may pursue, will have to be offset by deliberate regulation and intervention, sometimes despite men's legitimate expectation, to accord with our evolving sense of what it is fair for people to be asked to do and endure, our sense of the entitlement that must normally accrue to effort or achievement or inheritance or settled expectation or whatever and our untheoretic sense of the strengths of the differing classes of need claims. Justice here is only the lack of a certain sort of evil. (A theory of it does not need then to furnish a determinate paradigm for the legal and constitutional arrangements of a country.) And not only are there many other matters a society must concern itself with besides justice (the security of the state, economic survival etc.). And not only must these other considerations limit how just it is

186

possible to be. But also justice is itself a complex and many rooted idea, and can conflict with itself − or so our approach prepares us to expect − in ways for which there is no predetermined mode of resolution.

When it comes to applying such a conception of justice as this to social reality, whether in policy-making or in criticism, its practical application is at once direct, underdetermined and contextually constrained (leaving much to be decided by something like Aristotelian *aisthesis*[63]). There is no difficulty in seeing that certain things are clearly unjust. But room is left even for one and the same society at a given time to answer certain sorts of question in several different ways.

Nor is it a positive point in favour of accepting some other picture that it eliminates this under-determination, either within justice itself or in the competition between justice and other values. Even given a social morality as determinate as you like (as determinate even as such a thing can be), it is not demonstrably rational to look confidently for the elimination of essential contestability. But then, if we pause a little longer on the point, maybe we shall find not hopelessness but comfort − even some obscure hope for politics itself (does one *have* to think of one's political opponents as wicked or morally deranged?) − in the thought that I shall end by quoting from another colleague whom like Mackie I left it too late to consult about all sorts of things:

> The basic moral intuitions of mankind − which Right and Left
> alike cannot but take for granted as a premise for their moral appeal
> − provide no solution except in a prohibitive and limiting sense, for
> the permanent and topical problems of political organization and
> choice.[64]

ACKNOWLEDGMENTS

Sections 3,4,5,6,7 and 12 are adapted from work on needs which will appear elsewhere in another form (forthcoming *J. Medical Ethics*) under the joint authorship of Sira Dermen, to whom the author is greatly indebted, and of the present author, to whom the task has fallen of extending and rewriting joint drafts that date from the early and middle 1970s and of trying to update these materials in the light of books and articles that have been published or come to notice since then.

I have benefited greatly from letters that Bernard Williams and Ronald Dworkin most kindly sent to me about the penultimate draft. I am also indebted for advice and suggestions to Jennifer Hornsby, Susan Hurley, Robert Gay, Michael Smith, Margery Eagle and Anthony Price.

NOTES

1 'Bentham on legal rights', in *Oxford Essays in Jurisprudence* II, ed. Simpson, 1973, p. 200.

2 'Can there be a rights-based moral theory?' in *Midwest Studies in Philosophy* III, 1978, pp. 350–9; 'Rights, utility and universalization', in Frey (ed.), *Utility and Rights*, Oxford, Blackwell, 1984. See also his 'Rights, utility and external costs' (forthcoming).

3 *Critique of Gotha Programme* (towards the end of Marx's third comment on the document). For further references to Marx and Hegel, see Patricia Springborg, *The Problem of Human Needs and the Critique of Civilization*, London, Allen & Unwin, 1981. See also Agnes Heller's important study *The Theory of Need in Marx*, London, Allison & Busby, 1976.

4 Cp. Shakespeare, *King Lear*: 'So distribution should undo excess/ and each man have enough', 4.1.66. (Cp. also 3.4.28.) And for nineteenth-century pre-Marxian formulations of the abilities/ needs principle, L. Blanc's and others; see pp. 147–8, note 3, of Del Vecchio, *Justice: An Historical and Philosophical Essay*, Edinburgh, ed. A. H. Campbell, 1952.

5 Cp. Antony Flew, *The Politics of Procrustes*, London, Temple Smith, 1981, p. 117:

> An emphasis upon needs as opposed to wants cannot but appeal to those who would like to see themselves as experts qualified both to determine what the needs of others are, and to prescribe and enforce the means appropriate to the satisfaction of those needs.

Or compare Jeremy Bray, *Decision in Government*, London, Gollancz, 1970, p. 72.

For criticisms of a very different tone and tenor, see James Griffin, 'Modern utilitarianism', *Revue Internationale de Philosophie*, no. 141, 1982, pp. 340–3.

6 Although it is official ratiocination and argument rather than legislative enactment that displays the most frequent employment of the word 'need', it is by no means unknown even in Acts of Parliament. For instance, Clause 2 of the 1978 Transport Act requires County Councils in England and Wales to prepare and publish annually a five-year public transport plan reviewing existing services 'in relation to need'. (For the source of this use, compare the White Paper *Transport Policy 1977*, *Cmnd.* 6836, which lays it

down as one objective of official policy to 'meet social needs by securing a reasonable level of mobility'.)

Note that in the third example given in the sequel below we find as often, the form '*x* needs to be V-ed', which may be presumed to be a transformation from 'it needs to be that *x* is V-ed', which presumably comes from '[we] need to V *x*' or '[we] need *x* to be V-ed'.

7 Cp. Springborg, op, cit., Appendix. All else apart, the accusation concedes much too much to the word. There is no real contradiction at all in saying: 'This patient needs a blood transfusion. But she can't have one. The only suitable blood has been allocated to someone else.' (E. D. Watt in 'Human needs, human wants, and political consequences', *Political Studies*, vol. 30, 1982, p. 541, imputes the same error to K. R. Minogue, who wrongly characterizes a need as something that has by definition 'a right to satisfaction'. See *The Liberal Mind*, London, Methuen, 1963, pp. 46, 103.)

8 Or desires or preferences that I should have if I were rational? But who can say what it is rational for someone to want in advance of knowing what he needs? There must of course be many other ways arriving at rational wants otherwise than via needs; but in so far as rationality comes into the matter at all — i.e. rationality as conceived independently of given actual motivations — the idea of need surely has to be at least *coeval* with the idea of want, and should be accorded its own semantic identity.

9 See A. R. White's telling criticisms of the assimilation of needs and desires in *Modal Thinking*, Oxford, Blackwell, 1971, p. 114. There are numerous other ways of bringing out this sort of difference. But one way of making the distinction can and must be firmly dispensed with, and is certainly superfluous. This is the claim that a man who needs *x eo ipso* lacks *x* and ails without *x*, whereas a man who wants *x* may not lack *x*. The trouble with this is that it isn't true that I lack whatever I need: all sorts of things that I already have are things that I need. See again here White, p. 107. For the view, see e.g. S. I. Benn and R. S. Peters, *Social Principles and the Democratic State*, London, Allen & Unwin, 1959, p. 143.

10 The exceptions are (1) G. E. M. Anscombe, 'Modern moral philosophy', *Philosophy*, 1958, p. 7: 'To say that [an organism] needs that environment is not to say, e.g. that you want it to have that environment, but that it won't flourish unless it has it. Certainly, it all depends whether you *want* it to flourish! as Hume would say. But what "all depends" on whether you want it to flourish is whether the fact that it needs that environment, or won't flourish without it, has the slightest influence on your actions'; (2) Joel Feinberg in *Social Philosophy*, Englewood Cliffs, New Jersey, Prentice Hall, 1973, p. 111: 'In a general sense to say that S needs X is to say simply that if he doesn't have X he will be harmed'.

(Cp. David Miller, *Social Justice*, Oxford, Oxford University Press, 1976, p. 130; David Richards, *A Theory of Reasons for Action*, Oxford, 1970, Oxford University Press, pp. 37–8; Honoré, op. cit., at note 26 below, his p. 78.)

The main difference between these analyses or elucidations and the one we shall propose consists in the fact that we propose to see *need* as an explicitly modal notion, which leads us to insist that Anscombe's conditional be governed by 'necessarily'. For other works also presumably under the direct or indirect influence of Anscombe's formulation see D. Wiggins, *Sameness and Substance*, Oxford, Blackwell, 1980, p. 183, and J. Finnis, *Natural Law and Natural Rights*, Oxford, Oxford University Press, 1980, passim.

11 This is the common point in the otherwise very different (and differently modulated) accounts of Flew and White and Barry. See Flew, *Politics of Procrustes*, p. 120: ('If I say that I need something, it is never inept to ask what for. . . . There is always something hypothetically imperative about any need'); White, op. cit. ('To say that A needs to V is elliptical for saying that A needs to V in order to F [where to F is the end state] (p. 105), . . . a failure to notice the elliptical nature of statements about what A needs leads to arguments at cross purposes (p. 106) . . . "Does A need X?" is an elliptical not a normative question' (p. 106)); Brian Barry, *Political Argument*, London, Routledge & Kegan Paul, 1965, chapter III, §5a.

12 For more on this necessity see below §6. The three time variables t, t', t'', are all needed in the full form of the 'need' sentence as given without any ellipse or abbreviation (even though, evidently, they do not vary entirely independently). t'' need not be t', because the goal mentioned in the antecedent may be achieved later than the prerequisite mentioned in the consequent. t need not be t'', because the end-state, a child's having good second teeth for instance, may create an earlier necessity that certain measures be taken. And t need not be t' either, because it may be necessary *now* (t) that certain measure be taken next year (t') for the subsequent (t'') good of the second teeth — even though it was not necessary last year (before t) that these measures be taken at t'. Before t there was a chance of dispensing with these t' measures, e.g. by taking proper or better care of the first teeth.

It is well beyond our present scope to trace the relationship of the time indicators in this sort of elucidation to the tenses that appear in the various natural language forms that it seeks to elucidate.

One more caveat. Strictly speaking, it is necessary to add to the form in the text '. . . and having a suit is of concern to him'. The addition will be superfluous as soon as we supplant 'has a suit' in the antecedent by a sentence representing something he cannot

190

help being concerned with (as in the sequel, when we come to non-instrumental needing).

13 The hazards of claiming the strict lexical distinctness of senses are now familiar. We are claiming that the considerations in the text will suffice for a proof of distinctness of sense of 'need' that comes up to the standard proposed in David Wiggins, 'Sentence sense, word sense and difference of word sense' in *Semantics: An Interdisciplinary Reader*, D. Steinberg and D. Jacobovits, Cambridge, Cambridge University Press, 1971 or Bede Rundle, *Grammar in Philosophy*, Oxford University Press, 1981, pp. 14-5.

14 What might possibly confuse one is that if someone says that he needs something [absolutely] then he may perfectly well explain himself (as our equivalences indeed suggest) by reference to what he needs [instrumentally] to stay alive or avoid harm.

15 The feeling that this proposal imports a semantical singularity of some sort may be substantially reduced by reference to a certain more familiar and uncontroversial example of ambiguity, where there is a similar nesting of one sense of a word in the account of another sense of the same word: where 'V' holds a place for a verb or verb-phrase,

z has a [liberty] right to V iff z has no duty not to V; z has a [claim] right to V iff z has a [liberty] right to V and some person or agency has no [liberty] right not to secure to z the opportunity and ability to exercise his [liberty] right to V.

Cp. Joel Feinberg, *Social Philosophy*, p. 58: 'One can have a liberty which is not also a [claim] right but one cannot have a [claim] right which is not also a liberty'.

16 For instance, relativizing length, duration and motion and reformulating Newton's laws to render them relative to the reference frame of the observer and all reference frames in uniform motion with respect to him, and then qualifying the laws in certain ways suggested by the Special Theory of Relativity, made of a theory that was not previously unqualifiedly true a theory that may yet prove to be absolutely true.

17 Cp. David Wiggins, 'Towards a reasonable libertarianism', in *Essays on Freedom of Action*, ed. T. Honderich, London, Routledge & Kegan Paul, 1973 (amended edition, 1979), pp. 45-6, 59-60.

18 Note that we have already had implicit recourse to this thought in the discussion of the instrumental sense in so far as we allowed that N needed £200 to buy a suit. The fact that there is a future in which he has a suit without paying £200, because he steals one, was not allowed to count against this claim.

19 Thus for our conditional in §5 governed by the specially indexed modality the problem simply does not arise that the impossibility of the antecedent will make the conditional true vacuously.

For the reasons for preferring the 'harm'-formulation to a direct formulation in terms of 'flourishing' ('Necessarily (if z flourishes then. . . .)'), see below §12, on Aristotle.

20 'Basic' will be here, as in all the schemes we have encountered in other writers, a technical term to be grasped in the first instance by the definition of the category, and in the second instance by reference to the *point* of setting up such a category. (To forget this, and to dispute as if the categories were antecedently given, is to engage in the sort of logomachy that gives philosophy a bad name.) In particular, we would remark that our basic category is not the same in definition or point as the category of *survival needs*, or *biological needs* as Benn and Peters call them (op. cit. pp. 144–6; see also Rosen's criticisms in *Mind*, 1977, p. 88). Nor is it the same in definition or point as Benn and Peter's own category of *basic needs*, which simply concerns a decent standard of living; or the same as the modern Marxist category of *really human needs*, or *one's needs as a human being*, which are usually introduced to make a contrast with *false needs*. (A contrast we have partially but only partially absorbed by bringing out the full exigency of the truth-conditions of statements of need.)

21 Corruption flourishes in a special way when nobody quite knows what *counts* as corruption, and even honest men do not know what distance to keep from certain other men of entrepreneurial energy and flair. For one part of the reason for this state of doubt and confusion see §24 following below. This is a state of doubt and confusion that makes room for methods of persuasion and promotion that represent corruption in a further, moral or intellectual (not legal) sense. (Cp. Francis Gladstone, *The Politics of Planning* (London, Temple Smith 1976), p. 105 on rhetorical use of the 'have-not' as a means of dressing up the desiderata of those who 'have'.)

22 For the inherent indefiniteness of the subject matter of practice, cp. Aristotle, *Nicomachean Ethics* V.x. 4-5.

Somewhat similar remarks to those in the text ought probably to be directed at the Marxists' conception of 'truly human needs', needs that are 'expressive of human essence' etc. Countless needs, under any conceivable state of affairs, will always be both urgent and non-basic — i.e. put there by particular circumstances. And there will always be particular circumstances, however admirable the new condition of man. To the extent then that we cannot confront the problem that 'Under private property . . . every person speculates on creating a new need in another' (Marx *1844 MSS*, London, Lawrence & Wishart, 1970, p. 147) by insisting on the proper interpretation of claims of need, the problem of false needs is much too hard to be simply solved by identifying the class of basic or essentially human needs.

The poignancy of the contrast between the thin set of universal needs that *nature* will underwrite and the set of things that may be needed by a man placed in his particular situation is brought out, however obliquely to Shakespeare's intention, most vividly in *Lear* (2.4.262):

> Allow not nature more than nature needs,
> Man's life is cheap as beast's.

Plainly, there is no 'human need' to have a retinue of a hundred knights. But an abdicated king in Lear's position needed such a retinue – and, to judge by what happened to him, much else besides.

There is a closely related difficulty in bringing Rawls's theory of primary goods to bear upon the problem of needs, as I conceive this. For one of the things we have to be prepared to attempt here is to look behind social arrangements defined in terms of primary goods, and behind representative positions of representative kinds of person, to the actual circumstances of particular persons – all in a manner apparently forbidden by Rawls in *A Theory of Justice*. On this point, see Brian Barry *The Liberal Theory of Justice* (London, Macmillan, 1975), especially pp. 54–5, 114–15.

23 For some connected observations, based on the experience of developing countries, see Paul Streeten, *First Things First* (Oxford, Oxford University Press for World Bank 1981), pp. 190–1. I must however qualify the claims I make in the text. Under the right conditions – and especially when the *immediate* result is not in itself very costly – it may be heuristically indispensable to set the standard too high (even shameful not to). When anaesthetics did not exist, certain sorts of suffering and harm were inevitable. Yet there was a point in saying anaesthetics were needed; and, had our ancestors not felt some such thing, they would not have striven as hard as they did to make such things realistically envisageable or to discover them.

24 A good example of this is provided by modern transport planners' settled habit of speaking of 'mobility' (by car) as a standing need of western civilization. There is no doubt that with present tendencies towards concentration of facilities and dispersed patterns of development such mobility approximates to a short- or medium-term need with a considerable and rising degree of entrenchment. But, if alternative tendencies can be envisaged, we shall get a fairer view of all the available options if we realize that the right name for the standing, invariable need (the need that underlies the shorter-term need) is not 'mobility' but, more plastically and indefinitely, 'access [to facilities that are frequently needed]'.

25 Del Vecchio, *Justice*, op. cit., p. 148.

26 See his criticisms at p. 148 (note), somewhat mitigated at p. 143.

27 Cp. §21 below and cp. Mackie, 'Can there be a right-based moral theory?', op. cit. Note also the discrepancy with Mackie, who uses the notion of a right for what we use *right*, *counter-claim* and *need* together to accomplish.

28 The point is of course unaffected even if one supposes that the natural condition is *already* secretly modal. This would hardly make the modality indexed for time and circumstance, as in §6, redundant.

29 Cp. V. Pareto, *Les Systemes Socialistes* (Paris, 1901–2) vol II, pp. 167–8: 'La formule: *à chacun selon ses besoins*, devient . . . un travestissement métaphysique de la formule: *à chacun part égale, avec certaines corrections*'; Gregory Vlastos 'Justice and equality', in *Social Justice*, ed. R. Brandt, Englewood Cliffs, New Jersey, Prentice Hall, 1962; '"To each according to his need" . . . is in fact the most perfect form of equal distribution' (p. 40); A. M. Honoré, 'Social justice', in *Essays in Legal Philosophy*, ed. R. S. Summers, Oxford, Blackwell, 1970, p. 78: 'The principle of social justice . . . lays down that men have a claim to advantages and an equal share in advantages. Therefore the principle of justice according to need may be regarded as one aspect, or one corollary, of the principle of social justice. From the point of view of this principle, those who are in need are entitled to point to the fact that they lack advantages to which the principle of social justice entitles them'; Honoré quotes here D. D. Raphael, 'Justice and liberty', in *Proceedings of the Aristotelian Society* 1951: 'Thus the basis of the claim of social need is really a recognition of the claim to equality'; Feinberg, op. cit. at note 10 above, p. 111; A. Sen 'Equality of what?', in *Tanner Lectures on Human Values*, Utah/ Cambridge, Cambridge University Press, 1980, ed. McMurrin, especially pp. 217–19; David Miller, *Social Justice*, Oxford, 1976: 'One could say that the principle of need represents the most urgent part of the principle of equality' (p. 149). See also Peter Singer in *Reading Nozick*, ed. J. Paul, Oxford, Blackwell, 1981, p. 49; Flew, op. cit. at note 4 above; R. H. Tawney, *Equality* (London, Allen & Unwin, 1952), p. 42.

30 Cp. Williams, *Problems of the Self*, Cambridge, Cambridge University Press, 1973, p. 240 foll., and e.g. Vlastos, Honoré, Miller, cited at note 29.

31 It may be surmised that Ronald Dworkin would regard it as a hindrance, at least so far as elucidation goes. See 'What is equality? (Part One)', *Philosophy and Public Affairs*, vol. 10, no. 3, 1981. (Marx, having no patience with the idea of equality as such, is of course an exception to the general claim in the text.)

32 I lean heavily here, and below, on the useful formulations of Honoré.

33 And even perhaps inequality of respect? (Cp. H. L. A. Hart, *The Concept of Law*, Oxford, Oxford University Press 1961, p. 158.) Some may be tempted to say that equality of respect is a need. This is not something I shall deny. But note that if *this* is wherein the urgency of equal respect resides, then there is a danger, not that equality considerations will swallow considerations of need, but that the latter will swallow the former.

34 And if so, then here at least even some conservatives could afford to relax their guarded attitude towards needing. If the attitude towards need that I shall propose is taken just as it stands, and no more is then read into it by the force of habitual political association, then it is left open whether the proper province of state action or interference is wide or narrow, except in so far as there is strong pressure for such intervention from the quarter of otherwise unsatisfiable vital human need. But the final import of such claims of need will then depend on the totality of justice claims that are invoked. What is more, considerations of need will themselves suggest principles of limitation of the scope of action by the state. (See §21 below.)

Another point that needs to be stressed is that principles concerning vital need are not necessarily another gift to the dreaded experts (appointed, self-appointed or elected). Norms of flourishing and harm are not their intellectual property — unless what someone proposes is a system of government that makes these norms into their intellectual property.

Pareto writes in *Les Systems Socialistes* (op. cit.), p. 167; 'La formule: *à chacun selon ses besoins* se change ainsi en l'autre: *a chacun selon ce que decide l'autorité*; et elle vaut en general ce que vaut l'autorité'. This gibe has been repeated countless times in countless variants, even against opponents who, unlike Pareto's, do not propose 'To each according to his need' as part of some *supreme* principle of all justice. Outside that context, this is simply mud-slinging, or vilification by association.

If what someone fears is that expert opinion and/or some wide public consensus about what is a good or a wretched life might license massive interference in the freedom of those not party to the consensus, then there are two further points to make: first, that, in operation within a non-authoritarian, critical society in which discussion was both free and effective, some vital needs principle (cp. §21) might well *restore* freedom or choice or independence to classes whose freedom was in practice restricted and narrow, or had been diminished; and second, that, in my treatment at least, freedom, choice, and autonomy are themselves vital human needs, and must merit precisely the kind of protection that is accorded *qua* needs to other real needs.

35 This is not to say that, by simply knowing that the relevant feelings and sentiments were drawn from this store, one could determine the content or character of the claim for equal treatment. What matters for the argument is only that there should be some distinctive difference or other in the feelings characteristically involved in the making or the recognition of the two kinds of claim.

36 Cp. Del Vecchio's treatment of *alteritas* in *Justice*, Chapter VII. And compare H. L. A. Hart, *Concept of Law*, p. 155.

37 Strictly we need to add after '*seen*' some such words as these: *both*

within S and within any recognizable transformation of S that continues to define a point of view can be 'common to each man with others' as he departs from his 'private and particular situation'. (Cp. Hume, *Inquiry Concerning the Principles of Morals*, IX part 1, 222.)

Note that it suffices for this construction if, where there are interestingly different moral sensibilities to be discovered within a historically given culture, there is some minimal shared component or nucleus of differing sensibilities. Where not even a nucleus is available, political argument and even politics itself must be on the point of breaking down.

For the claim (neither required by nor inconsistent with anything that is urged here) that what is timelessly essential to the core of morality as such can be reached by factoring *ethos* out from morality itself, within what he sees as only superficially different moralities, see Aurel Kolnai, 'Moral consensus', *Proceedings of the Aristotelian Society*, 1969–70.

38 In connection with this whole approach, compare e.g. J. L. Mackie, 'Rights, utility and universalization', op. cit., J. L. Mackie, *Ethics*, Harmondsworth, Penguin, 1977, Bernard Williams, *Moral Luck*, Cambridge, Cambridge University Press, 1981, p. x and passim, e.g. 'Internal and external reasons', pp. 101–13. In so far as my treatment differs from Mackie's and Williams's, it is in respect of the crucial importance I should attach in these matters of motivation to judgments of value being what they seem to be, viz. statements about features of reality, albeit essentially anthropocentrically categorized, that are discovered to us by our interest in them. Cp. my 'Truth, invention and the meaning of life', *Proceedings of the British Academy*, 1977.

For certain aspects of social morality equally neglected by Williams, Mackie and myself, see A. M. Honoré, 'Groups, law and Obedience', in *Oxford Essays in Jurisprudence* II, 1973.

39 Cp. J. L. Mackie, 'Can there be a right-based moral theory?', op. cit.

> A central embarrassment for the best known goal-based theories, the various forms of utilitarianism, is that the well being of one individual should be sacrificed without limits, for the well being of others (352) .... Why should it not be a *fundamental* moral principle that the well being of one person cannot be simply replaced by that of another? There is no proof of purely aggregative consequentialism at any level. (354)

For a lawyer's formulation of what is almost the same point see Arnold Goodman, *Not for the Record*, London, André Deutsch, 1972, pp. 18–19:

> The popular proposition that we must sink our selfish self-interest in the public good ... requires the closest scrutiny and the strongest scepticism. For it is the proposition which can

justify any hardship or injustice to a private person, and the one most prone to ignore the arithmetical truism that the community is the sum of its individuals. That injury to an individual — inequitable or unrequited — is in the absence of strong contrary proof, an injustice to the community in whose name it is so lightly committed. But [this proposition] is invoked with monotonous ruthlessness by governmental systems.

40　States go to war, and in fighting them they have exacted the sacrifice of millions of lives. But states that deserve the loyalty of their subjects do not go to war 'to maximize the public good' — rather to avoid invasion or national humiliation or subjugation or to defend vital interests that subjects can identify with.

41　*A posteriority* is again what we ought to predict if we will allow that the relation between social morality and its embodying social institutions needs to be a reciprocal one. It needs to be reciprocal if the morality is to take up from *mores* and institutions the distinctive colouration and distinctive emphases that will shape and colour the communal ends and socially conditioned individual ends that the morality recognizes as intelligible ends of human endeavour and concern. (In fact, both logically and historically speaking, social morality and social institutions must come into being simultaneously.) To reject *a posteriority* here is to reject the idea that values and shared concerns need to have a historical aspect. But without a historical aspect most values and concerns that go beyond simple human survival are simply arbitrary and, in every relevant sense of this phrase, rationally unintelligible.

42　If we suppose that it is even a bit like something to opt into, then we immediately find ourselves forced to think that it ought to be possible to reconstruct the reasons (it is now as if) we once had for the choice that (it is now as if) we once made when we opted into it. Surely, though, if such reasons had to be found, none could possibly be provided. How could any candidate to be such a reason both show, as it would need to show, that this was the morality we would have been most *prudent* or *rational* to adhere to, and also respect the status as a morality of what it is as if we could have chosen? Any consideration at all that promised to be suitable to count as a reason of the required sort would either employ a notion of rationality and prudence that begged the question (this I insist is the innocent, fruitful way with the matter in all other connections), or depend on a conception of rationality that would show us as choosing virtue or justice not for what it is in itself but in the expectation of a return of some sort.

　　On all these matters, see further Schopenhauer, *On the Foundation of Morality*; and, for a well-known and needless exaggeration, going way beyond the key point, H. A. Prichard, 'Does moral philosophy rest on a mistake?', *Mind*, 1912.

43 Historically some have recognized rather fewer. But the reader will have guessed that I shall claim this does not matter. What people will put up with is an *a posteriori* question, and dependent on factors of human psychology and awareness that change gradually but constantly through time. These changes are for the most part irreversible. As in all matters of awareness, a kind of ratchet mechanism operates.

What people will put up with is also to some degree a moral question. For what people will put up with depends on what they think is fair to them. And what they think fair must depend however indirectly or minimally on what *is* fair. If our explanations in these sections were intended as reductive or eliminative, this would be fatal to them. But our aim here is only to exhibit the *interconnections* of the concepts *claim-right, need, participants' consensus, social justice....*

44 On claim rights, cp. note 15 above; and see also Alan Ryan 'Overriding interests', *Times Literary Supplement*, 22 April 1983, p. 411.

45 Cp. also Charles Fried, *Right and Wrong* (Cambridge, Mass., Harvard University Press, 1978), p. 122.

> The major objection to a theory of rights based on needs [is that] though needs and their satisfaction have an objective quality, the fact is that any commitment, via the recognition of positive rights, to meet need also makes us hostages to vastly varied and voracious needs.... How to contain this voraciousness? If needs create rights to their satisfaction, how are we to prevent them from claiming so much that there is no energy left to pursue other goals?

46 Cp. J. L. Mackie, *Ethics*, op. cit., pp. 175–6; and 'Rights, utility and universalization', op. cit. And for a relatively ancient statement of the relevant (still neglected) platitude, see J. von Neumann, *Collected Works VI*. 'Literally and figuratively we are running out of room. At long last, we begin to feel the effects of the finite actual size of the earth in a critical way.'

47 I am indebted to this formulation to Amartya Sen, *Poverty and Famines* (Oxford, Oxford University Press, 1982) and, later, to his persuasive contention that what famine dramatizes is not so much the power of natural disaster as the failure or weakness of systems of entitlement relations.

48 I say 'otherwise'. But of course they may do this anyway. And they may do it in a way that goes well beyond taking by force what they need. What is being urged here without prejudice to any of those questions is simply the weakest claim: that, if under these circumstances men combine to take what they need by force, then moral justification may be available for that, whatever condemnation may also be possible for whatever else they do.

49 For an illuminating account, see for instance J. N. Tarn, *Five Per Cent Philanthropy* (Cambridge, Cambridge University Press, 1973).

50 A citizen is taxed, surely, on what he has earned and made his own. He ought not to be deemed not even to have earned the portion he gives up. He cannot give back to society what is never his.

51 Consider for instance subsidized, publicly owned housing. Is this a better solution to the problem than subsidizing rents of those of low income in a flourishing, properly regulated private sector? For a powerful but wholly neglected argument that public or special housing was not the best or the only solution to the problem, see Jane Jacobs *Death and Life of the Great American City* (London, Jonathan Cape, 1962), pp. 323-7. And why in any case (we must always ask) are the incomes of some hard-working industrious persons doing essential work too low for them to be able to afford decent housing?

52 Cp. *mutatis mutandis* Sen's remark at op. cit., pp. 156-7 ('As a category for causal analysis the poor isn't a very helpful one').

53 Soberer theorists like E. Mishan have always been unequivocally clear that projects admitted on cost benefit analysis are 'consistent with transparent inequity', and that 'for a project to be socially acceptable it is not enough to show that the outcome of a cost-benefit analysis is acceptable . . . it must also be shown that no gross inequities are committed'.

Mackie had an idea which might seem to help here, in 'Can there be a right-based moral theory', op. cit.

> [We shall] not allow the vital interests of anyone to be sacrificed for the advantage of others, to be outweighed by an aggregate of less vital interests. Rather we might think in terms of a model in which each person is represented by a point-centre of force, and the forces (representing *prima facie* rights) obey an inverse square law, so that a right decreases in weight with the remoteness of the matter on which it bears from the person whose right it is. There will be some matters so close to each person that with respect to them his rights will nearly always outweigh any aggregate of other rights.

The mathematical model is suggestive, and it will be plain that I am indebted to it (though doubtful that it will work). But I fear it will provoke ingenious, disobliging persons to miss the whole point of holding some position such as Mackie's; and, if the model were transferred to my proposal (which complicates the picture by bringing in needs-based counter-claims as vital interests that do not necessarily correspond to rights), it would no doubt provoke the same persons to misunderstand the basis and intention of the Principle of Limitation. In my treatment, that principle is not, of course, part of an outline decision procedure but one of the several principles comprised in justice, with the special property of essentially contestably demarcating the area in which certain others can operate.

54 Yet nothing less than the possibility of refusing what was offered would have been sufficient in the case of many of the injustices that have actually been committed in this area.

It is instructive in this connection and in all sorts of connected ways to read command paper *Cmnd.* 5124 (October 1972), *Development and Compensation* — especially if one is moved beyond anything that is actively encouraged by the cool correct language of the document itself to try to remember or imagine the countless actions that eventually gave rise to the need for this, by the going standards, extraordinarily frank official confession of past injustice.

55 It may be well to give an example where common law rights give out before the concerns of justice can. When public works lay a whole neighbourhood waste and some or all of its inhabitants are all to be resettled, the only legal claim-right anyone has normally had to compensation has derived from the legal ownership of land or a house. But there are always many who own neither. It is true that in more recent times those who actually live there at a specified date have been given some legal right to be resettled by the local authority, and may even qualify under recent provisions for some grant for 'disturbance' (a sum that it was proposed in 1972, on the basis of some vague sense of its inadequacy, simply to double). These are improvements in justice, even though the local authority is not necessarily the landlord of their choice, nor will they necessarily be rehoused at the rent they paid previously. It is possible to imagine these and other deficiencies being remedied. It is even possible, I suppose, to imagine a code of compensation that made good in real terms what it actually took away from owners and non-owners who could be *identified*. Note however that even this would by no means exhaust those whose vital interests were actually affected, e.g. by the contribution that such public projects may make to shortage (pushing up rents and house-prices), to blight, and to the dereliction of local employment. An approach that will raise *this* question goes well beyond the concern with common law rights and codes of compensation.

56 A compromise might make provision for appeal against such procedures as Compulsory Purchase Order or Power of Eminent Domain, and might permit those directly affected to secure a formal hearing for themselves at which it was relevant and appropriate to refer to the Limitation Principle. Indeed I believe that the strong official predisposition in favour of the language of need, pointed out in §2, precisely rests on some inchoate, partial understanding of this appropriateness.

57 It is worth remembering here that if we allow ourselves to be forced by some imaginable but appalling circumstance to override the claim of justice, it will be better to say 'We had to be unjust'

than to say 'What we did was, in the circumstances, just' (or 'just in the circumstances'). (For a good statement of the impact of emergency upon criteria of vital need, see Finnis, *Natural Law and Natural Rights*, op. cit., p. 174.)

58 Nobody who does not already have some knowledge of the desolate scenes touched upon in *Cmnd*. 5124, op. cit., will want to take this on my say so. But to those who do I will remark how rare it is for a public agency bent on a large project with many direct and indirect consequences to pause to consider all the legal and moral obstacles that a private promoter would have had to face if he had tried to realize the same project as a commercial venture. Many public works no doubt pass this test. Yet it may be surmised that, if either this constraint or the Limitation Principle had operated in Britain or North America, then the face of the earth would now present a very different aspect from that which it has been given by some of the public works programmes of the last forty or fifty years.

59 It is not very useful to predict how people would behave, and what preferences they would thereby reveal, in a future state of affairs that inherits most of the unsatisfactory features they seek to escape from in the present. ('We always plan too much and think too little', as Schumpeter says, in another connection.) But of course to escape from *that* dead end, we must understand better on the levels of reason and constituent beliefs, desires, needs, vital interest. . . *what* people avoid or seek in the present, and what alterable features of the present *condition* these beliefs, desires, needs, vital interests . . . (and how they condition them). (See my *Sameness and Substance*, (Oxford, Blackwell, 1980) p. 180 ff.; also 'Deliberation and practical reason', in J. Raz, *Practical Reasoning*, Oxford, Oxford University Press, 1981.) And this may interest us afresh in considerations of justice that antedate phase three.

60 If subscribing to this principle is egalitarianism, and taking counter-claims seriously is socialism, then the writer must be an egalitarian socialist, however ill at ease with other paid-up members of this persuasion. But certainly the position here falls far short of other formulations. Consider for instance Richard Norman's 'Comprehensive egalitarian principle' in *Contemporary Political Philosophy: Radical Studies*, Cambridge, Cambridge University Press, 1982, ed. K. Graham, p. 102: 'satisfaction of the basic needs of all, plus equality of monetary incomes over and above that (though this might need further qualifying if it were desired to increase some incomes to compensate for particularly dangerous or unpleasant work)'.

61 Recall here Beveridge's five giants on the road of reconstruction: 'Want, Ignorance, Squalor, Idleness and Disease'.

62 Cp. *Sameness and Substance*, op. cit., chapter 6, with addenda for pp. 174–84, *Longer Note*, 6.36 §3; Peter Winch, *Presidential*

Address, Proceedings of the Aristotelian Society, 1980–81, stressing correctly the pre-rational character of this recognition.

63 Cp. J. R. Lucas, 'The lesbian rule', *Philosophy*, 154, David Wiggins, chapters 13 and 14 in *Essays on Aristotle's Ethics*, ed. A. O. Rorty, Los Angeles, University of California Press, 1980.

64 Aurel Kolnai, 'The moral theme in political division', *Philosophy*, 1960. For other references to Kolnai's thinking on this and related matters, see Bernard Williams's and David Wiggins's introduction to his *Ethics, Value and Reality*, London, Athlone, 1973.

IX
ETHICS AND THE FABRIC OF THE WORLD

Bernard Williams

John Mackie held[1] that values, in particular ethical values, were not objective, a denial which he took to mean that they were not 'part of the fabric of the world' (p. 15). He stressed that this was to be taken as an ontological thesis, as opposed to a 'linguistic or conceptual' thesis, and to arrive at it was, for him, a matter of 'factual rather than conceptual analysis' (p. 19). In this respect, he found a parallel between value properties and secondary qualities, as he did more generally, being prepared to say of both that they were 'projected' on to the world. The idea of 'factual analysis', and the exact contrast that he intended with conceptual analysis, are not entirely clear, and I suspect that he put it in this way because he closely associated the conceptual and the linguistic, and he wanted to stress – rightly – that the truth of what he claimed was not going to be determined by an enquiry into the use of ethical words. In any sense broader than that, it seems reasonable to hold, as McGinn[2] has argued, that the question of the subjectivity of secondary qualities is a conceptual question; and if that is, so will the same question with respect to ethical qualities (as I shall, for the moment, vaguely call them.)

Mackie's own arguments for his conclusion make it unclear how this could be a factual issue. One, the so-called 'argument from queerness', says in effect that the idea of ontologically objective values explains nothing and offends against parsimony: and the grounds of this criticism seem to be entirely *a priori*. The other, the 'argument from relativity', cites facts about the variation of ethical belief between cultures, and the plausible explanations of that variation that might be given by the social sciences. The facts about cultural variation can be accepted to be

203

factual facts, even though, as is well known, their interpretation leaves a lot of room for disagreement. But that does not make the conclusion which Mackie draws from them into a factual rather than (in the broader sense) a conceptual conclusion. Even if mankind displayed more unanimity in its ethical reactions than it does – or unanimity, one might say, at a more specific level – that would not seem to make the reactions more objective, on Mackie's view, but simply more like perceptions of secondary qualities. We shall see later that cultural variation does play a part in the argument, but it is at a different level.

Mackie was prepared to call his position 'moral scepticism', though he made it clear that this was not meant to imply any first-order indifferentism, or the rejection of moral considerations as bearing on practical reason. He described his account as an 'error theory' of moral judgments. (The error in question seems, very roughly, to be that of taking moral values to be objective.) Mackie himself said that the name 'moral scepticism' was appropriate (p. 35) just because it was an error theory: presumably because the theory exposes as false something that common-sense is disposed to believe. At the same time, however, he did not suppose that when this error was exposed, everyday moral convictions would properly be weakened or opened to doubt. I shall come back to the question of how these claims hang together. However, it is worth asking at this point why one should be more disposed, on the strength of the first of these claims (the error theory), to apply the name 'moral scepticism' to Mackie's view, than one is to withhold that name in virtue of the second claim – that everyday conviction is properly unshaken. That is not an obvious preference, and the fact that Mackie did choose to use 'moral scepticism' in this way reveals some assumptions. I take them to be, first, that scepticism is essentially concerned with knowledge or the lack of it, and, second, that in view of the error theory, there is no moral knowledge.

Particularly granted Mackie's own views, I do not think that this is the most helpful way to use this phrase. Scepticism is basically concerned with doubt, and not necessarily with (the denial of) knowledge. Where it is knowledge that is appropriately pursued in order to put an end to doubt, a denial that knowledge is possible will lead to a sceptical position; but in areas where, on a true view, there is no question of knowledge, and to seek it is inappropriate, this is not so. Scepticism will rather be whatever attacks conviction in those areas. On Mackie's view, which (as I take it) sees the moral as no candidate for knowledge at all, moral scepticism should rather be a position that upsets moral conviction, for instance by claiming that moral considerations have no place in practical reasoning. Of course, if the two claims, as I have called them, cannot after all be kept apart, there might be a good reason for thinking that the error theory was indeed a form of moral scepticism.

Mackie applied the error theory in ethics very widely. It is not simply a matter of those ethical perceptions that are nearest to certain aesthetic reactions, such as that certain people or actions are horrible. Many might agree that the perception of those characteristics can reasonably be assimilated in some degree to the perception of secondary qualities. Nor is it simply a matter of goodness. He says (p. 15) that in claiming moral values not to be objective, he intends to include, besides moral goodness,

> other things that could be more loosely called moral values or dis-
> values − rightness and wrongness, duty, obligation . . . and so on.

In the same spirit, he connects (p. 29) the denial of objective values with the rejection of a categorical imperative:

> So far as ethics is concerned, my thesis that there are no objective
> values is specifically the denial that any such categorically impera-
> tive element is objectively valid. The objective values which I am
> denying would be action-directing absolutely, not contingently . . .
> upon the agent's desires and inclinations.

This claim raises very sharply the question of what the objectivity is that Mackie is denying. It is not immediately clear what it could mean to say that a requirement or demand was 'part of the fabric of the world'. It might possibly mean that some agency which made the demand or imposed the requirement was part of the fabric, but, even if it were, that fact in itself would not be enough to make its demand categorical in the relevant sense. In purely logical or syntactic terms, of course, the demands of such an agent might be categorical, but so might the demands of any agent whatsoever. The person who peremptorily says 'get out of the way' speaks categorically. What he is telling you to do is to get out of the way, not to get out of the way unless you don't mind getting hurt: if you don't mind getting hurt, and stay in his way, you still prevent the state of affairs that he means to bring about. In this, his imperative is (logically) categorical, while the imperatives in the washing machine instructions (or most of them) are logically hypo-thetical, even though their antecedent, which is very obvious, is usually suppressed. But this, the question whether an imperative is *intended* categorically, is not the point. The question is rather about the status of some logically categorical imperative, whether an agent in some sense goes wrong who does not recognise it as a demand on him. Whatever that may turn out to mean, it cannot be the same as the question whether there is an agent 'in the fabric of the world' who makes that demand. If there is an exceptional agent in, or perhaps outside, the world whose demands do have that character, that will be because of his nature, not simply because he is 'out there'.

Consider another picture of what it would be for a demand to be 'objectively valid'. It is Kant's own picture.[3] According to this, a demand will be inescapable in the required sense if it is one that a rational agent must accept if he is to be a rational agent. It is, to use one of Kant's favourite metaphors, *self-addressed* by any rational agent. Kant was wrong, in my view, in supposing that the fundamental demands of morality were objective in this sense, but that is not the immediate point, which is that the conception deploys an intelligible and adequate sense of objectivity. It seems to have little to do with those demands being part of the fabric of the world; or, at any rate, they will be no more or less so than the demands of logic — which was, of course, part of Kant's point.

Kant's theory offers an *objective grounding* of morality which is not (as one might say) realist. Moral claims are objectively correct or incorrect, but when one gives a general explanation of what makes them so, that explanation does not run through the relation between those statements and the world, but rather through the relation between *accepting* those statements, and practical reason. There are other candidates for a theory that is objective but not realist, such as a theory which suggests that one must have the desires appropriate to the ethical life if one is going to be in good shape as a human being, where the idea of 'being in good shape' is one that can be explained at least partly (it need not be wholly) prior to the ethical life. This again would be objectivity, and there would be ethical correctness, but it would be basically a correctness of desire, and arriving at it would be a feat of practical reasoning; or if of theoretical reasoning, then, to a significant degree, of a non-ethical kind (establishing, for instance, the appropriate psychological truths).

Even if no theory of these kinds is sound, the possibility of them is important for the present discussion. This is not because it shows Mackie to have been looking for objectivity in the wrong place. The significant point is that under these possibilities we are *still* presented with the phenomenon that attracted Mackie's diagnosis, and they help one to understand what needs diagnosing. Suppose that the ethical life could be objectively grounded in one of these ways. One could come to know that it was so grounded, by developing or learning philosophical arguments which showed that ethical life satisfied the appropriate condition, of being related in the right way to practical reason or to well-being. But ethical life itself would continue to involve various experiences and judgments of the kind that present themselves as 'objective' — and what they present is not the objectivity which, on these theories, they would genuinely possess. They are not experienced as satisfying any such condition. This is notably clear in the Kantian case, and Kant saw the point himself. In acknowledging the categorical demand of obligation or recognising a moral requirement (the kind of thing expressed in saying, for moral reasons, 'I must'), one does not experience it as an application of the demands of practical reason, but as something more immediate than that, something presented to one by the facts. That is one reason why Kant found an empirical psychological surrogate of one's rational relations to morality, in the emotional phenomenon of the sense of reverence for the Law. That feeling does, on Kant's theory, represent objectivity. But it also misrepresents it, by making it seem something different from what it is.

It is reasonable to think that no experience could adequately represent an objectivity that lay in the Kantian kind of argument. That argument is to the effect that the requirements of practical reason will be met only by leading a life in which moral considerations play a constitutive, in particular a motivational, role. Moreover, that life is understood to be one in which moral considerations can, in contrast to other motivations, present themselves as objective demands. It follows that what it is for a consideration to present itself as an objective demand could never consist merely in its presenting itself as so related to that very argument. So, in the Kantian version at least, there is no alternative to the experience being a misrepresentation of genuine objectivity. The really important question that is raised here is how far such an experience of being confronted by an objective demand, has to be the central experience of the ethical life — indeed, how far it has to be part of it at all.

There would be a certain misrepresentation, then, in that experience of objectivity even if there were genuine objectivity in the form of an objective grounding. What if there were acknowledged to be no such grounding? This covers two distinct possibilities. One is that this kind

The grounds of gen obj. is not something you can experience

of grounding is an intelligible form of objectivity, but there is no convincing argument of this kind. (This is my own view.) This possibility raises much the same range of questions about the experience of objectivity as would be raised if the grounding argument were valid. If that argument is not valid, then we are to that extent the more deceived if we think that there is objectivity, but we are not any the more deceived *by the experience*; and whether the argument is valid or not, the same questions will arise about the necessity of that kind of experience to the ethical life.

The second possibility is to be found in the outlook of someone who agrees that there is no objective grounding, but nevertheless thinks that there is objectivity. Such a person (Prichard was one) will believe that it is mistaken to look for any argument of these kinds to yield objectivity; objectivity is, rather, something to be grasped through these experiences themselves. He thinks that objectivism gets its content just from the sense which these experiences embody, of confrontation with something independent. He construes objectivism as a kind of realism. This possibility is simply misconceived, and in relation to this idea, Mackie was right to detect error, since it takes the fact that an experience is demanding as sufficient evidence, indeed the only evidence, that it is the experience of a demand. It takes resonance to be reference, and that is certainly a mistake. The mistake, however, is not inherent simply in having that experience. Ot is not even inherent in having that experience and connecting it with objectivity. It lies in a theory which takes that experience to reveal all that one knows or needs to know about objectivity.

We can now go back to other kinds of what I earlier called 'ethical qualities', those that lie in the area of the good, the admirable and so forth, and also the more affective characteristics — the outrageous, the contemptible and the rest. In these last cases, at least, it is obvious to reflection that there is a relativity involved, and it is probable that there is some process of projection. It is tempting to see in this, as Mackie saw, some analogy to secondary qualities. However, there is a significant difference between the two cases; it lies in the conception that it is appropriate to have of 'the world' of which these various qualities are said not to be part. The fabric of the world from which the secondary qualities are absent (in their presented form) is the world of primary qualities, and (to take for granted the answers to several large and contentious questions) the claim that the secondary qualities, as presented, are not part of that world comes to much the same as the claim that they do not figure in an 'absolute conception' of the world on which scientific investigators, abstracting as much as possible from their various perceptual peculiarities, might converge.[4] There is nothing unnerving or subversive in the idea that ethical qualities are not part of the fabric of the world in this sense. They do not need to do better than secondary qualities.[5]

The subjective conception of secondary qualities rests on the notion that in principle the perception of (say) colours can be explained in terms of perceptual psychology, on the one hand, and the world as characterised in terms of primary qualities, on the other.[6] In the case of ethical qualities, however, if subjectivism holds that they are added to or projected on to the world, 'the world' has to be already construed in a psychologically and socially richer sense than 'the world' on to which secondary qualities are projected. Any conceivable explanations of variations in ethical reactions will have to include psychological and social elements in the cause. This would be so even if human beings as such converged in ethical reaction more than they do. However, the explanation of these variations can in fact be plausibly traced in many cases to cultural factors, and this is where we rejoin the 'argument from relativity' which earlier seemed not very relevant. It is not relevant, if (as I think Mackie had in mind) 'the world' is to be regarded in the same way for the two cases of secondary qualities and of ethics. But if this is not to be so, cultural variation and its explanations are relevant, because they help to make clear what kinds of convergence might appropriately be looked for in ethical thought, and how we might explain them.

The importance of those explanations comes out in the ways in which we might assess future processes of convergence in ethical thought. The mere fact that convergence occurred would not in itself be evidence of any kind of objectivity. What would matter would be the explanation of the convergence. Human beings might come to agree more on these matters than they do now just because of assimilation and a higher degree of interdependence, and that would tell us nothing about the status of ethical belief. It would be different if some argument for an objective grounding appeared to have gained increasing rational assent. Of course, what we think about the chances of finding an objective grounding will themselves affect and be affected by the ways in which we understand existing ethical variation: the relations, as one would expect, run in both directions.

None of these understandings, however, could make more plausible what I earlier called the *realist* version of objectivism. So, to summarise, the position seems to be the following. Realist objectivism, in that sense, is not an option and Mackie was right in rejecting it, though he was wrong in thinking that cultural variation was relevant to it. Cultural variation is relevant, but not at this point. It is so in virtue of the explanations that it requires us to give of ethical reactions, explanations which both affect our conception of 'the world' that elicits those reactions, and also are related to the prospects for objectivism in a different sense, that of an objective grounding of ethical beliefs and attitudes. The question of whether there could be such a grounding is not answered by Mackie's kind of critique, in terms of the fabric of the world; but that critique does nevertheless attack a feature of ethical experience, which, even if there were an objective grounding, would tend to misrepresent it − most starkly, as we have seen, in the Kantian case.

In referring here to the realist version of objectivism, I meant what I earlier called 'realism', the position which tries to conjure objectivity straight out of ethical experience. There are other positions that have been called 'realist', which involve the quite different idea that it is impossible to distinguish between 'the world' and what is supposedly projected on to it. They may deny this even for the supposedly absolute conception of the world in terms of primary qualities, or, alternatively, they may allow that conception, rightly point out that the fact that ethical qualities are not to be found in that is no great news, and then go on to say that when one tries to find a richer conception of 'the world' on to which values still need to be projected, one cannot find it. The first of these positions is, I think, that of John McDowell, while the second is perhaps taken by Wiggins. They raise wide issues that I cannot hope to pursue here.[7] In very bald summary, it seems to me that the approach makes a good point about certain substantive value-concepts, in rejecting a prescriptivist or similar approach to them: that is to say, it discourages the idea that for each such concept, one could produce a value-free description of the world that corresponds to it. The point helps to put some basic questions of objectivity (for instance, the possibility of ethical knowledge) into a more helpful perspective, but as to answering those questions, I think that it only puts off the evil day, because it fails to consider, first, the fact that some substantive ethical concepts may be replaced by others, and what needs to be understood is the process by which that happens; and, second, that any given substantive ethical concept may be criticised without using another such concept, through the use of very general notions, such as 'good' or 'ought', with regard to which this 'realist' line does not give much help.

I come back now to what I called earlier the 'two claims', that our ethical experiences involve an error, and that ethical conviction need not be upset by recognising that fact. It will be helpful to take the second claim first. In the case of secondary qualities, the discovery that they are subjective has very little, if any, effect on everyday practice, and it is obvious why that should be so. The psychological capacities that underly our perceiving the world in terms of certain secondary qualities have evolved so that the physical world can present itself to us in reliable and useful ways (it is an interesting question, discussed by McGinn, whether Kant was right in thinking that any world we could experience would have to present itself in terms of some secondary qualities). Coming to know that these secondary qualities constitute our form of perceptual engagement with the world, and how this mode of presentation works, will not unsettle the system. Indeed, in this case unreflective practice is so harmoniously related to theoretical understanding, that a good case can be made for rejecting Mackie's view that there is an *error* involved at all in everyday belief, though no doubt there is in naive philosophical theory about it.[8]

If we ask similar questions about ethical qualities and our experience of them, it seems that it is the second claim that is harder to accept. If the general direction of Mackie's critique is right, then ethical qualities are felt to be in some sense independent of us and our motivations, whereas in truth they are dependent on us and our motivations. Moreover, and more damagingly, this can be plausibly explained by supposing that ethical constraints and objectives have to be internalised in such a way that they can serve to control and redirect potentially destructive and unco-operative desires, and that they can do this, or do it most effectively, only if they do not present themselves as one motivation or desire among others, nor as offering one option among others. They thus present themselves as something given to the agent, but at the same time something from which he cannot feel himself entirely detached, as he could from some external, questionable, authority.

Similar experiences are involved when one's values come into conflict with other people's values. While one is involved in expressing one's own as against some other values, one cannot at the same time simply see those others as alternative ways of ordering society or of producing some very general kind of human good. One cannot, equally, simply think that, while as a matter of fact one sees the world from the perspective of one set of values, it might be more convenient if one could bring it about that one saw it from another; just as one cannot think it an acceptable way of dealing with some morally disagreeable phenomenon that one should stop being affected by it. It is for this kind of reason, indeed, that McGinn says that our moral consciousness is *not* like our experience of secondary qualities, since we readily accept that a way of changing the colours of the world could be to make a general enough psychological alteration. He may underestimate in this the momentum of our current conceptions of what colour things are: but, in any case, the consideration will not show that moral distinctions are not relative to our psychological and social constitution. It will only show how deeply entrenched they are.

If all this is so, then it is not easy to combine the two claims, and the consciousness of what the system is will not happily co-exist with the system's working. In this respect, it is not like the example of secondary qualities. The fundamental difficulty is to combine the efficacy of a social system with consciousness of what it involves. Moreover, if one believes, as I think John Mackie did, that it is a desirable feature of a society that its practices could in principle become as far as possible transparent to it (though not all of them could do so at once), then one must ask whether, on anything like Mackie's view of it, ethical experience could itself pass that test.

Despite his second claim, Mackie did not think that things would go on exactly the same if subjectivism in his sense became known. He recognised that if subjectivism is true, then acquiring values is not the process it is supposed to be under objectivism (p. 22), and it must surely follow that if subjectivism were not just true but known to be true, those processes would be consciously conducted in some different way. Sometimes (e.g. p. 106) Mackie was disposed to conclude that if his views were right, 'morality is not to be discovered but made: we have to decide what moral views to adopt. . . .' But, as so often when a conclusion of that kind is drawn from an ethical theory, it is unclear who 'we' are, and to what extent the process of decision is supposed to be individual or social or, indeed, concrete at all. It certainly cannot follow from Mackie's view that when we have come to realise what moral experience really is, we shall start to acquire our moral attitudes by self-consciously deciding on them, either individually or collectively. It is not clear that there could be such a process, and if there were, there is no reason at all to think, in the light of Mackie's theory itself, that it would be effective.

Mackie's theory, and any like it, leaves a real problem of what should happen when we know it to be true. I cannot try to take that problem further here. I shall offer just one speculation, that the first victim of this knowledge is likely to be the Kantian sense of presented duty. We have seen that it is the starkest example of objectification, and since there is virtually nothing to it except the sense of being given, it stands to suffer most if that sense is questioned. There are other ethical desires and perceptions which are better adapted to being seen for what they are. It is an important task for moral philosophy to consider what they may be, and into what coherent pictures of ethical life, philosophical, psychological and social, they will fit.

NOTES

1 *Ethics: Inventing Right and Wrong* (Harmondsworth, 1977); and first in 'A Refutation of Morals', *Australasian Journal of Psychology and Philosophy* 24 (1946). The page references that I give in parentheses are to *Ethics*. − I regret that John Mackie and I never had an opportunity to discuss the kind of question raised here, though we did talk about other issues in ethics, particularly utilitarianism. He would have certainly brought to the discussion of our disagreements the clarity, honesty and shrewd perception that he so notably showed on all occasions, and he would also have recognised that on these questions, the disagreements are rooted in a deeper agreement.

2 *The Subjective View* (Oxford, 1983), to which I am indebted at several points.

3 Some of the immense confusion that surrounds this subject comes from the fact that Kant, who started it off, expressed himself in terms of a logical distinction between categorical and hypothetical. Readers of the *First Critique* should not be surprised to find him using what seems to be logical distinction to make a different level of point.

4 See my *Descartes: The Project of Pure Enquiry* (Harmondsworth, 1978), esp. chs 1, 8 and 10; McGinn, op. cit., who well brings out how the absolute conception is not a perceptual one. For various formulations of the idea and assessments of their prospects, see N. Jardine, 'The possibility of absolutism', in D. H. Mellor (ed.), *Science, Belief and Behaviour: Essays in honour of R. B. Braithwaite* (Cambridge, 1980), pp. 23–42.

5 The point is well brought out in David Wiggins, 'Truth, invention, and the meaning of life', *British Academy Lecture*, 1976. McGinn

Bernard Williams

(p. 145 seq.) does think that ethical qualities, on our actual understanding of them, need to do better than secondary qualities: I shall
come back to this point later.

6   This is not to deny that variations in perceived colour may have
psychological causes, as they do by juxtaposition and in many other
cases. This is one area in which we invoke the difference between
real and apparent colours: it is generally thought that a difference in
the observer's expectations, for instance, cannot affect the colour a
thing is. It is not the same with smells; and certainly not with affective qualities. Whether a substance is perceived as food can affect
whether it *is* disgusting: the contrast with something's seeming
disgusting is drawn at a different level.

7   I discuss them in *Ethics and the Limits of Philosophy* (London,
Fontana, 1985), ch. 8.

8   McGinn, ch. 7. The issue involves the question of how the relativity
of secondary quality predicates shows up in their semantics. It is
not wholly clear what McGinn's view is on this: cf. pp. 119-20
with pp. 9-10. See also Wiggins, op. cit., and Williams, *Descartes*,
pp. 242-4.

A MEMORIAL ADDRESS
BY SIMON BLACKBURN

It is a great honour to speak today of John Mackie the philosopher.

The outlines of John Mackie's career will be well known to many of you. Born in 1917, he read Classics at the University of Sydney, where his teachers included the philosopher John Anderson, whom Mackie later described as the most important philosopher to have worked in Australia. Another teacher was Enoch Powell, who encouraged John to come to England after a characteristic episode: Powell had made a remark in class pointing out how difficult cultures relying on water-clocks must find it to recover a uniform measure of time from the variable levels and flows of water; John returned the next day with several solutions to the problem. John was awarded a Wentworth travelling scholarship, and entered Oriel in 1938, getting his First in Literae Humaniores in 1940. He remained proud of his classical education, whose distinctions included the Cromer Greek Essay Prize, which he gained in 1941, for an essay on Heraclitus.

After the war he held a lectureship in the department of Moral and Political Philosophy at Sydney, and then, famously, three successive Chairs, in Otago, Sydney, and at York, before his return to Oxford in 1967. It was in 1973 that he published his first book, *Truth Probability and Paradox*. This broke a dam. Including his last book, *The Miracle of Theism*, he wrote five more books in the following eight years. But he had published something over forty articles as well, twenty-four of which are to appear in two collections, under the auspices of the Oxford University Press.

In his last book he quotes with approval Epicurus: 'let us show our feeling for our lost friends not by lamentation but by meditation.'

Meditating upon his work tells us a good deal about philosophy, and about what it is to do it well. His merits are obvious, and well known to all of you. His industry was legendary. The breadth of his philosophical interests and knowledge was unrivalled. His papers range from the theory of Forms to Newcomb's paradox, from problems of textual criticism to those of special relativity. By his later years he had perfected a scholarly, sober style of great lucidity. He had a thoroughly professional way of absorbing and displaying complex argument, which he seemed able to employ when dealing with any subject. Many of us might enjoy relaxing with a book on biology and natural selection; only John Mackie, being given *The Selfish Gene* as a Christmas present, would shortly publish a paper on it, and one which has been described, by the author of that book, as making a contribution to biology. Many of us might feel that we knew vaguely what to say about, for instance, standard lines in the philosophy of religion. Only John Mackie would test such a belief by following up all the epicycles in the literature, patiently displaying them, and patiently finding them wanting. This catholic *appetite* for argument, allied with the most formidable industry and lucidity, is rare, and awesome.

He had a great admiration for science, and had what may perhaps be called a scientific attitude to philosophy. He believed in the right conduct of argument, and held that with rationality and patience the rights and wrongs of arguments and of positions depending on them could be made plain. This even, almost dispassionate, rationality is a notable quality. There is a sense in which even philosophers hanker after something different, as if the reasonable man is not quite so rational, or only reasonably rational. Part of us looks for the guiding vision, the metaphor or image of ourselves and our relations to truth, knowledge, or value, which can inform the arguments we mount. We want to fly beyond anywhere that the wings of argument will take us. John Mackie was not a man for such voyages. He was an empiricist, but one who looked to Locke rather than Berkeley or Hume. He had too much sense to land on the wilder shores of empiricism. When lines of argument began to lead to extravagance and paradox he was, as he described his teacher John Anderson, 'essentially and characterically in opposition'. This is not to say that he refused to recognize the forces leading to departures from good sense. It is just that he would not be unbalanced by them. He cites with approval Locke's warning that we must not let the difficulties in one hypothesis make us 'throw ourselves violently' into another, with equal or greater difficulties of its own. Of course, such even-handed rationality requires confidence in some concepts and some procedures: those which define the sensible world, from which we are not to depart too far. John Mackie had such confidence: in simple truth, in reason, in a real world of causally acting particular things. He maintained this basic stance from his earliest writings onwards. His famous 1946 article, on the 'Refutation of morality', puts moral truth outside the scientific pale: he maintained the stance, and for the same reasons, in his well-known book on ethics, and right into his last works. He was essentially out of sympathy with modern tendencies to see the basic simple category of truth dissolve or waver, either to the detriment of science, or to the advance of such things as moral and religious practice. Myself I do not know whether realistic empiricism always wins in the way he thought – whether, for instance, the propensity to see things as coloured or external which he allowed to give truth is so readily distinguished from the temptation to see them in other ways , which he did not.

He was absolutely at his best where the rights and wrongs of argument can be analysed out and exposed. Paradoxes and puzzles intrigued him, and any aspect of our subject which yields to patient rationality. They are aspects which some of us tend to fear. It takes intellectual courage to write on the Paradox of the Liar, or on the logic of conditionals, because there is little room for vagueness or evasion. Just this, it seems to me, is the ground on which John Mackie was happiest. He had great admiration not only for Science, about which he would have liked to know more, but also for Law: above all a discipline in which sober practices of enquiry lead to the truth, and in which wayward opinions and vain imaginings have no respected place, in which verdicts cannot be left in obscurity or metaphor. The energy and appetite for argument of which I spoke made him utterly formidable on such ground. Wherever the arguments become tangled he is a pleasure to follow; patiently, persistently unpicking the threads until he found one which could recommend itself to an acute and unbiased understanding.

He was not a controversialist. He never wrote with the slightest sign of rancour. He did not make a habit of writing about particularly modish issues, nor did he ever seem to write with the motive merely of refuting an opponent. But he was superbly informed, and must have been well aware of recent currents that oppose his blend of empiricism and realism, and his reliance on traditional conceptions of analysis and meaning, rationality and truth. Perhaps the most tragic consequence to the profession of his early death is that he never developed a synthesis of his views, putting together everything he said on different occasions, testing and weighing in his own way the concepts he relied upon. As I have hinted, I think the synthesis would sometimes have been difficult. But such syntheses are apt to be ponderous affairs, and perhaps John Mackie was always happier exercising his concept rather than building shrines to them.

Ultimately, his way of philosophizing is exactly that which justifies our place in society and our role as educators. We need pride in the theory and practice of criticism, in the patient and unbiased exercise of rationality. It is perhaps harder to maintain such pride and harder still to transmit it than it was when John Mackie started his career. Too many hostile winds blow. Pupils and now writers like the short cut, the instant attitude, while both continental scepticism and a Wittgensteinian mistiness can undermine the hope of solid and enduring philosophical theory. We can persuade pupils into modish views easily enough. But it is harder to alter their standards of argument, and to leave them with a permanent sense of the difference between reason and unreason. I can think of no philosopher better able to do that, than John Mackie was, by inclination and by example. It is for that that we should honour him today.

A MEMORIAL ADDRESS
BY G. L. CAWKWELL

I am going to speak of John Mackie as a Fellow of University College.

He became a Fellow in 1967 and for thirteen years we occupied adjacent rooms. So I saw a lot of him in a casual way. Not for me, of course, those earnest philosophical conversations echoed along the central heating pipes between our rooms, Gareth Evans, perhaps, insistent, and the quiet tempered response, but certainly a good number of lighthearted exchanges, so that his death is for me the loss of a companion. But a curious sort of companion, for I never had a 'personal' conversation with him, and from what a good number have said to me since his death, I suspect that hardly anyone ever did. He was universally liked and respected, his name was becoming celebrated, but he remained very much a private person.

However, there are things that can and should be said. First of all, he worked astonishingly hard, at any rate astonishingly long hours. He was in his room at all times of the day, often on Sundays and, like as not, on public holidays. 'The world's work', in his phrase, had to go on. This is partly why he was able to accomplish so much. If he was asked for his views on a paper, or on, perhaps, a disputed thesis (and the range of his competence was so great that he was frequently appealed to), he did what was asked of him without delay. One of my colleagues tells me that discussion over lunch could result in several pages of typescript placed in his pigeon-hole by sundown. It was wholly in character that he worked all through his illness.

Secondly, he was uncommonly duteous, as pupils, and especially graduate pupils, testify. There always seemed to be someone outside his door waiting for someone else to come out. He was restricted as Reader to six tutorials a week. He was not one for breaking contracts, but neither was he one for preferring his own interests or for teaching with his eye on the clock. One could not believe that he suffered fools gladly. He was much too clever and intelligent for that. But he certainly never showed it, and he spared himself no pains in doing what he could for his weaker pupils. Most of us being told that we would have to have at least half a term off, and possibly more, would be content enough not to be able to give our scheduled lectures. Not so John Mackie. Carried off to hospital in the first week of last term, he resolved to begin his lectures in the fifth week and most reluctantly accepted that he had to abandon them. Having published his intention to lecture, he could not think of not fulfilling it if he possibly could. An unphilosophical man, whose principal evidence about other people's conduct was the behaviour of John Mackie, would never dream of explaining it in the terms of the theory of 'moral scepticism'.

No doubt such discrepancy is more apparent than real. John Mackie was not given to neglecting the evidence. Indeed he was supremely rational, and his judgment was never overborne by passion or pettiness. If people did not agree with him, he did not get his own back with sly digs or innuendoes. His interventions in College business, although unfailingly fair-minded and in favour of just dealing, were not frequent, but there was one affair, which may be recalled, in which he took the initiative and which showed his character. Just over a decade ago he mildly surprised us by proposing that the College admit women. His arguments to the Government Body were admirably and dispassionately arranged and within the decade had come to be generally accepted as compelling. When at that time the Governing Body thought otherwise, John showed no resentment (and I imagine felt none), and when in time his colleagues almost to a man came round to his view, he was not heard to gloat. He was above such petty feelings.

If there indeed is, as Aristotle was moved to wonder, 'perception' after death, I imagine that John Mackie is at this moment chafing, or smiling wrily, at being represented as something of a moral hero, and although he was a man of principle and of honour, that is only part of what most of his colleagues in University College will remember. There were, for example, those strange silences in which one wondered what he was thinking, for it was unthinkable that he was not thinking. Small talk did not interest him. If, however, a real question was raised, the eyes would light up and he would engage, generally to the defeat of his opponent's argument. He enjoyed arguing seriously, and, one may add, he enjoyed winning. He also liked accuracy and took pains to get things right both for himself and for others. If one asked him 'What did Mill say about so and so?', he would give an exposition of Mill's views and within the hour one would find in one's box the relevant volume with bookmarkers in the places where one could read for oneself. He was indeed one for books, and seemed to have an uncommon knowledge of literature. This he could deftly deploy. At the time when I was responsible for commissioning for *The Times* obituaries of senior members of this University, he stopped me one day as I was entering my room to say that he had some verses which seemed to him apt to his position *vis-à-vis* myself and he quoted to me Kipling's lines:

> And there wakens in my bosom
> An emotion chill and gruesome
> As I canter past the Undertaker's horse.

He could also surprise in other ways. At any rate I was always mildly surprised to find him in the Common Room watching cricket or tennis on television. Whether this was because he liked watching his countrymen excel, or because he had in youth played the games or because games were a sort of ethics where rules could be adapted to improve the enjoyment of playing, for some reason I never enquired. He somehow kept such things to himself, under the indispensable Trilby.

One might wonder what impression it all made on his pupils, and it may be of interest if I quoted parts of a letter from one of them. He wrote:

'John's teaching had some startling aspects. One in particular was his astonishing power of textual recall. As a student I could raise a point concerning a particular philosophical text and he could go straight to the book and straight to the page and the passage to make direct reference to it. After this process, he would frequently mark the page with a slip of paper, as he said, "for future reference". Most books seemed to contain a substantial number of such pieces of paper. As it turned out he did not rely on them. He could go straight for unmarked passages with equal alacrity.

'Other aspects were touching, if at first also disconcerting. One in particular, was his habit, when reciting a particular text or observation from a book, of coming to kneel close beside you in your chair and (as he read) guiding you through the passage, with his finger.

'One other trivial feature. While listening to the reading of an undergraduate essay. John would lean back in his chair, close his eyes, and place his NHS glasses across his knee. Some astonishment in the mind of a young undergraduate, as I recall, that an already incisive mind was receiving additional support from a knee endowed with truly remarkable qualities!

'On more substantial points of appreciation, the first, clearly, was John's astonishing breadth of knowledge; embracing every aspect of philosophy (wide enough in itself) but also embracing fields outside pure philosophical enquiry, e.g. literature, foreign languages, the arts, and so forth. I cannot recall any subject coming up in discussion at parties at his house on which John did not have thoughts of recognizable wisdom.

'John was without any pretention whatever. He was, in my experience, entirely selfless. He went to great trouble to do things for his students. I recall writing to him during a vacation with some problems concerning a set book with which I was struggling. Within days I had a reply that ran to several pages of handwritten notes explaining the solutions to my problems. This was just one small instance of a generosity of nature that was surely extensive.'

Thus, a pupil. Others have written in similar reverent terms.

Now he has gone at an age approaching retirement but at the height of his great intellectual powers, and with a lot undone he had meant to do. This in itself is cause for sadness, but for me, and I doubt not for my colleagues, it is the man himself whose loss is most to be regretted.

THE PUBLICATIONS OF
J. L. MACKIE

Compiled by Joan Mackie

BOOKS

Truth, Probability, and Paradox (Oxford, 1973)
The Cement of the Universe – A Study of Causation (Oxford, 1974).
   Also paperback edition with preface, additional notes and additional
   bibliography (Oxford, 1980).
Problems from Locke (Oxford, 1976)
Ethics – Inventing Right and Wrong (Harmondsworth, 1977)
Hume's Moral Theory (London, 1980)
*The Miracle of Theism – Arguments For and Against the Existence of
   God* (Oxford, 1982)

LECTURES

Contemporary Linguistic Philosophy – Its Strength and its Weakness
   (University of Otago, 1956)
The Beginning of the Universe in Time – A Meeting Place of Science,
   Religion, and Philosophy (Sydney University Arts Association, 1961)
What's Really Wrong with Phenomenalism? (British Academy, 1969)
Do Moral Rights Determine the Law? (University of·Minnesota, 1977)

ARTICLES AND DISCUSSIONS

'A refutation of morals', *Australasian Journal of Philosophy*, 1946

'Scientific method in textual criticism', *Australasian Journal of Philosophy*, 1947

'The social background of Epicureanism', *Australasian Journal of Philosophy*, 1948

'"Psychological" errors in arithmetic', *Forum of Education*, 1948

'The logical status of grammar rules', *Australasian Journal of Philosophy*, 1949

'Critical notice: *Logic and the Basis of Ethics* (A. N. Prior)', *Australasian Journal of Philosophy*, 1950

'Logic and Professor Anderson', *Australasian Journal of Philosophy*, 1951

'Critical notice: *The Place of Reason in Ethics* (S. Toulmin)', *Australasian Journal of Philosophy*, 1951

'The nature of facts', *Australasian Journal of Philosophy*, 1952

'Critical notice: *Plato's Theory of Ideas* (Sir David Ross)', *Australiasian Journal of Philosophy*, 1952

'Thinking in school mathematics', *Australian Mathematics Teacher*, 1953

(with J. J. C. Smart) 'A variant of the "heterological" paradox', *Analysis*, 1953; also a further note on this topic, *Analysis*, 1954

'Critical notice: *Hume's Intentions* (J. A. Passmore)', *Australasian Journal of Philosophy*, 1954

'Evil and Omnipotence', *Mind*, 1955

'Has the universe a beginning in time?', *Australasian Journal of Philosophy*, 1955

'Responsibility and language', *Australasian Journal of Philosophy*, 1955

'Anderson's theory of education', *The Australian Highway*, 1958

'The rules of natural deduction', *Analysis*, 1958

'"This" as a singular quantifier', *Mind*, 1958

'The symbolising of natural deduction', *Analysis*, 1959

'Conditionally restricted operations', *Notre Dame Journal of Formal Logic*, 1961

'Philosophy – its place in the universities', *Vestes*, 1961

'The sustaining of counterfactuals', *Australasian Journal of Philosophy*, 1961

'Counterfactuals and causal laws', *Analytical Philosophy*, ed. R. J. Butler, (Oxford, 1962)

'Omnipotence', *Sophia*, 1962

'The philosophy of John Anderson', *Australasian Journal of Philosophy*, 1962

'Religion and the University', *Vestes*, 1962

'Theism and Utopia', *Philosophy*, 1962

'Are there any incorrigible empirical statements?' *Australasian Journal of Philosophy*, 1963

'The paradox of confirmation', *British Journal for the Philosophy of Science*, 1963

'Self-refutation – a formal analysis', *Philosophical Quarterly*, 1964

'Causes and conditions', *American Philosophical Quarterly*, 1965

'Rationalism and empiricism', *Australasian Journal of Philosophy*, 1965

'Proof', *Aristotelian Society Supplementary Volume*, 40, 1966

'Miller's so-called paradox of information', *British Journal for the Philosophy of Science*, 1966

'The direction of causation', *Philosophical Review*, 1966

'Mill's methods of induction'; 'Fallacies'; 'Westermarck, Edward Alexander'; in *The Encyclopedia of Philosophy*, ed. Paul Edwards (New York/London, 1967)

'The relevance criterion of confirmation', *British Journal for the Philosophy of Science*, 1969

'Aesthetic judgements – a logical study', *The Pluralist*, 1969

'The possibility of innate knowledge', *Proceedings of the Aristotelian Society*, 1970

'Simple truth', *Philosophical Quarterly*, 1970

'What can we learn from the paradoxes?', *Critica*, 1971

'Metaphysical common sense', *British Journal for the Philosophy of Science*, 1972

'The disutility of act utilitarianism', *Philosophical Quarterly*, 1973

'Locke's anticipation of Kripke, *Analysis*, 1974

'*De* what *re* is *de re* modality?', *Journal of Philosophy*, 1974

'The elusiveness of causation – a reply to Professor Flew', *Philosophical Books*, 1975

'Problems of intentionality', in *Phenomenology and Philosophical Understanding*, ed. E. Pivčević (Cambridge, 1975)

'Ideological explanation' in *Explanation*, ed. S. Körner (Oxford, 1975)

'Sidgwick's pessimism', *Philosophical Quarterly*, 1976

'The riddle of existence', *Aristotelian Society Supplementary Volume* 50, 1976

'The grounds of responsibility', in *Law, Morality, and Society, Essays in Honour of H. L. A. Hart*, ed. P. M. S. Hacker and J. Raz (Oxford, 1977)

'Newcomb's paradox and the direction of causation', *Canadian Journal of Philosophy*, 1977

'Dispositions, grounds, and causes', *Synthese*, 1977

'The third theory of law', *Philosophy and Public Affairs*, 1977

'Can there be a right-based moral theory?' *Midwest Studies in Philosophy*, vol. III (1978)

'Failures in criticism – Popper and his commentators', *British Journal for the Philosophy of Science*, 1978

'The law of the jungle – moral alternatives and principles of evolution', *Philosophy*, 1978

'Mind, brain, and causation', *Midwest Studies in Philosophy*, vol. IV (1979)

'A defence of induction', in *Perception and Identity – Essays Presented to A. J. Ayer*, ed. G. Macdonald (London, 1979)

'Die Ohnmacht moralischer Gottesbeweise', *Glaube und Vernunft*, ed. N. Hoerster (Munich, 1979)

'The transcendental 'I'', in *Philosophical Subjects – Essays Presented to P. F. Strawson*, ed. Z. van Straaten (Oxford, 1980)

'Konditionalsätze', in *Handbuch wissenschaftstheoretischer Begriffe*, ed. J. Speck (Göttingen/Zürich, 1980)

'Kant on personal identity', *Grazer philosophische Studien*, 1980

'The transitivity of counterfactuals and causation', *Analysis*, 1980

'Truth and knowability', *Analysis*, 1980

Comments in *Applications of Inductive Logic*, ed. L. J. Cohen and M. Hesse (Oxford, 1980)

'The efficacy of consciousness: comments on Honderich's paper, *Inquiry*', 1981

'Causal priority and the direction of conditionality', *Analysis*, 1981

'Five o'clock on the sun', *Analysis*, 1981

'Genes and egoism', *Philosophy*, 1981

'Obligations to obey the law', *Virginia Law Review*, 1981

'Propensity, evidence and diagnosis', *The Behavioral and Brain Sciences*, 1981

'Cooperation, competition and moral philosophy', in *Cooperation and Competition in Humans and Animals*, ed. A. M. Colman (Wokingham, 1982)

'Morality and the retributive emotions', in *Edward Westermarck: Essays on His Life and Works*, ed. T. Stroup (Helsinki, 1982)

'Empiricism and speculation', *Philosophical Books*, 1982

'Three steps towards absolutism', in *Space, Time and Causality*, ed. R. Swinburne (Dordrecht, 1983)

'Rules and reason', in *Law, Morality and Rights*, ed. M. A. Stewart (Dordrecht, 1983)

'Duress and necessity as defences to crime', in *Law, Morality and Rights*, ed. M. A. Stewart (Dordrecht, 1983)

'Rights, utility and universalization', in *Utility and Rights*, ed. R. G. Frey (Minneapolis/Oxford, 1984)

'Anti-realisms', *Logic and Knowledge* (Oxford, forthcoming)

'Bootstraps enterprises', *Persons and Values* (Oxford, forthcoming)

'Causation in concept, knowledge and reality', *Logic and Knowledge* (Oxford, forthcoming)

'The combination of partially-ordered preferences', *Persons and Values* (Oxford, forthcoming)

'Locke and representative perception', *Logic and Knowledge* (Oxford, forthcoming)

'Multiple personality', *Persons and Values* (Oxford, forthcoming)

'Norms and dilemmas', *Persons and Values* (Oxford, forthcoming)

'Parfit's population paradox', *Persons and Values* (Oxford, forthcoming)

'Popper's Third World — metaphysical pluralism and evolution', *Logic and Knowledge* (Oxford, forthcoming)

'Rights, utility and external costs', *Persons and Values* (Oxford, forthcoming)

'The three stages of universalization', *Persons and Values* (Oxford, forthcoming)

'Von Wright on conditionals and natural necessity', in *The Philosophy of G. H. von Wright*, ed. P. A. Schilpp, Library of Living Philosophers (La Salle, forthcoming)

BOOK REVIEWS

Society and Nature — A Sociological Inquiry (H. Kelsen), *Australasian Journal of Philosophy*, 1946

Soviet Education: Its Psychology and Philosophy (M. J. Shore), *Australasian Journal of Philosophy*, 1948

Towards a Socialist Australia (NSW Fabian Society), *Australasian Journal of Philosophy*, 1949

Social Pragmatism (L. Freed), *Australasian Journal of Philosophy*, 1950

Man for Himself (E. Fromm), *Australasian Journal of Philosophy*, 1950

Authority and Delinquency in the Modern State (A. Comfort), *Australasian Journal of Philosophy*, 1951

The Discourses of Niccolo Machiavelli (trans. L. J. Walker), *Australasian Journal of Philosophy*, 1951

The Strong and The Weak (D. Peyser), *Australasian Journal of Philosophy*, 1953

Bodily Sensations (D. M. Armstrong), *Australasian Journal of Philosophy*, 1963

The Anatomy of Inquiry (I. Scheffler), *British Journal for the Philosophy of Science*, 1965

The Conduct of Inquiry: Methodology for Behavioral Science (A. Kaplan), *Philosophical Quarterly*, 1966

Hypothetical Reasoning (N. Rescher), *Philosophical Quarterly*, 1966

Experience and Theory (S. Körner), *British Journal for the Philosophy of Science*, 1968

Gambling with Truth (I. Levi), *British Journal for the Philosophy of Science*, 1968

Boston Studies in the Philosophy of Science, vol. 3 (ed. Cohen and Wartofsky), *British Journal for the Philosophy of Science*, 1971

The Matter of Chance (D. H. Mellor), *Philosophical Quarterly*, 1973

Aspects of Language (Y. Bar-Hillel), *British Journal for the Philosophy of Science*, 1973

Pragmatics of Natural Languages (ed. Y. Bar-Hillel), *British Journal for the Philosophy of Science*, 1974

The Nature of Necessity (A. Plantinga), *Times Literary Supplement*, 1975

Causality and Determinism (G. H. von Wright), *Journal of Philosophy*, 1976

Sociobiology: Sense of Nonsense? (M. Ruse), *Erkenntnis*, 1980

Social Justice in the Liberal State (B. Ackerman), *Times Literary Supplement*, 1981

Anderson's Social Philosophy (A. J. Baker), *Australasian Journal of Philosophy*, 1982

A Discourse on Property: John Locke and his Adversaries (J. Tully), *Philosophical Quarterly*, 1982

The Creation (P. W. Atkins), *Times Literary Supplement*, 1982